IN BLACK & WHITE

IN BLACK & WHITE

PETER WILLIAMS

For Jo

Sir Patrick Abercrombie (1879 - 1957), pioneer planner who, in the 1920s, inspired and created the proposal to build a group of New Towns in East Kent, including Aylesham, to serve eighteen coalmines and a number of steelworks in the heart of the Garden of England.

CONTENTS

INTRODUCTION

Decades, like people, have their own peculiar characteristics, quirks and crises. The birth and life of the Kent Coalfield spans roughly ten decades – one hundred years – from the reign of Queen Victoria through the turmoil of two World Wars, to Britain's seismic shift away from an economy based on heavy industry.

This is a story of love and hate. The demanding relationship between Man, and a way of life that embraces hard work and boredom, comradeship and violence, danger and tragedy, moments of great triumph and crushing disappointment and, above all, deep political convictions. It is the story of a coalfield and a unique community with an accent of its own, drawn to Kent from all over Britain to hew its coal. It is secure in its own traditions and beliefs. It is a community proud to declare, today, that they are miners and miners' families, from mining stock.

Their stubborn creativity has survived two World Wars, a multitude of industrial disputes, the closure of the mines and the subsequent grinding poverty as fossil fuel that had founded the Industrial Revolution, gave way to new, people-friendly energy.

Coal was discovered in Kent by accident, in 1890, when men first thought of linking Britain to France though a tunnel. Today, after a hundred years of industrial struggle and successful production that ceased in 1989, there are people even in Kent who are unaware that a Kent coalfield ever existed. It is time that situation is rectified and that the contribution made by the families of both mine owners and miners, is finally on the record.

I am an 'incomer' myself. A Welshman, I was in the 1960s living in Bristol and working for the *Bristol Evening Post*. Television was the new kid on the block and I was eager to be part of it. My first job in television was in Dover, as a newsreader and reporter for the nightly magazine programme 'Day by Day', working for Southern Television as they opened their new regional ITV station for the south east. The region stretched from Brighton and Worthing to Reading and on to Margate and the Channel Ports. The studio was a converted bus garage. I came on a six-month contract and stayed in Kent 50 years and more.

During that first six months, I clearly remember noting that the unique story of the Kent Coalfield had never been properly documented. On reflection, that is an understatement because, at first, I was completely unaware that a coalmine even existed in Kent. Throughout a long career making documentaries for the major networks in the UK and overseas, I tried from time to time to persuade the major channels – BBC, ITV, Channel Four, Discovery and others – to commission a film on a century of coal in Kent. There were no takers.

In 2016, the Hadlow Group, who were the inspiration for the enlightened Betteshanger Project on the site of the old Betteshanger Colliery, produced the money to make a feature-length documentary on the subject. It has won awards from film festivals around the world. We called it 'A Century of Coal' – and a DVD of the film is available on-line at peter@pwtv.co.uk.

This book springs from the material assembled for that film, led by my wife, Jo, who thankfully, is one of the most highly-skilled and instinctive researchers in the business. It has been made possible by the generous support of our late friend, Sir Ronald McIntosh, and with the co-operation of the Kent Mining Heritage Foundation.

Peter Williams
Boughton-under-Blean
Kent 2019

FOREWORD

In Black and White spans several topics: local history, industrial history, political history... But terminology is to some extent misleading because it is too easily associated with facts and chronology. Peter Williams deals in both in his own way, but his book is first and foremost a multi-faceted account of a complex social experiment: the 20th Century migration of coal miners from Scotland, Wales and northern England to newly-opened collieries in East Kent.

These men, at first regarded with hostility, were able to adapt to their new surroundings and establish communities of their own, as they imported new rhythms of work, a new culture – almost a new language.

Appropriately, the book is full of voices. Long experience as an interviewer has made Peter Williams adept at putting people at their ease so that they can comfortably describe their experiences and feelings in their own language. These industrial migrants, their wives and their children, are vivid chroniclers, reaching beyond what they did, or what was done to them, to suggest how those happenings *felt*.

Many of their recollections are startling and distressing. To read this book is to become conscious of the fact that the daily hardships of *all* coal miners have been left virtually unreported and therefore unimaginable. We know less about life down in the mines than we do about the lives of elephants or insects. Peter Williams' many spokesmen evoke a literally crippling environment that, in terms of darkness, danger and physical demands, verged on the phantasmagoric. A range of life-threatening deficiencies and excesses were somehow permitted to continue unchecked, year after year, presumably for the sole reason that they were hidden half a mile below our 20th Century feet, far out of sight and hence outside public consciousness. A documented list of the 22 fatalities at the Chislet colliery *in the 30s alone* is a shocking revelation in itself. It is commendable that *In Black and White* puts such information on record before the mining industry lapses into the past like horse-drawn public transport, to be similarly erased from the collective memory.

The aptly named Malcolm Pitt deserves a paragraph to himself. The first member of his family to go to university he was later a school teacher, a member of the Communist party and a convert to Catholicism. But in a startling career change he chose to be a miner, and worked in the pits for 14 years, becoming President of the Kent area branch of the NUM. When he died he left behind notes and a manuscript which included detailed and eloquent first-hand accounts of life at the coalface. Williams rightly makes full use of this remarkable memoir.

Pitt's close-up descriptions, which appear in the eighth of the book's 16 chapters, are so absorbing that they bring the chronological overview that has previously shaped the narrative to a virtual halt. But that is a price amply worth paying for the quality of the material concerned. In any case, the story cannot be tidily sequential because Williams is obliged to move between the four Kent collieries and to respond to particular crises such as closures, strikes and war. And mere chronology has sometimes to be suspended elsewhere to create space for the inclusion of a variety of relevant background figures: Shinwell, Chamberlain, Bevan, Scargill, Mrs Thatcher, Lord and Lady Northbourne, Ianto Hill…

The cast list naturally becomes particularly extensive in a detailed, meticulous and chilling account of the great strike of 1984. Williams scrupulously avoids communicating his own views on these 'political' events beyond – at most – a hint here, a pointed chapter-epigraph there. The facts, some of them not publicly known at the time of the strike, are left to speak for themselves – and are eloquent. The subsequent abrupt and unheralded closure of the remaining Kent coalfields was a bitter final blow. But there was nothing the miners could have done to avert it. The Kent collieries had been highly productive in their day, but circumstances had changed. It wasn't merely that goalposts had been shifted. Growing awareness of air pollution and climate change meant that they had been removed altogether.

But the downfall of these collieries was only one of a number of major transformations in East Kent in the second half of the 20th Century. Traffic was re-routed, railway lines were closed, the traditional hop-picking all but vanished, many large stores ceased to trade and Kent Opera and the Hoverport came and went. On the other hand the Channel Tunnel was built, there is now a high-speed rail service to London, three new universities draw in thousands of students, a rebuilt Marlowe Theatre has opened in Canterbury, as has the Turner Gallery in Margate. In that context of change and adaptation, the final chapter of *In Black and White*, concerning the regeneration of Aylesham, offers some welcome reassurance. Here the 'immigrants', although retaining elements of their original identity, even of their original dialect, have in effect contrived to found a new town, with thriving small businesses, a vigorous community spirit and a host of leisure activities. After all, a cruel communal defeat can give rise to a communal recovery.

Michael Irwin
Professor of English
University of Kent
Canterbury 2019

CHAPTER ONE
In The Beginning...

*"This is what the people of Kent call
the Garden of England..."*
William Cobbett

Many of the greatest names and most critical events in English history have been in some way connected with Canterbury Cathedral. It is the mother church of English Christianity and its long and varied story is recorded in tomb and stone and window. Augustine and Ethelbert, Edward the Confessor and the Black Prince, Henry VIII and his rival the Holy Roman Emperor Charles V and, of course, Becket, whose martyrdom is still remembered annually with a dramatic and emotional service at the spot where he died, cut down by the Barons' swords.

An unlikely venue, then, to discuss coal and coal mines. Nonetheless, on July 24th 1926, in the precincts of Canterbury

Canterbury Cathedral (c 1925)

Neville Chamberlain

Cathedral and at the invitation of the then Dean George Bell, the great and the good of Kent gathered to hear a politician who would shortly become Britain's Prime Minister, Neville Chamberlain. He had summoned them because he had a plan. The plan was that Kent, the Garden of England, was to be asked to accommodate up to 18 coal mines, and perhaps three ironworks, to become, in effect, another Black Country. And Chamberlain's job that day was to break the news to an apprehensive assembly of the county's leaders, and to reassure them that Kent would not be irreversibly damaged by this forced industrial intrusion into a predominantly rural county.

Coal had fuelled Britain's industrial revolution, powered the rail networks and fuelled the Royal Navy that built and protected her worldwide empire. Coal was King. And behind the skilful speech that Chamberlain delivered lay a simple, economic impetus.

Coal had been discovered, by accident, in Kent. The nation's ever-expanding capital, London, was hungry for coal. Currently, every ton of coal had to be transported hundreds of miles either from South Wales or Scotland, Nottingham or Yorkshire. But Kent was only 60 miles away from London.

Coal from Kent had to be cheaper, in transport costs alone – and, besides, a new coalfield would present a fresh start after the bitterness that currently clouded relationships in every major coalfield in Britain in the aftermath of the 1926 General Strike, when the British miners had been among the Government's most trenchant opponents.

Chamberlain's audience knew that the Kent coal industry was as yet only in its infancy. Between 1906 and the outbreak of World War One, a new colliery had opened almost every year. Tilmanstone in 1906, Guilford in 1907, Snowdown in 1908, Wingham and Woodnesborough in 1910, Stonehall in 1912 and Chislet in 1913. But output was low and some pits had already closed. The sinking of a new, deep pit at Betteshanger in 1924 evoked this new optimism. Chamberlain left Canterbury that evening in 1926 having delivered his vision for the future and confident that he had convinced his audience that the economic argument would carry the day. But the Kent Coalfield had made a stuttering start over many years. And Chamberlain's grand plan was speculative to say the least...

* * * * * * * *

It was a railway initiative that led to the discovery of coal in Kent. Sir Edward William Watkin was at one time or another chairman of nine railway companies and trustee of a tenth. He was knighted in 1868 and made a baronet in 1880 for his pioneering work in helping to create Britain's rail network. Born in Lancashire, he had worked in his father's mills and later founded a newspaper, *The Merchant Examiner*. He was ambitious, a man of vision. He was an advisor to

Indian railways and those building the Athens to Piraeus rail link. He helped unite the Canadian provinces to create the transcontinental Canadian Pacific Railway.

His dream in Britain was to build a direct rail link from the North and Midlands to London and this he had achieved by 1899, with a grand opening of the Great Central main line at Marylebone Station, in London. Next, he planned to link Liverpool and Manchester to Paris by rail. He was already on the board of Chemins de Fer du Nord, a railway company whose headquarters were in Calais, and Watkin had constructed the Great Central main line from Sheffield to Marylebone with this in mind; its gauge would enable this British track to accommodate the larger-gauge continental trains.

But to fulfil this dream, a tunnel or a bridge would be needed to link Britain to France. Watkin, who was chairman of South Eastern Railway, chose the tunnel option and, in 1880, had sunk a shaft between Dover and Folkestone to enable a pilot heading to be bored. The borings were successful and Sir Edward formed the Submarine Continental Railway Company as a declaration of intent.[1] A second boring followed at Shakespeare Cliff, Dover and, in 1881, Watkin campaigned in Parliament for land on which he could begin to build a Channel Tunnel. History indicates again and again, however, that a relationship, be it political, economic or physical, between Britain and France, is fraught with difficulty. And so it proved in 1881.

Britain's politicians were more concerned about security than the *entente cordiale*. What if the French invaded through the tunnel? Watkin was asked how he would block the tunnel to prevent such an invasion. Fiercely he argued the trade

[1] A history of the Kent Coalfield, John Hilton, p1

and cultural advantages of a Channel Tunnel. He lobbied
the Prince of Wales, the Archbishop of Canterbury and the
Prime Minister at champagne receptions. But in April 1892,
the Board of Trade instructed him that boring must stop
until the military security of a tunnel was ensured.

Queen Victoria, it was reported, found Watkin's scheme
'objectionable'. The War Office Scientific Committee opposed
it. Watkin was left with a 'tunnel' 1850 metres long, and a
shattered vision. And it remained so for the next four years.
But the engineer to Watkin's tunnel company, Francis Brady,
had other ideas. In 1886, he suggested that the redundant
machinery might be used to look for coal. And he assembled
his evidence...

Across the Channel in France, there had been a Nord
Pas de Calais coalfield since 1852. There were collieries at
Lens, Bruay and Courrières. A scientific paper by Henry
Haversham Godwin-Austen in 1855 declared that, if you
extended a geological line from the established pits in South
Wales and the Forest of Dean, across the channel, to the Nord
Pas de Calais coalfields, there was every chance that there
would be coal in South East England, perhaps under the
rolling grasslands of Kent. He received little support for his
views but coal was the nation's primary source of energy and
in 1871, a Royal Commission on coal supplies considered
the suggestion again and agreed to a test boring. The 'Sub-
Wealden Committee' was set up and a test boring began near
Battle in Sussex. The boring reached a depth of 1905 – and
then the boring machine jammed. The operation had cost a
massive £7,000 and nothing had been proved. Undaunted,
geologist and soldier, Godwin-Austen, recommended a
second trial boring, this time not in the middle of Sussex

but near Dover, the closest point in Britain to the French collieries.

The Sub-Wealden Committee ignored the suggestion. But Watkin's engineer, Brady, urged that their redundant tunnelling machinery might indeed be used to seek out a coal seam, if one existed. Watkin agreed. Four years later, in 1890, 1180 feet from the surface, they struck a seam of coal 1ft 3ins thick. They drilled on. At 2221 feet, they found a seam 4 feet thick. He had proved that there was bituminous coal in Kent. The exercise had so far cost Watkin £10,000 but he was in no position to take commercial advantage of his discovery. Neither his Channel Tunnel Company nor his South Eastern Railway had a licence to dig coal. And Watkin was close to retirement. For the moment, coal in Kent would remain in the ground.

The discovery of coal became a political issue almost immediately. William Morris, designer of spectacular wallpaper, textiles and furniture, and a leading member of the Socialist League, forecast that Kent would become 'a manufacturing hell'. He went on: "They (the workers) have learned by this time that Sir Edward Watkin and his pals (the landowners) will stick to (keep) whatever swag they can filch out of Kentish Coal, which belongs to the people, not to them, and will only yield to the workers what they are compelled to yield."[2]

Despite the furore, Watkin's engineer, Brady, knew what he knew – he had proved that as he stood on Shakespeare Cliff, there was coal under his feet. His challenge, now that Sir Edward Watkin had retired, was how to turn this knowledge into cash. Enter, stage right, Arthur Burr. Burr is an unlikely fairy godfather, with a questionable record as an entrepreneur

[2] Those Dirty Miners, JP Hollingsworth, Stenlake Publishing, 2010, p4

behind him and an even more chequered financial career yet to be recorded. In his excellent essay on Burr,[3] JP Hollingsworth recalls that, on one of his frequent appearances in a bankruptcy court, the judge described him as 'a dangerous rogue'. Certainly, during his long and lively career, men died and others were stripped of all they possessed when they associated with Burr or one of his initiatives.

Arthur Burr

Arthur Burr was born in the London suburb of Islington in 1850. We know little of the first 55 years of his life; Hollingsworth describes him as 'an archetypal Victorian speculator...a basically agreeable and friendly man' about whom people had very different, often contradictory views depending on the experience of the acquaintanceship. He was probably 'a very skilled conman...with his cavalier methods of conducting business and perpetual optimism that maybe even he believed in.'

This was the man who approached Watkin's engineer, Francis Brady, in 1896, two years after Watkin's retirement. He offered to help Brady develop what he described as 'the Kent Coalfield'. Brady had considered setting up a syndicate

---

[3] Ibid

to do just that but Burr persuaded him to join his newly-formed 'Kent Coalfield Syndicate'. He gave Brady guarantees that favourable terms would be available to Sir Edward Watkin's companies, the South Eastern Railways and the Channel Tunnel Company. Brady received £2,000 in shares and £1,000 in cash from the Kent Coalfield Syndicate and became a director. For a few months.

In 1896, Brady instigated a resumption of exploration on the Shakespeare Cliff site and the 'Brady Pit' was dug 280 feet west of the existing workings. In July 1896, Arthur Burr decided to take over responsibility for the project. A great deal of water was then found at a depth of 360 feet and operations were suspended. A second shaft was sunk nearby, known as the 'Simpson Pit'. Almost immediately, there was a tragic accident. On March 6th 1897, 'there was an inrush of water from the greensand which suddenly engulfed the men working in the bottom...and eight men were drowned'.[4] Work went on and a third shaft was bored but all the pits were very wet. 'The total water that had to be dealt with at a depth of 450 feet was 54170 gallons per hour...with this amount of water coming in, the sinking was tedious. In 1899, progress became very slow...and financial difficulties intervened'.[5]

Increased flooding stopped the mining. But at the last minute a thick bed of ironstone was found. Allied to the coal deposit, Arthur Burr had something to work with and to influence others, to fund his dream. He publicly paraded the possibility of a coal mine (which was unworkable) and an ironworks (which was unproven). On October 14th 1897, he instigated a new company, The Kent Colliers Cooperation

---

[4] Ibid, p5
[5] Ibid, p5

Ltd. Its aim was to build, at the cost of £50,000, a colliery at Shakespeare Cliff, to produce 3000 tons a day by 1900. Costs rose to more than £1 million but no coal was ever mined in any commercially viable quantity.

By 1907, Arthur Burr was living with his wife and son, Malcolm, in a terraced Victorian villa in Church Road, Dover, with business premises at 58 Castle Street. Between 1904 and 1910 he began work on five more pits, none of which was a commercial success. The prospectus he wrote as he formed and discarded company after company, became ever more glowing. In 1897, he had declared the Kent Coal Exploration Company to be a vehicle for Dover coal to take advantage of the fact that it could be freighted to London four or five shillings a ton cheaper than Yorkshire or Midlands coal, and the company 'should for many years return large profits'. Ten years later, disappointed investors were still waiting.

There is a pattern to Burr's operations. First, he concentrated on the mineral rights, leases and freeholds to appeal to investors in a new company. Then, a separate company was floated to bore for coal. Next, a syndicate was formed to begin working and equipping the pits. A finance company was then added, and lastly a railway initiative.[6] All separate companies, each working with the others with no related accounts. Burr was usually chairman or director-general for life, taking 10% of trading profits. It was also a feature of the Burr groups that, if one company had money in the bank, some cash would be lent to less successful companies in the group. All these loans were negotiated for a fee through the East Kent Contract and Financial Company formed in December 1907 (Director-

---

[6] A History of Kent Coal, John Hilton, p15

General: Arthur Burr). The 1917 accounts reveal the Contract Company had lent:

- Kent Coal Concessions Ltd – £56,116:12:6d
- SE Coalfield Extension Ltd – £15,403:15:9d
- Extended Extensions Ltd – £10,232:4:11d
- East Kent Colliery Ltd – £15,819:7:10d
- Snowdown Colliery Ltd – £19,390:19:2d
- Guilford Syndicate Ltd – £42,736:16:2d
- SE Electric Power Co – £5,152:12:6d

But at the same time (1917), the East Kent Contract Company owed the following amounts:

- Intermediate Equipment Ltd – £29,041:8:7d
- Foncage Syndicate Ltd – £14,126:12:3d
- Sondage Syndicate Ltd – £4,577:19:1d
- Deal & Walmer Coalfield – Ext. £908:4:6d
- East Kent Light Railway – £8,886:14:0d

Like all the Burr companies, the truth was that the Contract Company was undercapitalised. The lendings to other companies were more than its issued share capital. Because of its position as a broker, and the constant lending and borrowing between companies, profits were high: 10% in 1908, 15% in 1909, 15% in 1910, 50% in 1911 and 20% in 1912. These dividends were very profitable to Burr; in 1912 he was paid £1,850.[7]

Yet Burr was a popular and respected figure in East Kent. In October 1912, the mayor and councillors of Dover

---

[7] Ibid

planned to honour him with a civic dinner. Unemployment in the Dover area was high, and Burr publicly offered to employ practically all the unemployed in his various companies, which indeed he did. He set up a 'Workmen's League' to improve the relationship between management and workers, to avoid misunderstandings and industrial interest. But, as Hollingsworth observes, his web of companies 'became so complex that it is amazing that Burr was able to keep his business going for the best part of 20 years. The strain of all his dealings must have been unimaginable'.[8]

But, for Arthur Burr, 1912 was a good year. The Tilmanstone pit had been sunk in 1907 and officially opened by Burr's granddaughter, Gabrielle, after whom the shaft was named. It didn't have a conspicuously successful start. It had flooded early on and work was suspended for a year. It claimed the lives of three miners when a bucket broke loose and fell down the shaft. It was underfinanced and the machinery needed to bore coal from the seam arrived nearly a year late.

But a second shaft, named after Burr's other granddaughter, Rowena, had been bored in 1910 and the installation of electric pumps to drain the water in 1912 meant that, at last, Tilmanstone was producing coal. Burr was ecstatic. He was unwell but insisted on going to the pithead carried by two burly miners.[9] In the same year at the Snowdown Colliery, in which Burr also had an interest, a rich coal seam was reached. A special train carried jubilant shareholders and company officials to the colliery and, as the first hobbit (bucket) of coal was brought to the surface, glasses of champagne were raised and emptied.

---

[8] Those Dirty Miners, JP Hollingsworth, p94
[9] Ibid, p25–26

However questionable Burr's business methods, there was no doubt that he, and coal, had brought fresh business to Dover and East Kent. On February 4th 1913, Arthur Burr was made a Freeman of the Borough of Dover. His acceptance speech lauded one man – Arthur Burr. The coal mining industry in Kent had been a 'one-man show'. No Board of Directors would have carried through the enterprise. 'They would have killed it because they would not have taken the risk'. Burr was presented with a loving cup, which cost the town 250 guineas and the mayor praised him as 'one of the greatest benefactors Dover has ever known'.

During this explosion of praise, Sir Arthur Conan Doyle, creator of Sherlock Holmes, declared that Dover was destined to become 'the Liverpool of the South' and 'one of six biggest cities in Britain'.[10] Burr did not challenge this assessment and prepared his next business prospectus.[11]

Arthur Burr had reached the peak of his career. He now embarked on a series of negotiations embracing land and mineral sales and company mergers. It perturbed shareholders. They invited Burr to a private meeting in May 1914 'to give account of his stewardship'.[12] His supporters 'began to smell a rat and Burr was accused of being a conman'.[13] They produced £30,000 to pay immediate bills and began proceedings against him and his son, Malcolm, for fraud and misuse of funds. Undeterred, Burr continued to conjure up coal-related businesses until 1918, at which time he still owned nine companies. Burr's life moved rapidly to its end. In March 1919, he was declared bankrupt;

---

[10] Ibid
[11] Ibid
[12] A History of the Kent Coalfield, John Hilton, p19
[13] Those Dirty Miners, JP Hollingsworth, p95

there were judgments totalling £80,000 against him. Mr Justice Sergeant said of the Concessions Company: "Mr Burr appeared to have this company in the hollow of his hands and, I am sorry to say, he appears to have held similar powers with regard to associated companies…. He has acted in a most unscrupulous manner." It emerged that Burr had been bankrupt three times before – in 1874, with liabilities of £80,000, in 1880 (£6,000 liabilities) and in 1891 (£35,000 liabilities).[14]

Arthur Burr died in 1919. He was 70 years old. For all his faults and machinations, he had been seminally involved in the birth of the East Kent coalfield. Boreholes, nearly 50 in all, had been dug all over Kent by more than 40 companies and coal had been found in a rough triangle, with the towns of Dover and Deal at its base and Canterbury at its apex. There had been encouraging signs at 12 sites:

- Adisham, a village six miles south of Canterbury where plans for a colliery were never pursued.
- Cobham, which, in the 18th Century had been an opencast mine (and where, in 1947 and for six years, a small amount of coal would be produced).[15]
- Guilford, part of the Earl of Guilford estate, at Coldred, near the Dover-Canterbury road. Good coal was found in 1909 in the parkland and was mined, on and off, until 1920. It was never commercially viable and this coal seam was eventually mined from the Tilmanstone Colliery.

---

[14] Ibid, p94
[15] Those Dirty Miners, JP Hollingsworth, pp 19–24

- Woodnesborough,[16] south of Sandwich, colliery constructed in 1911 but a shaft was never sunk. The buildings were used as stables for the cavalry during World War One.
- Maydensole,[17] at East Langdon, near the Dover-Deal road, explored in 1910 but never worked.
- Stonehall, near Lydden, lying west of the A2 Dover-Canterbury road, where three shafts were dug in 1913. No coal was found.
- Wingham, a historic village between Canterbury and Sandwich, where shafts were sunk by 1910 by another company headed by Arthur Burr; they flooded and there was no money to buy pumps.
- Goodnestone, on the Canterbury-Sandwich road, on land whose owner was related to Jane Austen, where three shafts were dug, one to a depth of 4,000 foot but no coal was found.
- Fredville, on the estate of HW Plumptre, where exploration stopped in 1908, probably due to financial difficulties.
- Barham, south of Canterbury, where coal was found but not developed.
- Waldershare, just north of Dover, where a number of seams were found but never worked.
- Nonington, where, again, coal-seams were found but never developed.

Arthur Burr was involved in at least five of the companies that carried out these explorations. The birth of

---

[16] Also known as Hammill Pit, ibid, p19
[17] Those Dirty Miners, JP Hollingsworth, pp 19–24

the Kent Coalfield had been protracted, painful and clouded in controversy. But by 1914, three pits were producing coal – Tilmanstone, opened in 1906, and five miles inland from Deal; Snowdown, near Aylesham in 1908; and Chislet, near Canterbury in 1914.

The first phase of the Kent Coalfield was complete. The second phase would be led by a man whose pedigree and methods were a complete contrast to those employed by Arthur Burr. He would bring stability and credibility to the Kent Coalfield. He was Australian and his name was Richard Tilden Smith. But, first, a world war would intervene…

CHAPTER TWO
World War One – Underground Warfare

*"You can't say civilisation doesn't
advance – for in every war, they kill
you in a new way."*
Will Rogers, 1949

At the outbreak of World War One, there were only a few hundred coal miners employed in the Kent Coalfield, working at three collieries – Tilmanstone, Snowdown and the newly-opened Chislet. Coal was crucial to the war effort and initially miners were not encouraged to answer Kitchener's call to

A time for reflection after a WW1 explosion at Messines Ridge

arms. But by the end of 1914/15, the picture had changed. However fiercely the opposing armies fought, the rhythm of the war had been quickly set – a repetitive advance and retreat over much the same stretches of land in Belgium and Northern France. Hundreds of thousands of men were dying in pursuit of stalemate. The Western Front stretching from the channel coast through Belgium into Western France, was virtually static.

All-out war inspires ingenuity in the skills that both take life and save it. As the paralysis on the Western Front set in, both the Allies and the Germans considered tunnelling under opposing lines and blowing up the enemy with huge amounts of high explosives. To dig the holes, they would need miners. The Germans first attacked in this way at Ypres in December

Major John Norton-Griffiths

1914 and early in 1915. The British promptly retaliated and by June 1916, there were more than 30 tunnelling companies in the British sector, totalling 21000 men.[18]

The inspiration behind the British effort was Major John Norton-Griffiths,[19] named 'Empire Jack' because of

---

[18] Patrick Bishop, 2014
[19] Later, Lt. Col. Sir John Norton-Griffiths

his often-expressed patriotism.[20] Norton-Griffiths had mined gold in South Africa and, through a successful business career in construction companies, had dug sewers in London and tunnels beneath Manchester.[21] He wrote to the War Office in 1914 suggesting he assemble a company of 'moles' – a description he insisted on using to describe a workforce of miners – in preparation for underground warfare. His letter was ignored until the British realised they had no retaliatory force to oppose the Germans. He recruited his men, his 'clay-kickers', from every mine in the country – coal, slate and clay.

Those men recruited from Kent didn't have to travel far for their training. Chatham, the headquarters of the Royal Engineers, was the assembly point for all the miners recruited

by Norton-Griffiths and they were then trained at Hythe, near Folkestone, whose dockside became the last sight of Britain for so many millions of soldiers as they left for

Smiling WWI miners underground

---

[20] Beneath Flanders Fields, Barton, Doyle and van der Walle, p61
[21] With the London Southern Sewer Company in 1910 and 1913

the Western Front. Norton-Griffiths was in a hurry. He had drawn some of his 'moles' from army units which they had voluntarily joined on the outbreak of war in 1914. Most of his first 'company' of 'clay-kickers', however, he knew from personal experience. One Friday, he plucked 20 employees from his own tunnelling company, as they dug beneath the city of Manchester. By lunchtime the following Monday, the men were in uniform, equipped with thigh-length gumboots, a knitted khaki balaclava helmet, a cap and a sleeveless leather jerkin. They had received no military training, couldn't march or drill and "were more likely to call an officer 'mate' than 'sir'."[22]

Lance-Corporal Harvey Moseley, then a teenager, remembers:

"I was a National Reservist, a clay-kicker. I was a lad of 16 and worked on building the railway from Leeds to Huddersfield. They showed me how to clay kick for laying drains and so on underground. I volunteered and went into the King's Own Yorkshire Light Infantry. We were training at Hythe. Norton-Griffiths came. All the men paraded to 'Take two paces to the front' and he called out some names. I wondered where he'd got mine from. We stood out and were mustered – we were all miners. Norton-Griffiths went round each company calling out names, and the men stood out. They put us on parade then, and marched the others away. He told us to get ready as we were going away and that we were going to be specially enlisted tunnellers for a job that he knew we could do. We were the people he wanted. We weren't volunteers. We all jumped at it, though, when he told us the figure we were going to get – an increase from a

---

[22] Beneath Flanders Fields, Barton, Doyle and van der Walle, p61

shilling a week to six shillings a day! I got six shillings a day right from the start. I was in the first tunnelling companies to go to France."[23]

Harvey Moseley was not a typical 'mole'. Norton-Phillips preferred older, wiser workers and he scoured the units and the mines for such men. He believed that experienced men were likely to react better in crisis situations – and, as they were to discover, that was not infrequent. Captain Matthew Roach[24] remembered his first day at the front:

"The road was torn and rutted by shellfire and transport traffic until it almost resembled a cart track on the Karoo. On either hand was a countryside of indescribable desolation. Where once had been green, smiling pastures and well-tilled fields was now a dreary waste of weeds; an unkempt wilderness of yellow grass and cankerous undergrowth. Here and there, piles of debris, brick and plaster and protruding beams, marked where the homely cottages of the peasantry once stood. Now not a peasant was to be seen. They had fled before the terrible, all-destroying tidal wave of war and the little homes which had sheltered them for years had been pounded to shapeless heaps by the roaring guns. Everywhere was solitude, dreariness and ruin."

Unlike most army units, Britain's tunnelling companies were allotted specific areas of the front line and they stayed there. The need for these specialist men to have a rest, relief from the familiar and ever-present danger, was balanced against the advantage for the tunnellers of knowing intimately the land into which they would burrow. So the British tunnellers stayed put.

---

[23] Lance-Corporal Harvey Moseley, 170 TC, RE
[24] Capt. Matthew Roach MC, RE, killed in action, July 2nd 1916

The Germans decided otherwise. Their tunnellers, named *Pioniere*, moved with their units. Many German tunnellers, therefore, remained infantrymen. They were to prove less effective than the British in this new underground warfare.

Both armies used similar mining methods, standardising the dimensions of the tunnels they dug, matching the shape of the face ahead to the shape and size of the wooden 'setts' (supports) they would insert in the tunnel before they moved forward. The tunnel was perhaps four feet high. The men worked in appalling conditions, in foul air and often dripping wet from flooding. Men who had been in a crouching position for hours were unable to stand when they emerged from their shift. While they were underground they listened, they dug, they hammered, and then they listened. They invented a sign language to communicate. Both sides used stethoscopes to try to hear if there were tunnellers from the other side digging towards them, from above or below. And they were ready to attack their opponents, below ground, either by blowing them up, or by breaking into the rival tunnel, and killing the enemy. The nightmare quality of such actions, and there were many of them, can only be imagined.

Bill Hodgson, recruited from Betteshanger, never spoke about the horrors of this warfare. The Hodgson family had come to Kent from Nottingham and his grandson, Vic Stevens, remembers visiting him at his home in Minster. "Granddad was badly disabled and, after my gran died, we became quite close. I did his shopping for him at the weekends. Granddad would chat about anything – but one subject was off-limits. That was the years he spent digging tunnels in France to blow up the Germans."

The miners usually worked in four 12-man shifts, each of six hours a day; four men on face work, four on removing the spoil, two men on hoisting and two on pumping the air through to the miners in the often lengthy tunnels. The crude judgment on whether work could continue on the face at the end of the tunnel was made by watching the flame of the candles that made work possible. If they quivered and went out it meant that there was not sufficient oxygen to keep them alight. Nor, presumably, for the miners to breathe. Later, candles were replaced by rechargeable storage batteries. Blacksmiths' bellows connected to long lines of stove pipes and pumped continually by two men, supervised by a junior officer, took air to the toiling miners, sometimes hundreds of metres away underground. Tunnellers on both sides made a major contribution to the Battle of the Somme in 1915/16. The British placed 19 mines beneath the German lines at La Boisselle before the battle, and a further line of charges to create a channel to protect the allied troops as they advanced. The miners, by now named the 179th Tunnelling Company, knew the German tunnellers were also digging towards their trenches. They created further tunnels beneath and above the German excavations. Huge charges, an estimated 18400 kilograms of ammonal in a single tunnel, exploded as, on the ground above, the allied advance began.

Tunnellers on both sides were killed. In 2011, the bodies of 28 British miners were found entombed in the collapsed tunnels at La Boisselle. It was, according to military historians, 'a classic example of mining and counter-mining on both sides'.

Tunnels were dug defensively, to discover and deter enemy movements below ground, as well as offensively, to gain a military advantage. Tunnelling sapped the morale of the infantry who were waiting to do battle, while aware of the underground activity, perhaps beneath their feet. As Norton-Griffiths put it, "You couldn't expect Tommy to be shot at on the surface, bombed from above and blown to hell from below."[25] The casualty rate among his 'moles' was high. More than a thousand died every month in 1916/17.[26]

Though the stalemate on the Western Front continued through 1916 and 1917, the tempo of the underground war in France quickened. The Messines Ridge, protruding into the Allied lines, had long proved an advantage to the Kaiser's forces. In February 1917, the British started to dig a network of 21 tunnels on a 10-mile sector. Under what would become known as Hill 60, the workings were so complicated that up to 50 listening posts were set up to monitor rival activity and guess at the objectives. On June 17th 1917, the Germans discovered what the British had been planning. War correspondents watched from a distance as 1.2 million pounds of high explosives were detonated. One described it as 'the most diabolical splendour I have ever seen'. Ten thousand men died. A German who survived wrote about the experience of being blown up:

"Throughout the afternoon, the English had maintained their slow but effective gunfire of all calibres upon the German positions. Then suddenly at 8 o'clock in the evening there was a tremble and a swaying of the ground; then a shudder. The sentry, who was standing in position at his loophole with whistle in mouth, was hurled against the revetment and lay there stunned. Another was

---

[25] Ibid, p99
[26] Historian Patrick Bishop

thrown over the breastworks. Dugouts collapsed, burying and crushing those inside. Suddenly we were enveloped in darkness and the air was full of soil and dust. From the skies came huge clods of earth, timber, wire pickets, human limbs and whole bodies; everything swirling in confusion. Trenches are flattened by the falling mass. Those who are dazed and half-conscious and cannot dig themselves out are suffocated. The English have exploded a mine – and what a mine it must have been! The central sector was about 100 metres wide and the two platoons within it were either blown to pieces or buried alive."[27]

World War One, and the attritional way it was fought, scarred both those who were part of it and those who observed it. Poet Wilfred Owen was among the talented group of men who did both and were able to express their feelings. 'Miners' is one of his most widely-read works (see Appendix). He set out to write a poem on the Minnie pit disaster that rocked Staffordshire on January 12th 1918, in which 155 men and boys lost their lives as a result of a firedamp explosion. At that time, Owen was on leave from the Western Front and had had a spell at home. He was now back on duty in Scarborough, with the 3rd/5th Battalion of the Manchester Regiment, staying in a hotel in Clarence Gardens, now named the Clifton Hotel. Although the subject of his poem is a mining disaster, the images he conjured that day, and set down, drove him more and more to the horrors of his traumatic experiences on the front line. On the Western Front, many of the men in his platoon had been miners, 'hard-handed, hard-headed, blond, coarse, ungainly, strong, 'unfatigable' (sic), unlovely, Lancashire soldiers. Saxon to the bone…'

---

[27] Beneath Flanders Fields, p153

Owen's poem compares murmuring coals with the moans of the dying men "writhing for air"; it recalls the slaughter on the barbed wire and the heaps of 'white bones' in the fire's ashes underground, the miners' 'muscles charred'.

These words will have had a special significance for those brave men who dug and paused, and listened for the enemy, deep beneath the mud of the Western Front. The casualty rate among the army's miners on both sides was high. As Owen sub-titled his poem – 'How the future will forget the dead in War'.

Norton-Griffiths wrote in 1917 that the devastating effect of these huge mines would mean that the Allied troops would be able to walk to the top of the Ridge 'smoking their pipes'. It was not quite like that. Hundreds died in hand-to-hand fighting. After the Allied victory at Messines, the tunnellers turned their attention to building vast, deep dugouts capable of accommodating thousands of troops. They constructed hospitals, kitchens, workshops and canteens, all artificially ventilated and lit by electricity. As for Norton-Griffiths, he was not there to see the triumph of the initiative he had launched in 1914. He had been temporarily detached from the Western Front to go to Romania, an ally of Germany, to mastermind a campaign to blow up and disable the Romanian oil wells that were fuelling the German forces. He is credited with destroying 70 refineries and 800,000 tons of oil.

Throughout the war, Norton-Griffiths maintained an almost manic enthusiasm for working with miners in the task he had set himself. He did it with style. His wife, Gwladys, owned a Rolls-Royce which Norton-Griffiths persuaded the War Office to buy, so that he could drive it to the army units which he approached seeking men or favours; the car always carried

*Major John Norton-Griffiths with his
Rolls-Royce at the front line*

whisky, port, champagne or claret, to help persuade resistant company commanders. Almost single-handed, he inspired a massive underground campaign that terrified the enemy, as Peter Barton writes in his excellent and comprehensive book *Beneath Flanders Fields: The Tunnellers' War*:

'Despite his exasperating eccentricities and disregard for protocol, most of the staff at GHQ realised the value of the work 'Naughty' was doing, and that he had unique capabilities. They recognised knowledge derived from experience, and knew that no one else had either the drive or contacts to make things happen as swiftly as he could.'

Norton-Griffiths was awarded the DSO[28] in 1916 and become a baronet in 1922. His construction company prospered after the war until it became involved in a scheme to raise the height of the Aswan Dam in Egypt. There were financial problems. On September 30th 1930, Sir John Norton-Griffiths went for a swim. He took a rowing boat from the

[28] Distinguished Service Order

beach at the Casino Hotel, near Alexandria, and headed out to sea. The boat was later discovered, empty. Sir John's body was recovered with a bullet wound in the temple. No weapon was ever found but the coroner recorded a verdict of suicide. His body was brought back to England and he is buried at Mickleham Church, Surrey. He was 59.

The face of war was changing and Norton-Griffiths had played his part in the process. The art of killing, and of defence, was becoming more sophisticated. Machine guns had increased the number and frequency of bullets that could be fired into thousands of human bodies. Tanks would soon appear, crushing troops beneath their tracks and bringing the war to an end. In 1917, mechanisation was on the march. In the three pits that made up the Kent Coalfield, the miners who had not joined Norton-Griffiths on his crusade had spent four years hewing coal for the nation's war effort. They had banded together to form the beginnings of a 'trade union' called 'The Miners' Federation of Great Britain'. Conditions in the Kent pits were among the worst in the country. They were promised improved working conditions, including increased mechanisation below ground. In July 1919, 1200 Kent miners lost patience; they went on strike.

At the end of the war, politicians had promised 'a world fit for heroes'. The miners of Kent felt the world they inhabited wasn't even fit for purpose. Not for the last time, they decided to flex their industrial muscle.

CHAPTER THREE
Mechanisation and Tilden Smith

*"Be wary of engineers – they begin
with sewing machines and end up
with atomic bombs."*
Marcus Pagnol, 1973

The traditional image of a miner is of a man in coal black, perhaps kneeling in helmet and knee pads, hard-muscled, sweat gleaming. It is reflected in statue, portrait and photograph. Mining involved hard work over many hours. No wonder then that men have sought to ease this endemic physical pain by embracing machinery wherever possible. Just as in World War One the tank was revolutionising the pattern of war, so human ingenuity was attempting to improve the passage of coal, from mine to customer.

At the end of World War One, three pits in Kent were commercially producing coal. All were eager to explore better methods of transporting the coal to the customer. As early as 1907, proposals had been made for a railway line to serve the coalfield. Amid the welter of documents issued by Arthur Burr in his various guises, was a prospectus that envisaged 'the development of what appears...likely to prove to be a second South Wales Coalfield (in Kent) within a short distance of London'.[29]

It was a time of optimism. The East Kent Light Railways Company had been launched in 1910, heavily promoted by the Burr-led Kent Coal Concessions Company. The first line linked the existing South Eastern and Chatham railway at Shepherdswell with the Tilmanstone Colliery. It opened in December 1911. The Kent railway system was planned in the form of a Y, with Eastry at its junction and Canterbury, Shepherdswell and the new port of Richborough at its extremities.[30] In November 1912, the first hobbit[31] of coal was raised from the Snowdown Colliery. Four months later, Tilmanstone produced its first coal but, in March 1914, the roof at Tilmanstone collapsed and the pit flooded at the rate of six gallons a minute. Tilmanstone closed for six weeks. At the same time, smaller collieries at Woodnesborough, Stonehall and Wingham closed. But, despite all these difficulties, the new railway line opened in October 1916. There were stations at Shepherdswell, Eythorne, Tilmanstone (both for the colliery and the village), Eastry, Ash Town and Wingham. The trucks carried freight and coal and there were four coaches for passengers (first and third class).

The coal companies had high hopes of exporting Kent coal. They listed a choice of ports through which the export traffic could flow:

Queenborough, on the Isle of Sheppey, but it was 30 miles from the nearest colliery; Faversham, which had already handled small amounts of coal, carried on barges;

---

[29] United Coalfields of Kent, 1912
[30] Map of East Kent Light Railway, 1912 in Appendix
[31] Hobbit – a hoist bucket of coal

Birchington and Deal, where negotiations were unsuccessful; and Sandwich, where, after a ceremony graced by the mayor and corporation, a cargo of coal had left by barge to London in 1914. Richborough, developed by the government for war-time traffic, and Dover which, with a minimum depth of 26 foot could be used for coaling 24 hours a day, were also possibilities for development.

The railway company tried to reach out to all the possible competitors. But by 1920, Dover appeared to be the port of choice for the export of coal. Six vessels were regularly leaving for Calais and Boulogne. Most of the coal carried by the railways in these early years was produced by the Tilmanstone Colliery and the war effort stimulated the growth of the Kent coal industry. There was a direct correlation between the coal production at Tilmanstone and activity on the East Kent Light Railway. In 1913, 1914 and 1915, Tilmanstone produced an average of 50,000 tons a year. In the next three years, the partnership of pit and railway flourished:

	Tilmanstone Output	Rail Tonnage
1915	41,546 tons	15,886 tons
1916	103,040 tons	70,896 tons
1917	135,350 tons	132,275 tons
1918	129,600 tons	129,604 tons

Tilmanstone's success was attracting ambitious speculators and shrewd businessmen. Richard Tilden Smith was Australian and a banker and had already made one fortune. Before he was 21 he owned five million acres of land in Australia and a 75,000 herd of cattle. He had also mined gold in South Africa and coal in the highly successful South Maitland Colliery in New South Wales.

In 1893, a bank crisis had dramatically reduced his assets and he set out for Europe

Richard Tilden Smith

to seek a second fortune. He became a founder-member of the British Bank of Northern Commerce, which would later amalgamate with Hambros Bank. When he arrived in England, Smith took a keen interest in the Kent Coalfield. He joined Arthur Burr in his Kent Collieries Company, which owned the Shakespeare Colliery, and he positively assessed the potential of the coal deposits lying beneath Kent. Simultaneously, he pursued other initiatives – a colliery near Swansea in South Wales and a nearby spelter works,[32] which produced zinc. He had earlier reopened old mine workings at Namtu, Burma,[33] serving on the board beside Herbert Hoover, soon to become President of the United States. While working with Authur Burr in 1904, Tilden Smith had unsuccessfully tried to buy the Tilmanstone Colliery. He now sold his shares in South

[32] Spelter – with copper an important constituent of brass
[33] Now Myanmar

Wales and Burma and formed the National Metal and Chemical Bank. Through a Trust, he bought shares in the East Kent Colliery Company. He had identified his prime target: the Kent Coalfield. He forced the Colliery Company into liquidation, became interim general manager of Tilmanstone and immediately set about reconstructing the colliery.

For all his faults, Authur Burr had been the lynchpin of the first phase of the development of the Kent Coalfield. Tilden Smith now assumed that role, his methods as different from Burr's as chalk is from cheese.

The 1920s began badly for the British coal industry. They also started badly for Tilden Smith and Tilmanstone. The Kent miners had been on strike over pay and now there was a dispute over whether an engine man had fallen asleep on duty. Tilden Smith immediately faced negotiations with a disgruntled workforce. He laid out the facts as he saw them – currently Tilmanstone was not financially viable and he could not afford it. It was losing £100 a week. In 1924, a cut in the miners' wages led to a dispute and the temporary closure of the Tilmanstone and Chislet pits. In the end, the miners gave way and the Tilmanstone men went back to work on Tilden Smith's terms, much to the disgust of the Chislet miners.[34] Tilden Smith remarked that he 'did not regard the miners as his employees but as his associates'.

At this time, Tilmanstone was key to the success of the coalfield. The annual output at Tilmanstone in 1925 was 229,000 tons. This was 65% of the total output of the Kent Coalfield. Tilmanstone employed 854 miners – 41% of the Kent Coalfield labour force. Tilden Smith took stock and

---

[34] A History of the Kent Coalfield, Hilton, p36, p38

shared the strategic picture at a meeting with his workforce. First, he said, the price of producing a ton of Kent coal was 18 shillings 9 pence; the price of coal from other British pits was 16 shillings 4 pence – more than two shillings a ton cheaper. Second, at Tilmanstone in the three weeks running up to Christmas, the output had been 14,712 tons. It would have been 1,000 tons higher if Southern Railway had supplied enough trucks to carry the coal. Third, the distance to London was 74 miles; the distance to Dover 9 miles. Economies, he told his workforce, must be made in the transport of Kent coal. It must become more efficient. There was no reason why Tilmanstone should not be profitable if miner and mine owner could work together.

Nationally, in 1925, the relationship between miner and mine owner could hardly have been worse. It was only eight years since the Russian Revolution, and there were many in Whitehall who feared that, as the British workforce asserted itself, with the miners leading the way, this was the beginning of a British revolutionary movement.

Tilden Smith saw the rise of communism in Russia and listened as the Kent miners praised and compared the conditions there with those they experienced in Kent. He chose two miners, one of them a convinced communist, and invited the local schoolmaster to accompany them on a fact-finding tour to Moscow. The three men went, unannounced, and visited the Russian coal miners. When they returned, at a meeting held to hear their findings, the miners declared 'there would be hell to pay' if British miners had to work in the conditions they had seen in Soviet Russia. Tilden Smith also offered free passage to any other miner and his family who might wish to go to work in the Soviet Union.

Overhead Coal Aerial Ropeway

There were no takers.

To increase efficiency, Tilden Smith then embarked on one of the most curious examples of mechanisation in the history of the Kent Coalfield; he decided to link Tilmanstone Colliery directly with the vessels waiting to be fed with coal in the port of Dover, a distance of seven and a half miles. He would do so with an overhead ropeway. In 1926, the General Strike was declared and Britain came to a standstill. Tilden Smith coped with the withdrawal of labour in his own way[35] and continued to refine his plans for Kent's overhead ropeway. In September 1926, he applied to the Dover Council for permission to go ahead with his scheme. They prevaricated. Southern Railway opposed the ropeway because it would deprive them of business. Dover Harbour Board was less than supportive. Tilden Smith pressed ahead; he had calculated that, not only would coal be transported from Kent more efficiently, but the ropeway could also be profitable if used by others. The cost, he calculated, of getting

---

[35] Tilden Smith contributed £100 every week to provide food for the miners' wives and children

a ton of coal to Dover on the ropeway would be 1 shilling and 9 pence a ton. He would be charging Dover Harbour Board 5 shillings and 9 pence a ton, matching the figure that the Southern Railway charged the port to transport his coal to the dockside. At a Public Inquiry, the Dover Harbour Board eventually backed Tilden Smith's proposal and work began on the ropeway. It would be 12,300 yards long, with 585 buckets, and would transfer 267 tons of coal every hour. The ropeway would be supported by 177 concrete trestles, 30 feet high and 75 yards apart, each weighing 3½ tons. It would cross 15 roads and two railways, each road crossing protected by 100 foot-long bridges. The whole operation would be driven by a 200 horsepower Robey engine, and the speed of travel was 4¼ miles an hour. The ropeway would be finished by January 1930. And so it was.

But, on December 18th 1929, Richard Tilden Smith died suddenly. He was in the House of Commons, pursuing his long-held belief that all collieries in Britain should be amalgamated into a single 'coal board' which would enable the industry to speak, powerfully, with a single voice, and would ensure its independence. It had been a good meeting. As the group left for lunch, Tilden Smith collapsed and died on the steps of the House of Commons. He was 64.

But the overhead aerial ropeway was complete. It now straddled the Kent countryside for seven miles, crossing green fields and hop gardens, before sliding through two tunnels and arriving dockside at Dover. Tilden Smith had at least seen the opening of the first stage of his ropeway three months earlier, in October 1929, when guests travelled in the hoist buckets the short distance from Tilmanstone to Pineham. The formal opening ceremony took place on February 14th 1930,

Tilmanstone Miners 1947

three months after his death, when Tilden Smith's eldest daughter, Mrs Pip Eldridge, officially started the ropeway. It was a quiet affair.

The first ship to be loaded with Tilmanstone coal was the *Corminster.* The hoist buckets emptied their loads into the hopper at the Dover quayside and, from that, the coal was dropped directly into the vessel. The consignment was bound for Barking Power Station.[36]

Tilden Smith was a key figure in the history of the Kent Coalfield. He also made a significant and far-sighted contribution to the national debate on coal and coal mining. He carried the voice and needs of Kent to Westminster. He thought strategically about communities for the miners who worked for and with him; he had just overseen the building of another 100 houses in the village of Elvington when he died. It is very possible that his plans would have seen the

---

[36] The aerial ropeway operated until 1939 when it became vulnerable to enemy air raids. It wasn't dismantled until 1952. Parts of it are believed to have been sold to a company in India

industrialisation of Kent and the immediate growth of the port of Dover into one of the largest ports in Europe.[37] But he died at the very moment the debate over the future of the Kent Coalfield became a national issue. The Baldwin government had recognised the potential of the billions of tons of coal now confirmed in Kent; the coalfield was closer to London by far than any other coalfield, and coal in the 20th Century was the prime source of power sustaining Britain's economy and political ambitions.

Westminster decided it was time to give priority to the future of Kent. Would it remain predominantly a place of peace and tranquillity, its orchards and hop gardens undisturbed? Or would it become a new Black Country, part of the industrial impetus that would drive Britain and its Empire for the remaining years of the 20th Century? The debate would make startling progress in this critical year, 1926.

[37] Those Dirty Miners, JP Hollingsworth, p95

East Kent Planning Scheme, containing Sir Patrick Abercrombie's credo

CHAPTER FOUR
The Great Experiment

*"If we survey the whole of England,
there is no portion of it more abundant,
or more calculated to captivate the eye,
than the county of Kent."*
WH Ireland, 1818

The two books look frail and battered now as they lie on the desk. Like the hands of an old man, they bear the marks of ageing, in stain and blemish. As books go, they are not big – more ledger than tome. Even their title is mundane: *East Kent Regional Planning Scheme*. But their combined 180 pages foreshadowed 'a crisis in Kent's history'.[38]

In July 1926, Britain was still emerging from the effects of a nationwide General Strike. It had officially ended on May 12th but many trade unionists had not gone back to work, including the Kent miners who would fight on for many months. It was in this febrile atmosphere that the East Kent Regional Planning Scheme was launched at Canterbury Cathedral, on July 24th, at the invitation of the then Dean of Canterbury, George Bell. Bell was an inspirational Dean, believing that the church's voice should be heard giving

---

[38] Neville Chamberlain, Canterbury Cathedral, July 24th 1926

spiritual leadership on temporal matters. During his four years at Canterbury, he would initiate the Canterbury Festival of Arts, welcome Mahatma Ghandi, reach out to other religions and, later, as Bishop of Chichester, oppose the blanket bombing of Germany in World War Two, much to the annoyance of Winston Churchill.

In 1926, then, it was wholly natural that he should involve himself in this major social initiative and offer the Cathedral and Deanery to accommodate such a seminal conference on the future of Kent.

The keynote speaker was Neville Chamberlain, then Minister of Health, soon to be Britain's Prime Minister. Chamberlain was a businessman and a shrewd politician; he knew that the message he was about to deliver to the great and the good of Kent was tricky. His task was to convince the assembled audience that a future as a new Black Country would be good for them.

He ended his speech with these key sentences:

"It is a very interesting experiment you are all engaged upon…it will be watched critically by many who come from the Continent…and from further afield. I believe you realise the responsibility which lies upon you. I feel confident that, with goodwill, perseverance, patience and persistence…you will succeed in showing England and the world what we can do."

Chamberlain was asking Kent, the Garden of England, to prepare for the arrival of 18 coal mines, eight new towns and an unspecified number of ironworks in the next decade. This, in a county with no industrial heritage nor expertise, and an economy based firmly and traditionally on agriculture and horticulture. Chamberlain started his speech cautiously.

He concentrated on his portfolio as Minister of Health. It was necessary, he said, to avoid the errors of previous generations who had created slums through lack of planning, and had 'jammed together' so tightly 'houses mixed between factories and railway embankments, with high walls shutting out light and air'. Generations of children in Britain's towns had 'stunted physiques...deprived as they are of fresh air and sunlight'. Britain, he said, was due 'an awakening...if only we have the will, we have got the power to control our development'. He argued at length the value of regional and strategic planning; he condemned the haphazard development of the past. Then he spelled out the advantages Kent possessed and the risk that the county was now facing.[39] He recalled his train journey from London to Canterbury that morning:

"As I looked out of the windows...and gazed upon all that wealth of orchards, and flowers, and fruit, and woods; and then, as I came into this wonderful, ancient city, with its marvellous buildings and all its historical associations with the early days of our race, I could not help thinking to myself: 'Here, in this Garden of England, we possess an inestimable treasure – something unparalleled, not merely in this country, but in the whole world, something which, if it once were destroyed, never, never could be replaced; but which yet might be destroyed, as surely and as certainly as if we were overwhelmed by some great catastrophe, some earthquake or some eruption.

"We are, ladies and gentlemen, in the presence of a threat. I fancy that when, years ago, it was first bruited about that there was coal in Kent, a good many hearts sank. A great many people who, perhaps, had seen what had happened to

---

[39] Ibid

some of the most beautiful valleys in Wales, to great stretches of land in Yorkshire, to the Black Country from which I come, and to many other parts of the country asked: is that to be sacrificed to the march of commercialism?"

Chamberlain had recently visited Wales where miners were 'a people by themselves…with nothing to think about but mines…and nothing to do in (their) leisure time'. He said:

"The development which is suggested here in East Kent is something different from that. You are getting away, on the one hand, from that straggling kind of development to which I have alluded; and, on the other hand, from those pit-head villages which I think are such an unfortunate feature of many of our mining areas. You are proposing a series of towns which are not to be at the pit-heads, but which are, nevertheless, near enough to serve them; and you can give the miners who will occupy these towns a social life of a far fuller, wider and more interesting character than they can ever hope to get in those mining villages in Wales."[40]

A report accompanied Chamberlain's speech, published by PD Estates and Co Ltd, a Canterbury printer (price 6 pence, post free) gave precise details of the plan. It said:

'There is no need to enlarge on the importance of this part of Kent as a piece of typically beautiful English country and as the scene of many of the most epoch-making events of our history. The Roman remains are numerous and striking, Richborough Castle (Rutupiae) being one of the most impressive in the country. Canterbury and its Cathedral are the natural metropolis in every sense of the region, as well as being the ecclesiastic metropolitan of England. Scarcely less interesting are the two Cinque Ports of Dover and

---

[40] Ibid, p10

Sandwich – the former with its castle, the real gateway to England from the Continent; the latter an almost perfectly-preserved market town. There are also a series of old villages as completely English as can anywhere be found, parklands of unrivalled beauty, and the white chalk cliffs of the coastal scenery, on which are placed many of the most famed seaside towns in the world. This countryside, moreover, is redolent of the two authors that epitomise old England – Dickens and Barham, of the Ingoldsby Legends.

'Into this quiet countryside has been suddenly dropped the disturbing element of coal, with the special significance of coal within 60 miles of London. Under these chalk downs lies a coalfield which has hitherto been concealed, seeing that nowhere do the coal measures outcrop.'

The report then named four pits, including the infant Betteshanger Colliery, whose first shaft had been sunk in 1924 but where the first seam of coal would not be reached until 1927:

1. Chislet, near the northern outcrop, worked by the Chislet Colliery Co., Ltd;
2. Snowdown, on the main line from Canterbury to Dover, worked by Messrs Pearson & Dorman Long, Ltd;
3. Betteshanger, to the west of Deal (not yet productive), worked by Messrs Pearson & Dorman Long, Ltd;
4. Tilmanstone, the first pit continuously to produce coal, worked by the Tilmanstone (Kent) Collieries, Ltd.

'In addition to these, there will be probably 14 other pitheads; 10 out of the 18 will be situated in the Rural District of Eastry, and these will be among the earliest to be worked. Although coal was first discovered on the southern extremity of the region near Dover, the easiest worked seams of coal are from the middle, northwards. A comparison of coals of similar analyses elsewhere shows that the Kent seams are equal or superior to the corresponding qualities in South Wales, Yorkshire and Lancashire.'

It assessed the potential of the pits that would be involved in this new coal-related traffic, and the steelworks that would be built close by. The report continued: 'The ultimate destination of the coal, whether it is to be converted into electric power in Kent and transmitted by cable to London, or reduced by low carbonisation process to a smokeless fuel, or shipped raw to London and abroad, is by no means settled as yet. With this is bound up the question of the port or ports. Dover, with increased siding accommodation, is the natural outlet for Continental and foreign purposes. Richborough, the wartime mystery port, suggests itself as suitable for barge traffic to cross the Channel and penetrate the canals of Northern France and Flanders. There is also the possibility of reviving the Roman port of Reculver, near Herne Bay. This would entail opening up the old channel of the River Wantsum by means of a canal which could be made accessible to a large number of pits, and from which it would be possible to ship coal direct to London by river barge without the necessity of rounding the North Foreland.

'The most suitable place for the blast furnaces and steel works is also bound up with the choice of a port, which is necessary not only for exporting the finished steel, but for importing the foreign ores necessary to mix with the native ores.'

Lastly, it looked at the growth in population which would be needed to serve this industrial development, and the new towns that would be built to accommodate it (see Appendix). The population of East Kent in 1926 was about 300,000, living mainly in Canterbury and the seaside towns. New

Sir Patrick Abercrombie

industry would 'within 30 years produce an additional population of about 280,000 people'. These 'new' people would not be 'scattered (about) the region in a series of housing schemes attached to pits and factories' or in ribbon developments along the main roads. They would be grouped in 'eight or nine new towns, of which the largest would be about 36,000 inhabitants (the size of Folkestone or Ramsgate), four towns of about 25,000 (rather larger than Canterbury) and three of 12,000 (about the size of Deal)'. The first would be called Aylesham, designed to serve two pits – Snowdown Colliery and another pit to be sunk near Adisham.

In nine short pages the blueprint for the future of East Kent was set out. It promised disruption but also prosperity and a complete change in the characteristics of the community. The author of the East Kent Scheme and the man chosen to give substance to this dream was Professor Leslie Patrick Abercrombie, from the Department of Civic Design at the University of Liverpool.

Patrick Abercrombie was 47 when he was given charge of this 'great experiment'[41] in Kent. He was the ninth child of a Manchester businessman, educated at Uppingham and, as a youngster, interested in music and geology. He had only one eye, having lost the other during a bout of diphtheria in his teens. He had a privileged upbringing but had experienced relative poverty when his father's business career faltered.[42] He was 'an old-fashioned liberal...he cared about people'.[43] He cut an imposing figure: monocled, urgent in speech, with a thin, reedy voice. He was articled to a Manchester architect from whom, he said, he learned nothing. Yet it can be argued that Patrick Abercrombie, first at Doncaster and then in Kent, invented and inspired strategic regional planning in Britain. He would later describe the East Kent plan as 'the most challenging' he ever had – and given the brief handed to him by Neville Chamberlain that day in Canterbury, with the sociological uproar that he feared, it is easy to understand why. Given his interest in geology, Abercrombie understood that flexibility would be necessary in any plan he drew up. For a quarter of a century, boreholes had been dug over much of East Kent in the hunt for coal.[44] As long ago as 1858, Godwin-Austen had traced a great anticline[45] across the South of England from Pembroke in South Wales across the Mendips, past Maidstone, along the North Downs towards Folkestone, into France at Cap Gris Nez and along the hills of Artois. It was a buried mountain range and, from experience, coal

---

[41] Neville Chamberlain, Canterbury Cathedral, July 24th 1926
[42] Professor Gerald Dix, conversation with author, 2018
[43] Ibid
[44] Map of Boreholes, see Appendix
[45] Science Progress, 1908, p379

should be found nearby. By 1926, the coalfields of South Wales and Northern France were providing the motive power for rapid industrialisation and all the evidence was that, here in Kent, lay the missing link in a chain of coal that ran from the West of Britain under the English Channel, and into the Nord Pas de Calais.

One of Abercrombie's challenges was to try to second guess the sites of the 18 pits that Chamberlain forecast. He knew that Chislet and Tilmanstone, Snowdown and the infant Betteshanger already had commercial investment behind them – but, the other 14 pits might be sunk inland near Maidstone or near the coast at Deal, to the north of the county around Sandwich or Thanet, or to the south, towards Dover.

Nine months before, in an article on Town Planning, he had outlined the dilemma that had faced him as he thought about the task ahead: "Which part of the Garden of England is to be disturbed, and the answer is clear. A line drawn from the coast north-east of Deal to Blean Woods near Sturry, and then turning south by east to the coast just east of Folkestone, will include the coal deposits of Kent. Dover, Walmer, Deal and Sandwich are included, but Canterbury may slumber in peace, and the clean pure air of Thanet need lose none of its ozone. Alas, however, for charming medieval Sandwich, loved of artists. Every effort must be made to keep Sandwich uncontaminated by lust for coal.

"Some 28 borings out of 39 have revealed workable coal, and it is thought that 18 pits may develop into useful mines. At the present time, those at Tilmanstone, Chislet, and Snowdown, between them produce nearly 5,000 tons weekly, and it is calculated that the whole field may last four centuries, and produce six thousand million tons of coal."[46]

He pointed out that iron ore had also been found and that 'a like calculation (showed that) in a century 30 million tons of metal could be produced.' With coal and iron ore (see Appendix) on the spot, he said, it was "inconceivable but that many other industries will not find their way to East Kent".[47] He revealed the mathematics involved in the challenge of planning for 18 pits each employing 2500 men.

"These men will bring their families, so that, reckoning four to a family, there will be a mining population of 10,000 on the average around the pit, i.e. 180,000 in the district, besides perhaps 20,000 working in iron and steel. Moreover, a large ancillary population always follows in the wake of industrial development to supply their various needs, and this, in the opinion of the writers, will increase the mining population by 70,000 thus bringing 250,000 newcomers to East Kent; besides the iron and steel workers and their followers, another 27,000. The present population of the region being 300,000, it will thus be nearly doubled when the pits and furnaces are in full work, not to mention the natural growth of the population, which in thirty years may be 100,000. Indeed, it may well be that by 1955 or 1960 no less than 700,000 will occupy the space now held by 300,000."[48]

In the eight new towns that would be necessary to accommodate them, he suggested a ratio of 12 houses or 60 persons to the acre. He reflected: "Most of the mining towns and villages of this country grew almost by accident and are suffering today from a lack of vision in those who founded or

[46] East Kent Regional Plan, Patrick Abercrombie and John Archibald, 1925
[47] Article Garden Cities and Town Planning, PS King and Sons, October 1925
[48] Ibid

enlarged them...Never previously in our long island story has it been given to one generation to plan the erection of eight new towns in a single county..."[49]

Abercrombie used instinct and his core beliefs to match the challenge he faced – which is probably a major reason he was entrusted with the job. Planning, he wrote,

Professor Gerald Dix

'simply means proposing (a course of action) and then doing it, following it through in an orderly, related and rational way, having in view an end that is expected to be beneficial'.[50] He believed in small towns, new communities for the miners. If the miners had to travel further to work, it was a small price for them to pay relative to the community benefits that they and their families would experience. 'Town Planning', he said, 'should offer a guiding hand to the trend of natural evolution...as a result of careful study of the place itself and its external relationships.[51] Planning was 'more than... structural engineering, or satisfactory hygiene or successful economics'. The result should be 'a social organism and a work of art'.[52] East Kent was his canvas. His priority in his

[49] Ibid
[50] Patrick Geddes, town planner, writing to his daughter, September 1922
[51] Abercrombie, Town and Country Planning
[52] Ibid

new towns would be better housing, shops, schools and open spaces, better access for the miner to his work, better views of the unspoiled countryside to enjoy as a miner and his family strolled through the streets of the towns he would build.

He outlined the first new town, Aylesham. Abercrombie's curriculum vitae qualified him to face the task ahead with confidence. He had already designed a small 'workstown' near Redcar called Dormanstown. He had designed the village of Kirk Sandall for Pilkington Brothers, the renowned glassmakers.[53] With Henry Johnson, he had, in 1922, drawn up a regional plan for the Doncaster area, covering 169 square miles, for a population of 139,940. It was Britain's first, comprehensive regional plan, creating a template for those who would follow, for there was no national policy for new-town planning. Abercrombie's strategic thinking would lead his assistant and colleague, Professor Gerald Dix, to describe him as 'the world's foremost prophet and practitioner of town and country planning'.[54] The profession's trade publication, *The Architect*, described his Doncaster plan as 'a model of the manner in which, if applied to other districts in the course of development, would enable (Britain) to avoid the errors of the past and leave our successors an infinitely better country'.

Abercrombie applied his beliefs to his plan for Kent. If any of the 16 regional schemes, which were written in Britain between 1923 and 1935, can be said to mark a major step forward, it was that which Abercrombie prepared for East Kent.[55] It would not seek to improve an area largely

[53] Pilkington Brothers Garden Village Ventures, by Barbara R Penny, University of Liverpool, July 1976
[54] Pioneers of British Planning, by Gordon E Cherry, chapter by Gerald Dix, p103
[55] Ibid, p109

spoiled by industry, or one that was derelict; it would instead try to avoid the destruction of a region untouched by industrialisation. It was to be 'preventative medicine rather than surgery'.[56] His strategy was to concentrate on carefully-placed developments, allied to a stout defence of the green spaces in-between. Only in this way could the ambition of the coal industry be reconciled with a proper consideration of the landscape. He observed in the East Kent Planning Scheme survey:

'Of course, the rural seclusion of East Kent must go – but this has largely departed already…the peaceful lanes are already penetrated by the charabanc and the main roads are served by the regular motor bus…(the discovery of coal and iron) is the biggest happening in England of this quarter-century. Kent is not Durham or Lancashire or Glamorgan – distant spots glamoured in gloom; it is in the eye of the world…at London's door, and not at the back door either…Kent could supply four times the present amount of power used in London and still have enough for local industries as well.'[57]

In preparing his plan for the future, Abercrombie examined every aspect of life in East Kent, natural features such as rainfall and topography, the ports, the population, existing communications by road and rail, open spaces, water supplies, electric power, social and educational considerations, the arts and community activities, even smallholdings and allotments. He worked closely with John Archibald, surveyor to the local Eastry Rural District Council, co-author of the survey, and with Frederick Cloke, the council's clerk and partner in Cloke

---

[56] Ibid, p109
[57] East Kent Regional Planning Scheme, 1925, pp xx, xxi

and Tucker, solicitors in Sandwich and known locally as 'Cloak and Dagger'. Fred Cloke acted as Abercrombie's clerk when he worked in Kent and Abercrombie stayed with the Clokes at their home, the Long House, near the river in Sandwich.[58] As always, Abercrombie immersed himself in his work. He suggested a need for a Kent university. He assessed, as far as he could, the potential of the existing coal industry in Kent. Then, he laid out the plan – including the likely position of the coal mines which would depend not only on the natural topography but also on commercial considerations such as the appetite for Kent coal and the determination of investors to pursue the seams currently being explored. Thus far, 39 boreholes had been driven into the East Kent landscape, from Pluckley and Brabourne in the west to Mattice Hill, Sandwich; from Canterbury and Bishopsbourne in the north to Dover and Folkestone.[59]

Abercrombie produced a map of the 18 pits that were planned, neatly identified alphabetically A to R. It also showed the probable extent of the iron deposits, overlaid on the anticipated shape of 'the economic coalfield'.[60] He 'zoned the county into three sections – a low-lying zone unsuitable for housing; a neutral zone, where housing should be placed on higher ground; and an agricultural zone, which could be 'transferred to residential use'.[61] He identified the sites of the

[58] David Steed, grandson of Frederick Cloke, conversation with author. Frederick Cloke was awarded the OBE in the 1929 Honours List, Civil Section

[59] Boreholes listed Ibid p30 and in Appendix, East Kent Regional Planning Scheme, map, etc

[60] Map plate ii, facing page 22 and xiii facing page 28, on pages 22 and 28 of the East Kent Survey

[61] Plate xxxii, facing p92, East Kent Survey

eight new towns, allocated each a population, and estimated the acreage needed:

Chislet	8,000	133⅓ acres
New Littlebourne	12,000	216⅔ acres
New Wingham	20,000	458⅔ acres
Ham (near Sandwich)	31,000	600 acres
Nonington	20,000	350 acres
Martin Hill	20,000	400 acres
Shepherdswell	24,000	483⅔ acres

Eight new towns, requiring 2,842 acres of Kent countryside. Abercrombie declared: 'These new towns, planned from the first with some idea of their ultimate size, should not exhibit the makeshifts and meanness of scale of the old places which have had greatness thrust upon them. Civic centres, shopping areas, local open spaces, school sites etc, can all be located with confidence, and on an ample scale…the best skills should be used to plan these towns'.[62] He assumed that in five years' time, five pits would be active – Chislet and Tilmanstone, Snowdown and Betteshanger, and Guilford. He calculated a need for 10,000 houses in the next five years.[63] He acknowledged his ambitions for this Kent plan were high but they were also realistic:

'…there is no excuse for the monstrous ugliness of certain standard houses which have been illustrated of late. Well-proportioned windows and doors cost no

---

[62] Ibid, pp73–76
[63] Ibid, p83

more than ill-proportioned ones; and a little thought and architectural knowledge in the spacing of these features will make all the difference between repeated houses which plumb the depths of ignobility and the quiet interest and charm such as is found in the Georgian parts of our old towns and villages'.[64]

Two years later, Patrick Abercrombie wrote a progress report. Sadly, he reflected that, as so often happens, progress did not match his expectations. 'It would have been attractive', he wrote in 1926, 'to have shown...plans for all the new towns as approved...but progress has not been sufficiently rapid...only one of the completely new towns has been actually located and begun, namely Aylesham...and two existing communities, Chislet and Elvington, have been added to'. But Aylesham was taking shape. The first 402 houses were complete, a further 100 in the course of construction on a semi-circular road in a conurbation that echoed the wheel at the pithead of every colliery. The houses grouped around 'a shopping square'. The dwellings had two or three bedrooms with a bathroom upstairs or, predominantly, downstairs, each with a living room and most with a parlour. The housing, he said, had a 'faint Flemish flavour...characteristic of houses built in the district in the late 17th and early 18th Century.' There was a railway station, three churches or chapels, a pub and plans for an open air market where a space had been left at the centre of the town.[65] The reasons for these frustrating delays involved personalities as much as any lack of determination.

---

[64] East Kent Survey, p84
[65] Abercrombie's original plan for Aylesham. See plate facing page 50 Final Report, East Kent Regional Planning Scheme, 1928

Lord Milner who had championed the Kent plan, and to whom Abercrombie acknowledged 'an incalculable debt', died suddenly as did a number of other leading members of the joint planning committee. It affected the impetus of the scheme, momentum was lost and Aylesham, the first of the eight new towns, would never be completed in Abercrombie's vision. Industrial unrest, economic difficulties and another World War would see to that.

Abercrombie went on in years ahead to be entrusted with some of the most important planning briefs in Britain – the rebuilding of the blitzed cities of London, Plymouth and Hull. Gerald Dix, who would work with Abercrombie in his later life, identifies a strong strand of realism in his approach to planning. "I worked for him on a major project in Addis Ababa, and his plans in the city were much praised. As we walked up the steps of one of the great buildings, a senior official confided in him: 'It is marvellous but I doubt if it will all be carried out. Maybe 20 percent…' Pat (Abercrombie) turned round straight away and said: 'Twenty percent, ten percent, that would be quite good really'. Pat was a pragmatist…"[66]

Dix sums up his character thus: "Shrewd, caring, thorough, sometimes autocratic – but a visionary. He was one of the best architectural draughtsmen of his day. The responsibility he took, post-war, in planning the rebirth of London, Plymouth and Hull, and his advocacy for the Council for the Preservation of Rural England, indicate the dedication he had for his chosen profession. When he died in 1957, he had probably done more for planning than anyone else of his time. No-one else had the same

---

[66] Conversation with author, 2017

breadth of professional versatility and competence. Clough Williams-Ellis described Abercrombie as 'a genial wizard'."

Patrick Abercrombie may have had only one eye, but that eye didn't miss much…

CHAPTER FIVE
The Gibbs and Scotland

*"Pressure is working down the pit;
pressure is having no work at all.
Pressure is not the Cup Final. That's
the reward."*
Bill Shankly, football manager

Louie and George Gibb are churchgoers. At the heart of the Christian doctrine lies the instruction to 'love thy neighbour as thyself', not simply the family next door but everyone else in the world. Challenging though that is, Louise and George do their best and they certainly love each other.

*Gibb Family gathered for George and Louie's
70th wedding anniversary*

The Roundhouse, Bowhill – favoured by 'The Body Snatchers' Burke And Hare

Their bungalow is in Mill Hill, a suburb of what was the fishing village of Deal when George first came to Kent from Scotland in 1928. He was two years old and, in all, there were 17 Gibbs in three families who made the journey south – George's grandfather and grandmother, three brothers, their wives and two daughters – and George.

The mechanics of this mass exodus of the Gibb family from Scotland were simple. The manager of the Kent Coalfield was Scottish and, as he needed to recruit miners, he turned first to those he knew in Scotland. He wrote to George's grandfather, George Birrell Gibb, and invited him and his sons to 'help open up the coal seams'. It was a new opportunity, and a new challenge, and grandfather George accepted it on behalf of the entire family.[67]

For the Gibbs, it must have been like emigrating to the other side of the world. None of them had ever crossed the Scottish border before. They were a Fife family, tucked away on the north-east coast of Scotland, locked into a tradition of sons following fathers into the crowded cages for the long drop down to the coalface to earn a living.

---

[67] George Birrell Gibb when working in Betteshanger was awarded the British Empire Medal in 1942 for his services to the mining industry

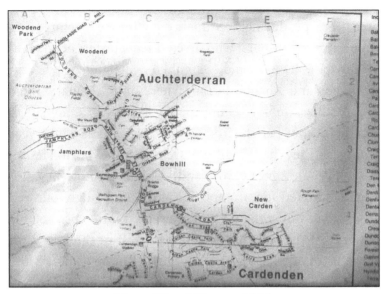

Map of Bowhill area, 1920s

An ancient lease tells us that the first miners in West Fife, in 1291, were monks in the local monastery. The first mine shaft was dug in the 1600s. The only other industry in the area was salt production. Until 1799, the salters and the miners were virtually slaves to the mine owners. Certainly, they were bonded men who were contracted to the mine owners and they were pursued and harassed to return to work if they tried to escape from the bondage. The relationship between the miner and mine owner, then, was uneasy, more so even than across the border in England.[68]

The Gibbs lived close to the pit where they worked, Bowhill in Fife.[69] By the mid-1800s, scores of mines in the

---

[68] The Scottish Act of Parliament of 1799 served to release the men from their bondage. Ironically, the mine owners were instrumental in driving the Act through Parliament as they saw the price of coal dropping and wished to renegotiate lower working terms and conditions, to increase their profits

[69] One of the most remarkable buildings in Bowhill was the Roundhouse

area were producing top quality coking coal, employing thousands of miners who lived in a cluster of villages – Bowhill, Dundonald, Jamphlars, Balgreggie, Cluny, Lochgelly and Auchterderran, where on 4th January 1864, grandfather George Gibb married Sarah Campbell in Auchterderran Parish Kirk. George was 24, his wife a year younger. They had four children, George born (1900), Hugh (1904), Agnes (1907) and Uphiam (1909). They also had an adopted son, Campbell. George and Hugh followed their father down the pit and life settled into a predictable pattern. At the start of the century, most of the houses in this cluster of villages were built by the mine owners – the Bowhill Coal Company and the Fife Coal Company. Many were as alike as peas in a pod – single storey, one room, a kitchen, a scullery and an outside toilet.

The main street of Bowhill was crossed by a railway line from the colliery, noisily accommodating the thousands of trucks that came to bear away the coal torn from the hills of Fife.

Beside it, ran the River Ore. Here, generations of boys and girls were taught to swim using bunches of reeds for buoyancy. They did so in pools created by blocking the running water with what became known as 'dookie dams'. There were four of them – Wallace and Glen dams to the east of the road bridge, Coos Dip and Brighills to the west. Going for a swim became 'going for a dook'. The water was icy and hardly crystal clear. Those who swam in it risked contracting ringworm. But, together, the children learned to swim.

(pictured opposite). Once a tollhouse it was used by the infamous body-snatchers, Burke and Hare, as a store for the bodies they had exhumed from graves on the way to Edinburgh hospitals for dissection

This was a community determined to survive. Later, in the 1920s and 1930s, every worker would volunteer to deduct one penny, every week, from their wages, to build a proper swimming pool. There would be cinemas in the town, three of them, where you could pay for a seat with an empty jam jar which would then be recycled, and there would be dances on a Saturday night. Every village would have its own football team and there would be leagues of men who played quoits competitively.

The whole world, it seemed, was at play – at least, that part of the world that could afford it. Flappers flapped, Lindbergh flew across the Atlantic and Marlene Dietrich dispensed glamour and mystery in the talking pictures. The Prince of Wales who would become Britain's uncrowned King, partied harder than the next man – and the crowds adored him as a 'prince for the people'.

But, in Bowhill in the 1920s, simple day-to-day pleasures were to be disturbed by industrial action that was to change the life of the Gibb family for ever. During World War One, Britain's miners had been state-controlled. They were still controlled by the state two years after the war ended but the Government then decided to hand that control back to the mine owners. The mine owners issued an ultimatum – that mining would continue only if miners accepted reduced wages. The miners refused. What followed in 1920/21 was either a strike or a lock-out, dependent on one's point of view. No miners or safety men went to work. The Fife mine owners tried to keep the pits viable and dry by employing scab workers. Hundreds of striking miners then marched on every pit, one by one. There were violent exchanges involving miners, scabs and the police. There were injuries on both sides. Miners were arrested as they slept, hauled from their beds in Cowdenbeath and Lochgelly. They were tried on public order offences and imprisoned for up to 12 months. Bus-loads of soldiers and marines poured into the two towns. A miner wrote to a friend:

'The West Fife mining communities were now under military occupation for the rest of the summer. Mass meetings and marches are banned.'

The miners' houses were built in rows, with grassed areas in-between, known as 'the backs', which were criss-crossed by the families' washing lines. The Gibbs lived in a street called Front Row. Living conditions became so bad that a concession that had been won earlier from school boards[70] to provide modest free meals for miners' school children during prolonged industrial stoppages, was again implemented, and was extended into the weekends. The mine owners flexed their muscles. They cut off the water supply to the miners' homes. Women and children trekked to The Old Institute, which had an independent water supply to fill their buckets and bowls. At Cardenden, Fife, a former pupil recalled how, in 1921:

"I used to get my dinner at school. You went down and got a penny roll in the morning. Then you got two slices of bread and a bowl of soup at dinner time, in the school playground. It was made at the school. When you came out of school – two slices of bread and jam. And on a Sunday you got a boiled egg, your mug of tea and a slice of bread or toast."

The community closed ranks. Local farmers, shopkeepers and other sympathisers gave the strikers food. Many of the men went poaching for rabbits and fish. Poultry and sheep

---

[70] Local education authorities from 1919

also went missing from some farms, although miners generally observed a code of honour whereby friendly and helpful farmers were not harassed. In addition to centralised kitchens, soup and meat were often cooked in scrubbed-out boilers in the scullery of miners' houses. Queues of hungry men, women and children waited their turn.

Mrs Galloway, who lived in the row of houses behind Cardenden School, made soup in her boiler and regularly handed it over the

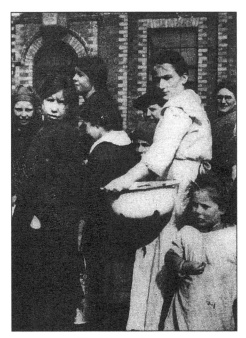

The Water Queue

There was no room for sentiment in 1921 as there was to be none in 1926. The dispute and lock-out of 1921 came as the conclusion to a growing period of restlessness within the coal industry when the coal owners flexed their muscles in an attempt to break the power of organised labour.

The picture shows the frequent ritual of fetching water when the water supply had been cut off from the miners' rows in Bowhill by the Fife Coal Company. Women and children mostly made the trek back and forth to the Old Institute with their pails and bowls. Along with Gammie Place, the Institute had a water supply independent of the coal owners

dyke to the children at dinner break. Kind gestures lightened the industrial storm. When a baby was born to a striker's wife, the local police often took round a parcel of food to the family. Farmers gave sacks of potatoes and other vegetables for the soup kitchens.

Ironically, the striking miners ran out of coal to warm their homes and stoke the scullery boilers. Some farmers had small old pits or outcrops of coal on their land and, through the union, they allowed the miners to dig the coal. The arrangement was called 'bag-a-boot' – one bag for the farmer, one for the soup kitchens, and one for the miner himself.

In July 1921, after months of penury and near starvation, the miners went back to work and this long-drawn-out industrial conflict ended. But the ill-feeling lingered on. Work was scarce. Many pits did not resume full production. Wages had been driven down below their pre-1914 level. Times were hard.

The Gibb family shared this experience. They had watched the funerals of those who had died in cold, ill-lit homes, as they wound their way behind coal-black horses through the village streets and on to the cemetery. Industrial strife had become a way of life.

The bitterness of the 1921 dispute served only to ensure that the arguments would be pursued again, and soon.

Nationally, the Miners' Federation had been calling for state ownership of the coal industry since the Sankey Commission had produced four conflicting reports in 1919. Sankey's advice was ignored. Instead, the Government offered the miners three concessions: a shared involvement in the daily management of the pits, a levy which would be spent on improved working and living conditions, and miners' representatives on Area Boards that would control the industry. But, crucially, the pits would remain in the mine owners' hands.

The Miners' Federation also rejected Sankey's proposal. So did the mine owners. With the profits from coal dropping, they declared they needed to make cuts in pay and increase working hours. In the next few years, union pressure for the nationalisation of the coal industry would grow. In the 1920s, it was only three years since revolution had rid Russia of the Czar and its ruling class. There were those, and not only in Whitehall, who saw 'revolution' in every move, every demand made by an increasingly vocal working class. The miners cried:

'Not a penny off the pay
Not a second off the day'

It was also a slogan that within four years would lead them into the General Strike of 1926. That strike lasted nine days from May 3rd until May 12th. It was called by the Trades Union Congress in an attempt to force the British Government to stop the mine owners reducing miners' wages, and to encourage them to improve the miners' working and living conditions. It was unsuccessful.

Those bare facts fail properly to reflect the chasm that had developed between management and worker in the years leading up to 1926, or the determination of some miners, particularly in Wales and Scotland, to pursue their aims even if it prolonged the dispute.

Young miners were impatient with what they saw as the impotence of their leaders. But the greater, unifying force was the outrage they felt over the failure of the owners and the Government to recognise the justice of their claims. Much had happened in local politics in Scotland in the five years between 1921 and 1926. Many parish councils were now dominated by Labour or Communist candidates. At Wemyss, for instance, 13 out of 15 councillors were now of the Left; the remaining two were nominees of the mine owners.

Councillors felt that they now had a mandate to support their mining constituents. The Cooperative movement had made a huge contribution to feeding the miners and their families as the 1921 dispute dragged on. Labour and Co-operative candidates now stood against the Conservatives and Liberals. The Co-op, as it became familiarly known,[71] had extended debt for its customers, provided cheap food, and enabled its members to survive during this long-drawn-out collision between management and miners. In 1926, their generosity was about to be tested again. The General Strike collapsed within nine days. The railway unions, the transport unions, the printers and several others gave in; they signed agreements with management and the Government, admitting that the General Strike was 'a wrongful act'. But the miners fought on – for another nine months.

Cardenden, 1930s

[71] Cooperative shops had first opened in Britain in 1850

The prime task of any reporter is to put what they are seeing, sometimes what they're feeling, 'on the record'.[72] Living in Cardenden in the 1920s was a man of many talents – Joe Corrie – miner, writer, poet. Though he wrote articles for the local paper, the *Lochgelly Times*, it was his poetry and plays that led to TS Elliot describing him as 'the best Scots poet since Burns'. At 14, in 1908, Corrie had become a miner. Corrie wrote: 'My school days from the beginning were marred by poverty'. His father was an invalid and there was no other breadwinner in the family. He worked underground and at the pit top. He was an odd-job man, an all-rounder and he was a fierce advocate of miners' rights. On being a miner, he wrote 'The Image o' God', comparing the miner crawling below ground to an insect, watched by God from above:

Crawling aboot like a snail in the mud,
Covered with clammy blae,
Me, made after the image o God –
Jings! But it's laugheable, tae.

Howkin awa 'neath a mountain o stane,
Gaspin for want o air,
The sweat makin streams doon my bare back-banes,
And my knees aa hauckite and sair.

Strainin and cursin the hale shift through,
Half-starved, half-blin, half-mad,

---

[72] A favourite saying of journalist Martha Gellhorn, which became her credo. Gellhorn made her name as a war correspondent and was, for years, a mistress of Ernest Hemingway

And the gaffer he says, "Less dirt in that coal
Or ye go up the pit, my lad"

So I gie my life tae the Nimmo squad
For eicht and fower a day.
Me! Made after the image o God –
Jings! But it's laughable, tae.

In 1926 he wrote his best-known play, *In Time o' Strife*. The play told of three Cardenden families, the Smiths, the Baxters and the Pettigrews. Mrs Pettigrew starves to death during the play, sacrificing herself for her children. Her grief-stricken husband Willie turns to drink. "It was a work," said Corrie, "that reflected life as I saw it, with very little exaggeration."

Corrie formed a group of local amateur actors, The Bowhill Players. A member of the cast, Mrs King, remembers: "We travelled with *In Time o' Strife* every Friday and wherever we went we topped the bill." After some months they were spotted by Hugh Ogilvie, a Scottish theatre agent; this bunch of miners and miners' wives and families virtually became professional actors as they took their message all over Scotland. Mrs King continues: "It was a good life. I left school at 14 and worked in a warehouse near Dunfermline on embroidery machines. I earned 7s 6d a week. I joined the Players at 17. And when we were travelling, I earned £5 a week so I was able to pay for my 'digs', send money home and buy all my clothes. We toured Scotland and then ventured into the North of England but we had to 'Englify' the play in Newcastle. They still couldn't understand us.

"But they loved Joe. In Dunfermline, we played the Opera House – my goodness, what a crowd. They were even sitting on the roof."

The Players became a family – and it included Corrie's own family, his sister Violet, who worked in an ice cream parlour and his girlfriend, Agnes Beveridge. The message was political but it was also polished in performance. It changed lives. Margaret McLean, a Bowhill housewife and a mother of five joined Joe and toured with the company. Ned Murdoch, a leading union activist in the 1926 strike, had twice been sent to prison; he found acting 'an easier way of bringing what we felt to those who weren't necessarily sympathetic to what we were going through'.

In Time o' Strife ran for months, twice nightly, six days a week. It made Hugh Ogilvie a rich man. He confided that, in touring the play, he made twice as much money in one year as he did with his usual programmes of variety acts and pantomime.

Bowhill 1930s

And miner, Joe Corrie? He never went back to the mines but continued to write strikingly good poetry. Cast member, 'Misty' Thompson, remembers:

"Joe was more than a gentleman. He was a working-class man. Every man was his brother, every woman his sister. The higher-ups were nothing to him. All he was interested in was the life of a miner. He worked hard for them; he portrayed their life."

But like so many in the 1930s, Joe Corrie left Scotland to move south with his wife Mary and daughter Morag. He went to live in Surrey.[73]

George Gibb, now 92 and living with his wife Louisa ('Louie') in their bungalow in Deal, Kent, remembers nothing of those grim years in the 1920s. What he does recall are the stories his father told him of life throughout the 'twenties and in the aftermath of the General Strike – how the strike had begun with the unions at Conference on their feet to sing *The Red Flag*:

With heads uncovered swear we all
To bear it onward till we fall
Come dungeon dark or gallows grim
This song shall be our parting hymn

Yet the strike had lasted only nine days. The Trades Union Congress and major unions conceded that Stanley Baldwin's government could hold out longer than the workers. The short-lived strike which they described as 'a brilliant failure', was just that – a failure. Leaders of the Left claimed that there had

---

[73] In 1958, Joe Corrie returned to Fife, to Glenrothes. In 1967 he went to live with his daughter Morag in Edinburgh. He died there on November 13th 1968

never been a better example of labour solidarity. Politicians in the House of Commons and the House of Lords again stirred uneasily at what they saw as the potential for revolution. George Gibb recalls that his father, a strong man and a leader underground, recognised the increasing power of the miners' voice in the affairs of the nation, "but he was more concerned about putting bread on the table so that the family could survive," says George. "After the General Strike, and remember the miners in Scotland didn't go back for nine months, there was no guarantee that the mine owners would take all the men back.[74] The price of coal had dropped. The owners said they needed to make economies. They were offering reduced wages.[75] So when the letter came from Betteshanger in Kent it was a godsend in many ways. It was a huge step for the family to take but, after the months and years of struggle in Scotland, this was a chance for a fresh start."

George Gibb was born in Bowhill in 1926, the year of the General Strike. When the three Gibb families first moved to Kent, they lived together in an old farmhouse at the bottom of Marley Lane in Finglesham, which was about three quarters of a mile from the pit. The manager, Mr Beeton, was a good friend of George's grandfather and he paid for the families' journey by rail from Scotland to Kent.

"My father, Hugh Campbell Gibb, was a very hard man. Once he'd made his mind up, that was it. He gets the 'Campbell' from my grandfather, who was a Campbell. Soon after we arrived, my father went to sign on in the little village Welfare Club; it was a corrugated iron building and when he

---

[74] The strikers went back even though the Government stated it had '*no power to compel employers to take back every man who had been on strike*'
[75] Over seven years, miners' pay per week had reduced from roughly £6 to £3.90

got there, there was a chap sitting behind the desk collecting the money and writing down the details.

'Right' he said, 'What's your name?' Dad said: 'Hugh *Campbell* Gibb'. He said: '*Campbell* Gibb? You'll only become a member of this club over my dead body'. So my father said, 'That can be arranged'. And he turned over the table and there were fisticuffs.

"The man behind the table was a MacDonald. The Scots have got long memories – the Massacre of Glencoe and that. Anyway, my father joined the club."

Rivalries crossed racial barriers. Betteshanger was a cosmopolitan pit, mainly Welsh but large numbers of miners were from Scotland, Northumberland, Newcastle, Lancashire and Derbyshire. They used to say that, on a Saturday night, blood used to run down the streets of Mill Hill as scores were settled. George was five when he saw his father involved in the argument.

"One Saturday, five or six Scots fell out with the Welsh and it was decided they would meet on the Sunday morning to settle it. Now my father wasn't there. He was in bed with a cold. But somebody came to fetch him and he went over. By the time he arrived, there were about 20 or 30 Welshmen gathered and Father was the only other Scot. They nominated a gentleman called Phil Davies as their champion; he was a mountain fighter. Now, Father had had no part in the dispute but he accepted the challenge, one to one – until someone said that Phil Davies would need a second for this fight. My father said: 'No, just me and him'. So the fight came to nothing. I remember it well; I was proud that my father was the chosen champion. But, if the fight had happened, I don't think I would have wanted to be there."

George Gibb's childhood in the Garden of England is remembered as an uneventful series of routine engagements with authority at Deal Council School and in the community. He was a good pupil at the local school. He worked hard. He was also lucky; they were about to enter a local orchard to scrump apples and cherries when they encountered half a dozen farmers on a day's shooting. "We all bolted. They came to the hedge and shot at us. We could feel the pellets on our back but they didn't go through anything. You had to be quick…"

Like many mothers, Mrs Gibb didn't want George to follow his father into the pit. There was a baker in Mill Hill who was a Scot. When George left school at 14, he was given a job in the bakery. George helped bake the bread and delivered the fresh loaves on a stylish bicycle with a pannier on the front.

But in 1939, Britain declared war on Nazi Germany. Kent was now in the front line of a Europe-wide conflict which was nothing new for the community closest to Europe. A 20-mile military exclusion zone was created along the Kent coast and official papers were necessary to enter or leave that zone.

George's father was anxious for the safety of his family and sent his wife, three sisters and a brother back to Scotland to stay with friends and relatives. George and his father stayed in Kent but moved to his grandmother's home in Finglesham, where young George continued to work in the Deal bakery, pedalling the seven miles there and back every day.

"One day I said to my father, 'Look Dad, this is not on. I want to go down the pit'. The money was better and I just fancied it. So my father allowed me to apply and I got a job on the pit top because Mam didn't want me to go underground.

But the job was on the screens and it was the worst job I ever did – noise and dust and the metal sheeting clanging away as you picked the rocks out of the coal on the conveyor belts. You couldn't hear yourself speak. We used sign language. Hours after you finished shift, you couldn't hear properly because your ears were ringing. I stuck it for weeks. Then an overman came into the room and said he needed three lads for underground. My hand was the first to go up."

George Gibb was 15 years old. There were now 16 members of the Gibb family working underground. Because of the Scottish tradition of an eldest son taking his father's Christian name, four of them were named George Birrell Gibb – George's grandfather, uncle and cousin, in addition to himself. Which made for some confusion on pay day. With Britain now at war, George and his father stayed in Kent while his mother, brothers and sisters were despatched to the relative safety of Scotland. George's father was less than happy. On a visit to Bowhill to see his wife and family, he got a job at an airfield. He worked there for a week and he wanted to stay but, as George remembers, being a miner was a priority for a nation at war and George's father was directed back to his job in Kent. This time the family came too, and they returned to their old home in Mill Hill. They were together again "and," says George, "I remember how good that felt."

Kent was bombed throughout World War Two. The coal mines didn't escape. In 1941, young George was trapped underground for 18 hours when the Betteshanger pithead was struck by high explosive bombs. The fan house was destroyed so no fresh air could be circulated to the miners trapped 2000 feet below. The entire ventilating system was out of action. It was a Sunday morning and the shift had been whitewashing the steel rings that kept the diggings secure.

"We were so deep we didn't feel a tremor. But the lights went out. We thought we'd damaged the electric cables but we checked and it was obviously more serious than that. Anyway, some men eventually came along and said the Germans had bombed the pit and our best chance was to make for the pit bottom. So we scrambled to number 2 pit-bottom and we tried to make ourselves comfortable because the pump winding house was out of gear. There was a phone connection and we knew that men had been killed in the fan house and we couldn't get out. We got some rations – small tins of meat paste and hard biscuits and water. And we waited – 60 or 70 of us.

"Because the phones were intact, we knew they were trying to get us out. Eventually, they got an auxiliary motor over from Snowdown and they said they were going to try one more time to get us out. And it worked. There was a crowd at the top of the shaft. We'd been underground since six in the morning and now it was after midnight."[76]

Among the 70 men who shared the experience with young George was an older miner, Kent-born John Phyall. Within three years, young George would marry his daughter, Louisa.

Margaret Louisa Phyall, one of four children, was the second daughter of John and Maude Phyall. John Phyall, though born in Kent, was working in Wales when he had met Maude, a fellow miner's daughter, and he had cycled the 300 miles from South Wales to get a job in Kent. When the Phyalls had first arrived, they lived in huts in the pit

---

[76] The collieries were targeted on five occasions during World War Two. Several of the estimated 25 bombs dropped, damaged parts of the pithead machinery, including the powerhouse; *Deal Mercury*

yard. And that was where Louisa was born. Her father sang in the Welsh miners' choir in Kent and he joined the colliery social club; Louise attended Northbourne School and Sandwich Central School and was 'as good as gold'. She delivered the village newspapers door-to-door to earn pocket money and, in 1941, she remembers sheltering with her bag of newspapers in a porch as a German plane swept down the main street. "I could clearly see the face of the pilot. He was smiling. There was a big bang and the front door of the porch where I was taking shelter blew open. The lady inside was deaf but even she must have heard it. There were people injured in that raid."

At 17, Louisa joined the Land Army, as did her sister Lilian. She looked after cows on a farm at Herne Bay 'washing their udders and backsides' and lived in a Land Army hostel.

"Most of the male calves were sent for veal. There was a bull, of course, and he was a big fellow. I was put in charge of him and I would take him out of the stalls on a halter. I was filling a bucket for him one day and he decided he wanted to explore. I was only a little thing and off he went, dragging me with him. I wouldn't let go and eventually a cowman heard the uproar and together we walked the bull back to the cowsheds. Even after that, I still trusted the bull, we got on famously."

Young George Gibb regularly cycled the 25-mile round trip from the pit to Herne Bay to see his sweetheart. George lived in Mill Hill, Deal, but both his grannies and most of his cousins lived in Betteshanger, and it was on one of these Sunday outings on the bus that George says he 'spotted Louie' through the bus window. "There were some girls skipping in the road and I saw this very dark-eyed girl and she had something about her and I thought, even then,

Louie Gibb with bull

'She's the one for me." They didn't meet again for three years. Louisa was sent back to Wales, away from the bombs to stay with her relatives. When she returned, they bumped into each other at a bus stop, after a Saturday night dance at St Clement's Hall, Sandwich. George remembers: "I was with my two ginger-haired pals and we chatted up Louie and her sister. In fact, I gave her a piggyback around the park as we waited for the bus." Louie says: "I thought you were quite rude. You were lucky I went out with you after that."

George Gibb married Margaret Louisa Phyall on August 3rd 1946. George has always called Louisa 'Louie'. They had five daughters – Carol Ann, Kathleen, Margaret, Marilyn and Pauline. As with most families, they have tasted joy and sorrow. Marilyn lived only a few days. In 1949, their eldest, Carol Ann, was killed in a road accident near their home. She was two-and-a-half. George remembers:

"I was called from the pit, still in my black, and I went straight to my mother's house where I had dropped Carol Ann on my way to work. In those days, we would order

George and Louie Gibb with their daughter, Carol Ann

our fresh fish to be delivered on the local bus straight from Deal. What had happened was that Carol Ann was with my mother going to get the fish and was coming back to Betteshanger when Carol Ann spotted her cousin across the road. She dashed across the road and this van hit her. And that was it."

It is through their daughter Pauline that George and Louie found their strong belief in Jesus Christ. In her teens, Pauline had joined the Baptist Chapel near the family home in Deal and decided she would like to be baptised – which, in the Baptist Chapel, means full immersion. George says: "I was against it. I'd given up going to church when I was about 14 and I thought our Pauline had fallen in with a young, dedicated crowd and was being indoctrinated."

But he said 'yes' and went to Pauline's baptism.

"We couldn't let her down – but I cried because I thought we were losing her. I thought she was going to be a missionary or something and I didn't like the idea."

Pauline went to the University of Leicester and qualified to become a doctor. George and Louie proudly went to

Leicester, stopped in the halls and met her friends. Next morning, Pauline said she was going to church. She asked her parents, "What will you do?" George looked at Louie and said, "Well, I think we'll come along with you to church." Afterwards they had a meal together.

"On the long motorway back to Kent, Louie was very quiet," says George. "I said to Louie 'You know, we've got to do something about this Christian thing' and Lou said 'No, you have to decide what you want to do about it'. So I said 'Alright - **I** have to do something about it' and she said 'Well, I've been thinking exactly the same'. So when we got back, we went to this Chapel round the corner and we've been there ever since."

Walmer Chapel is small and welcoming. George is an elder and he and Louie worship together. Often, the chapel is full; sometimes they pray or sing with only a handful of the faithful. They agree they have had a good life together, even though mining can be such a dangerous job. Did Louie ever try to persuade George to give up being a miner?

"I did. Once. And he said 'Lou, I don't want to come out of the pit. I look back and I see what I've done and I feel very satisfied'. And, after that, I gave up. And God has blessed us because he'd had good health all the way through." George explains: "You see, once I was in the pit, that was my life." And Louie adds: "George was very respected in the pit. I've been told that by other men. He was very fair. And I was very proud of him." And there are tears in her eyes.

She says: "The secret to our marriage is that we have always shared everything. The pay packet and our thoughts. It was hard sometimes but we always had enough money to buy the children a pair of shoes when they needed them and we worked our budget out over the years and saved to pay all our big bills. What we have had in our hands, I believe we have used wisely. Obviously, we did suffer. We still miss the children but God promises to be with you when you're going through deep waters, and I believe he is our strength. In God's eyes everyone, all his children, are equal, and we never forgot that, both as a comfort and a duty."

All men are equal... which was also the firm belief of George's father, Hugh, when he came to Kent in 1928, for George's father struck up an unlikely friendship with Lord Northbourne, the man who owned the Betteshanger mine and who employed so many of the Gibb family. It all began through dog walking. Hughie Gibb loved dogs. He always had one or two, a bull terrier or an Alsatian, and he would exercise them quite legally, on footpaths across Lord Northbourne's land. Miner and mine owner would sometimes meet each other and pass the time of day. One day, Hughie Gibb asked Lord Northbourne if he minded him walking the dogs on his land in this way; Northbourne replied that he rather liked it 'because the sight of him and the dogs kept the robbers away'. Hughie Gibb's daily vigil became a routine – "and the potato pickers," says George, "would often leave a bag of spuds for Dad, which I know had the approval of Lord Northbourne."

There is also concrete evidence of this relationship. Traditionally, there was right of way from Betteshanger Colliery across the marshland to the main Deal Road. It was a regularly-used shortcut. To improve the transport of spoil from the mine to the tip, the mine owners put in conveyor belts. This blocked the short cut. One afternoon, Hughie Gibb pointed this out to Lord Northbourne. With no short cut, the miners and their families had to walk a considerable distance further. Man to man, was he, Lord Northbourne, happy about this?

Within three months, there was a footbridge over the lines and the short cut was restored. There are some who call it 'Hughie's Bridge'.

CHAPTER SIX
The Northbournes and Betteshanger

*"Never speak disrespectfully of society
– only people who can't get into it do
that."*
Oscar Wilde, 1895

Walter James, 2ⁿᵈ Baron Northbourne

Christopher George Walter James lives in a fine Victorian house at the end of a long private drive, with alpacas on the lawn. It used to be three farm workers' cottages but when the family moved here from the big house, Northbourne Court, they amalgamated their cottages into one stylish home. Christopher James, the 5th Baron Northbourne, is now in his 90s, and lives there with his wife, Lady Marie Sygne Northbourne, daughter of Henri Paul Claudel, a French poet, playwright and diplomat; they married in 1959.

The Northbourne family owned the youngest of the East Kent pits, Betteshanger, until they sold the lease in the 1990s. They still own the land that

4ᵗʰ Baron Northbourne (Christopher Northbourne's Father)

surrounds the site which, as part of an ambitious scheme of regeneration, is being developed into a heritage museum, a healthy living centre and a sustainable energy park.[77] Lady Northbourne has chaired the fundraising group that has helped this development, yet there is an irony in the Northbourne involvement in this initiative.

For the family had, for generations, made a living shipbuilding and coal mining in the North East, where Christopher's great-grandfather had been a Member of Parliament for Gateshead. They had moved south, to Kent, in the 1850s, driven by a desire to get away from the clamour of industry in general and coal in particular.

Christopher Northbourne recalls the moment in the 1920s that forced the family to consider again an involvement in the coal industry. It was breakfast time at Northbourne Court and a weighty letter arrived, addressed to Christopher's great-

---

[77] See Chapter 16

grandfather. "It was from the industrialists, Dorman Long. They had been exploring for coal locally and wanted to rent our land on which boreholes had been made – and, later, to buy the rights. Great-grandfather was not frightfully pleased. The family had, after all, just moved to Kent to get away from coal mines. Now, someone wanted to start mining on our doorstep.

"Anyway, he did let them come and look at the fields to assess the possibilities. They were permitted a restricted area of land and, very quickly, they offered a very substantial sum, which he accepted, and they started digging."

The Betteshanger Colliery was officially opened at a luncheon in the huge fitting shop at the pithead on May 19th 1924. It was a grand affair. Everyone who was anyone in Kent was invited, and a special train of seven Pullman carriages left London Victoria at 9.40am carrying an additional 200 guests. The band of the Royal Marines greeted them at Betteshanger and the chairman and directors of Messrs

Christopher Northbourne

Dorman Long, shook each of them by the hand. The Archbishop of Canterbury, the Right Reverend Randall Davidson, offered a prayer of dedication and, according to the *Kentish Observer* of May 22nd that year, 'inaugurated the sinking of the down-cast pit by exploding a charge in the shaft.

The interesting ceremony was followed by Lady Northbourne starting the winding engine, lowering the master sinker and his men into the pit to send out the first 'official' hobbit of earth'. The Minister of Mines, Emanuel

Lord and Lady Northbourne wedding day (1920s)

Shinwell MP, presented a special licence to the Archbishop, enabling him to fire the inaugural shot, otherwise he, the Archbishop, would have been breaking the law. There was much laughter. The mine owners' chairman, Sir Hugh Bell, assured Mr Elks, secretary of the Kent Miners' Association, that although the Archbishop was wearing black, 'he is not a blackleg' (more laughter). The occasion glowed with bright optimism. Earl Beauchamp declared that an estimated 1,500,000,000 tons of coal could be mined in an area of 80 square miles of East Kent, and pits would soon be open at Wingham, Fleete, Woodnesborough, Stodmarsh and Deal. He was one of three speakers who looked ahead at the challenges the mine owners would face. Betteshanger could provide work for 10,000 – he said houses would be needed to accommodate them.

The Mining Minister, 'Manny' Shinwell, embarking on a career that decades later would embrace the nationalisation of the coal industry, foreshadowed a change from private ownership, 'though we may have to wait a long time before the social order is transformed…(in the meantime) you could make life happier and more tolerable for the great mass of people under your control and supervision…with housing conditions and social amenities which would obviate the laying of charges that you were despoiling the countryside'.

Lord Northbourne regretted, and argued against, industrial and social conflict in the coal industry. Why couldn't there be in mining the same 'personal relations and mutual confidence which obtain (as a rule) between us farmers and the workmen we employ?' There was a shared appreciation of the difficulties experienced by employer and employee. Socially, he warned: 'You are bringing great change to our countryside…no invasion has ever been truly successful unless the invaders have absorbed and adapted something from the invaded…Naturally, we look forward to learning a great deal from you and your people…' Perhaps, he added, 'the invaders' might also learn from 'the natives'.

Lord Northbourne's great-grandson, Christopher, the present Lord Northbourne, was born in 1926 and the first coal seam at Betteshanger was struck a year later. His early memories are ones of slight irritation. "I had a nanny and a nursery maid and at Northbourne Court, we lived over the hill from the digging so we could actually see the workings. They had a little steam engine to carry waste material to where it could be shipped on to the main Southern or East Kent Railway. So there were perpetual noises – bub, bub, bub when the trucks ran into each other. Chuff, chuff, chuff and a whistle when the train was moving. I must have been four or five. The noise didn't upset me; my nanny put me into bed and I felt safe because I could hear her talking to the nursery maid in front of the fire as I fell asleep.

"Do you know, I don't think we ever went to look at the mine. That's odd, isn't it?"

Christopher, the 5th Baron, farmer and businessman, is the son of Walter Ernest Christopher James, the 4th Baron Northbourne, who, in 1940, coined the phrase 'organic farming' in his book *Look to the Land*. It was a strategic document written ahead of its time, which argued the need to manage farms 'as an organic whole'.

When World War Two broke out, the then 4th Baron Northbourne, Christopher's father, was asked to develop an agricultural plan for Kent. Britain's farming industry had been neglected for the past two decades; now, suddenly, the country needed all the food it could produce as German U–boats and surface vessels threatened Britain's worldwide supply routes. Christopher's father was the obvious choice for the job. He was a published author; he understood farming and his views on food production were fresh but pragmatic.

"He worked very, very hard. Fourteen hours a day, every day of the year because the economics of farming were very bad between the wars. And the country's need was great. He relaxed, I remember, only for two hours every Sunday, when there was a music concert on BBC Radio. He would paint a watercolour while he listened."

The Northbourne family have always recognised their responsibilities to the community in which they live. They built the local Northbourne School for the children of the miners and the agricultural workers who toiled on their land. They supported the local parish church and, later, would set up Northbourne Park private school in what had once been the family home, Betteshanger House. Particularly, when times were hard at the pit, they employed miners' wives

The Northbourne family home, now Northbourne Park School

and families on their land – but, for the Northbournes, agriculture, not mining, has been the priority. "It was an interesting relationship between the two industries," according to the present Lord Northbourne. "We were mine owners but, in our home, all the talk was of farming. It was easier for us to help in those days when miners' families were experiencing difficulties because there were always jobs to do in the seasons – picking potatoes or Brussels sprouts, apples, cherries and soft fruits.

"We had a large workforce – 32 on the estate. How many does my son have now? Two. That's mechanisation for you."[78]

Christopher went off to school at Eton College, a transition which coincided with the outbreak of World War Two and a fundamental change in the lives of everyone in Britain, including the Northbournes. If Hitler were going to invade, it was likely to be across the short sea route from France to Kent. A 20-mile exclusion zone was set up along the East Coast. No one under the age of four could stay in East

[78] Conversation with author

Kent. So Christopher's mother and his sisters went back north to a house they still owned on the border of Northumberland. Christopher did not go. In his holidays he came back from Eton to be with his father, at Northbourne Court. "It was exciting – and, besides, I wanted to play my part in the war effort. As a teenager, I worked all day on the farm, up on the ricks at harvest time, sharing the jokes with the men. They would pitch the sheaves up and we would lay them out on the top of the stack and rope them down – and if one fell off, they'd laugh and say: 'That'll cost you a pint of beer'.

"I was rather proud to be allowed back into the exclusion zone. There were troops and barbed wire fences everywhere; it was a huge military operation and I was often stopped by the police to check my age and our papers.

"My grandmother absolutely refused to leave Northbourne Court to go back to Northumberland. If Mr Hitler was going to come, she said she wanted to be here to tell him what she thought of him.[79]

Wartime Kent – clifftop barbed wire

---

[79] Ibid

"We did our bit. We gathered up waste paper every Thursday and baled it up for the war effort. We collected and gave money to the Spitfire Fund, to build more Spitfires. I remember only one thing: we were determined to win.

"And by 'we', I mean everyone. We worked together. If one has benefited through inheritance and luck, one has a duty to work with the less well off. It was 'normal' in my father's time, and I hope during our time, to be helpful and constructive. I would expect that to be the case."

The Northbournes have practised what they preached. Christopher Northbourne, 5th Baron Northbourne, was a cross-bench member of the House of Lords; moderate and popular, he was one of only 90 hereditary peers elected to remain in the Lords after the passing of the House of Lords Act in 1999. He was spokesperson in the Lords for families and children,[80] chair of Toynbee Hall and a governor of Wye Agricultural College: he retired from the House of Lords in 2018. Every year, for decades, he welcomed children from London's East End to stay on his estate.

Lady Northbourne was for many years chair of the Kent Community Housing Trust, which cared for the community's elderly. She inspired the formation of Kent Opera,[81] a brave and innovative regional opera company, unfairly killed by the then Arts Council which withdrew all funding in 1989. Her charitable work in East Kent has brought her into contact with many mining families; the lives of the men, she says,

---

[80] Lord Northbourne was a patron of the Stepney Children's Fund and welcomed needy children of all races, colours and creeds, to spend weeks at a time at Northbourne during the summer months

[81] Kent Opera was founded in 1969 and was the first regional opera in the UK. The Marlowe Theatre in Canterbury was built from an old Odeon Cinema to accommodate Kent Opera and the Canterbury Festival

have been visibly shortened by their years in coal mining. Latterly, the Trust took on the responsibility of caring for the children of immigrants when they arrived, homeless and often helpless, on the shores of Kent.

With her husband, she welcomed over many years disadvantaged children from London's East End who came by the score to spend a few sunlit weeks of summer with them in East Kent.[82] They picked fruit and drove tractors and, occasionally, asked about the spinning wheel of the pithead, just over the hill.

Betteshanger Colliery became the largest in the Kent Coalfield. Dorman Long, the company which had first approached Christopher Northbourne's great-grandfather for the mineral rights to the land, merged with S Pearson and Sons and also became the owners of the Snowdown Colliery.[83] Like most Kent pits, Betteshanger was handicapped by flooding and the shafts were consolidated by sealing the sides with cement. The development and growth of Betteshanger coincided with the fall-out from the General Strike of 1926[84] and its arrival was welcomed both by the miners and by Pearson and Dorman Long. It was a rivulet of good news in an ocean of unrest. The General Strike had occurred because the coal owners wished to cut wages. More than a million miners had rebelled and were locked out, 'prevented from working', said the Trade Union Congress (TUC). The TUC had watched as the nation's essential services were maintained during the short-lived strike by the Government,

---

[82] "I left the ignition keys in my parked car one day and looked up to see it being driven away. One of the young lads had decided to go for a joy ride. I've never run faster in my life. I did stop him." Lady Northbourne, conversation with Jo Taylor, 1990

[83] The company became Pearson and Dorman Long

[84] See Chapters 5 and 7

using mainly middle-class volunteers and the army. They rapidly admitted defeat. But many miners, embittered by the confrontation with management and disappointed at the sudden collapse of the committee, refused to go back to work. The nine-day strike, however, had enabled the mine owners to identify the miners' leaders in their workforces. Each employer drew up a list of 'troublemakers'. And they used the law ruthlessly to punish the strikers.

The mine owners had no obligation to employ any of the men who had gone on strike. Those they didn't want they put on a blacklist. There was no job for them in their home pit. But there might be a job in Kent. After all, it was a new coalfield, wasn't it? Out-of-work miners converged on Kent.[85] Their reputation preceded them and Betteshanger would become one of the country's most militant collieries – a reputation it would never lose.

Few could afford the train fare and they came by bicycle and on foot. Many walked hundreds of miles, with no job guaranteed at the end of their marathon journey. Some gave false names as they sought work at Betteshanger in case they had been blacklisted by their former employers. Mostly, they travelled without their families. Their incentive was a full-time job in a coalfield with higher-than-average wages. Unemployment in traditional mining areas was as high as 50%. Here, in the Garden of England, was a chance of a fresh start, whatever had gone before.

In the ten years between 1925 and 1935, coal output rose sharply. So did the working population of the Kent Coalfield; 2044 in 1925 and 7409 ten years later. Almost overnight, the seaside town of Deal and the villages around it, were

---

[85] See Chapter 5

overwhelmed in the 1920s by the arrival of some 1500 men looking for lodgings.[86] As one miner, John McEwan, put it:

"There was fellas on the road for debt – they'd had the 1926 strike, grocery debts, rent, and different debts, and there was fellas on the run from kids and wives. Some of the real best come down 'ere and some of the worst, but a lot of them couldn't face it. Men were breaking down with boils, pimples and carbuncles – the heat. Well, they was working in 98 degrees – 100 degrees was nothing. There was a hell of a lot walked down here. There was a fella tramped from Durham, took him seven weeks to get here, and he got his job on the Monday night. He sat down at 2 o'clock and said, 'I do feel bad' and the next thing there was, he just keeled over – as dead as doornails."[87]

He wasn't the only man completely exhausted when he arrived in Kent.

"Some of them simply couldn't work, they were too weak. They were in such bad stress after walking down. They eventually got the sack, they'd have a note on their lamp and they'd have to see the manager. He'd stand them off and then they'd walk back. It was terrible. They didn't have much help off us either – it was dog eat dog. You didn't have the money."[88]

John Jones walked to Kent in the 1920s. His father, also a miner, had died of silicosis at the age of 33. His widowed mother brought up five children, including John. He fought in World War One and, when he came back, there was no work for him. He went on the dole. That's why he walked to

---

[86] Those Dirty Miners, JP Hollingsworth, p83
[87] John McEwan, born 1904 in Lancashire, worked in nine pits
[88] Mrs E Sidwell, wife of Nottingham miner, who worked at Tilmanstone

Kent, doing odd jobs on the way in order to eat. It took him four months.

When the men arrived, they were not always welcome. The local Deal Mercury was soon carrying warnings in the small ads offering rooms to let – but excluding newly-arrived miners. They were perceived as rough and dirty. They spoke with accents the locals could not understand and they were not trusted. Signs went up in the windows of boarding houses, pubs and cafés: 'No Miners'. One miner walked through Deal pushing a pram containing his family's belongings, carrying a sign which read 'Home Wanted.'[89]

"You used to see it in the paper, regular as clockwork: 'House to Let', or 'Rooms to Let – no miners, no dogs, no children'. You used to see that every week and they just wouldn't take you in if you was a miner".

When the Betteshanger pit closed in 1989, it was Jim Davies who switched the lights out and closed the door for the last time. He was a Deputy at the colliery and his family, like so many, had made the trek to Kent, in his case from South Wales. Jim has served his time at the Betteshanger coalface and was respected both by miner and management. He has lived through the toil and turmoil, prosperity and final closure at Betteshanger, and he says: "My father was as tough as they come, but he always said that the early years in Kent were among the hardest of his life."

These men who came to Kent in their hundreds had left their families and the surroundings in which they had been brought up, to seek a new life. They were arriving in what might just as well have been a foreign country. They were immigrants.

And immigration is never easy…

[89] Those Dirty Miners, JP Hollingsworth

CHAPTER SEVEN
Immigration and the Welsh Connection

*"Give me a place to stand on, and I
will move the earth."*
Plato (287–212 BC)

The 1930s were not conspicuous for their moments of joy. The decade began with the Wall Street crash that brought poverty and unemployment to all the world's leading industrial nations. It signalled further misery when Adolf Hitler was democratically elected as Chancellor in Germany; it reeled with the attack on China by an expansionist Japan, and it succumbed into world conflict with the invasion of Poland in 1939 and Britain's subsequent declaration of war against the invaders, Nazi Germany.

Suddenly, whole populations were on the move, from countries that were being invaded, to countries which promised some security in a violently-changing world. Forced migration, for whatever reason, has its problems as history repeatedly tells us. The influx of thousands of miners and their families into Kent was no exception. In seeking new opportunity, the immigrants shared the worst aspects of leaving one community for another – fear, unfamiliarity, homelessness, discomfort, language difficulties and communication.

At its peak, the Kent Coalfield employed nearly 8,000 men. The vast majority of them came from parts of Britain that contrasted dramatically with the green fields of Kent. Their families came with them and they settled into the houses which were provided for them – to rent, of course, for they were owned by their employers. They were the raw material that an expanding coal industry needed and which, without their skill and dedication, the mines would not thrive. They were also consumers who would add to the community's economic prosperity. But that is true of all immigration, even that forced by circumstance.

The miners who came to Kent in their thousands were as unfamiliar with the Garden of England as any Iranian taking his first steps on an English shore. Many had not travelled beyond the limits of their home town or, at best, to the nearest seaside resort during the summertime Factories Week, when commerce closed down in the North and the Midlands.

Jim Davies, historian, archivist, miner

For all their kith and kin bravado, they feared discrimination in an unfamiliar world. Their families, particularly some of the wives, were homesick for the terraced, back-to-back contact over the garden fence that had been part of the daily round. They were

Blackwood High Street 1920s

uneasy, often defensive in their dealings with the people who had lived in Kent for years, and this was a sensitivity that sometimes surfaced as aggression. They spoke a different language – English, certainly, but with rhythms and a resonance very different from a Kentish accent. It was the search for accommodation that brought them face to face with all these difficulties.

Jim Davies' family came to Kent from South Wales, the mining village of Blackwood in the Sirhowy Valley, Monmouthshire. The guidebooks of those days describe Blackwood as 'a village in a beautiful valley which is lighted with the gas from the council's own gas works'. In fact, Blackwood is a single-street town and always has been. It is a street where grocers and solicitors, banks and booksellers trade side-by-side with, these days, charity shops that fill the gaps left by a long-dead industry. It is still a busy town, however, busier than many and faded less than brethren towns in the Rhondda, Rhymney, Tawe and other valleys.

Blackwood has no castle. Nearby Caerphilly has a castle but the footfall in Blackwood is heavier than in poster-pretty Caerphilly. At least, that's what Granville Hall says and he's president of the local Conservative Party. Bluff and friendly, and not a man to be overlooked, there's nothing much he doesn't know about Blackwood and Oakdale and the other shafts driven into the green valley of the Sirhowy River. The echoes of the past are still loud. In its heyday, Oakdale pits had 54 coalfaces producing coal. The headquarters of the Oakdale and Blackwood Miners' Welfare Institute may now be in nearby St Fagans but the colourless concrete block that is the local miners' headquarters in the town still holds its place in the main street. On this grey day, the lights are still on. Bedwellty Urban District Council administers one side of the valley; 22 chapels thrive there (9 Baptist, 5 Methodist, 7 Congregationalist and 2 Presbyterian). There's a landmark on the hill, on the right-hand side as you go out of town. It is a sculpture that recalls the years of coal. The words engraved on the flat, slate memorial read:

'Out of darkness, let there be light
In memory of the miners who dedicated their lives for the benefit of the nation'

The memorial stands beside the new Islwyn High School, built on the former slag heaps, a statement of glass and optimism, energy neutral and very 21st Century. Those who live in Oakdale and Blackwood, beside the Sirhowy group of pits, are determined that their mines and miners will not be forgotten.

The valleys of South Wales cascade south to the ports of the most industrial of Welsh counties, Glamorgan, where sits the nation's capital city, Cardiff. Perhaps more than any other British coalfield, the story of Welsh coal is blighted by major disaster – Risca (1860 and again in 1880) when a total of 265 men died; Abercarn (1878) when 146 men were killed; Abersychan (1890) 176 deaths; Cilfynydd (1894) 276 deaths; Senghenydd (1913) 431 deaths and Aberfan (1966) when 116 children and 28 adults were killed as a coal spoil tip collapsed on the local school. The Sirhowy Valley takes its name from the river that flows through it, in Welsh, Afon Sirhywi. As is so often the case in mining communities, the industries of iron and coal grew side by side and, by 1921, 250,000 men were employed in Welsh coal mines.

As in the coalfields of Scotland, Yorkshire and the North East, the General Strike of 1926 and the subsequent economic slump brought hardship to South Wales, particularly because, as a result of underinvestment by Welsh coal owners, productivity was low and costs were high. By 1930, the mining workforce had halved. As always, the Welsh expressed their emotions in words and music. Idris Davies, a miner from the age of 14, was injured in the McLaren pit at Abertysswg and, during four years' unemployment following the General Strike of 1926, his poetry reflected his determination to record the agony and anger within his community. He wrote:

> Send out your homing pigeons, Dai
> Your blue-grey pigeons, hard as nails
> Send them with messages tied to their wings
> Words of your anger, words of your love
> Send them to Dover, to Glasgow, to Cork
> Send them to the wharves of Hull and of Belfast,

To the harbours of Liverpool and Dublin and Leith,
Send them to the Islands and out of the oceans
To the wild, wet islands of the northern sea
Where little grey women about in heavy shawls
At the hour of dusk to gaze at the merciless waters,
And send them to the decorated islands of the south
Where the mineowner and his tall, stiff lady
Walk around and round the rose-pink hotel, day after day.

Send out your pigeons, Dai, send them out
With words of your anger and your love and your pride,
With stern little sentences wrought in your heart,
Send out your pigeons, flashing and dazzling towards
the sun.
Go out, pigeons bach, and do what Dai tells you.[90]

Jim Davies' family carried this message with them as, disillusioned, they set out for Kent.

Jim Davies' mother, Thelma, and father, Arthur, had met in the Tredegar Arms public house in Blackwood where Thelma was working. "My father was always known as 'Bingo' Davies; we had a family tradition of nicknames. The Tredegar Arms was a rugby pub, where all the players gathered and my father was a bit of a star, at full-back or fly (outside) half. My mother, like so many Welsh girls, went into service when she left school at 12 and she got a job in Weston-super-Mare. But when she was 17 or 18, she came back to Blackwood and that's when she met my father."

The Davieses came to Kent in the 1930s. Thelma

---

[90] From The Collected Poems of Idris Davies, ed Islwyn Jenkins, Gomer Press

Davies was hurt by the reception the family received and never forgot it. Jim Davies says: "She was still scathing about it even just before she died. The Kent people were really hostile – and, in return, the mining families dismissed locals as 'cherry pickers'. Mam and dad didn't have a house to go to and they were looking for rooms. It was really difficult. There were notices in the papers and in the windows of boarding houses that said: 'No miners, No dogs, No children'. They just wouldn't take you if you were a miner." Even if a miner's family found rooms there was no guarantee that they could move in. A Betteshanger wife, Mrs Owen, remembers she went with her sister to collect a key for a house in Dover which they were going to share. "We went to the landlord on the Monday and my sister had put down on the form that her husband was a miner. The agent turned round and said: 'I'm very sorry, you can't have the key because your husband's a miner'. And he had a big roaring fire in his grate and my sister said: 'Where would you be without my husband digging that coal? I've a good mind to get a bucket of water and throw it all over that fire!' Ooh! She was mad!"[91]

There were no pithead baths until 1934 and the miners were conspicuous in the community in their coal-black clothes. They were less than welcome on the buses as they made the seats dirty; they felt discriminated against in the shops. As another Betteshanger wife remembers: "They wouldn't talk to you because they didn't like miners. Deal people still don't like miners, but it was the miners who made this place. They'd look at you as if you were – well, I don't know what, and none of them was brought up as strict as

---

[91] Mrs Watkins from South Wales, 2013, Oral History

what I was brought up. They used to put out streaky bacon, you know, fatty bacon, and they'd put a label on it: 'Miners' bacon'. I think it was horrible – 'miners' bacon' indeed."[92]

Rejection and hostility emphasised the alienation many women felt. While the men buried themselves in their work, the wives had more time to reflect on their new lives. The Betteshanger miners settled as a community in Mill Hill, a suburb of Deal, which expanded to accommodate the thousands of newcomers. Mrs Cox remembers: "Ooh, was I homesick! I said to Ted (her husband) 'I think I'll go back. I don't like it here'. And I would've if there'd been a train coming. We were such a big family, such a close family but I cried and cried. I hated every minute in Deal. Even my children wanted to go home. I didn't like the seagulls squawking. They used to squawk and I used to cry."[93] Understandably, this imposed a strain on relationships but most marriages survived in a society where divorce was rare. Mrs Cox's husband, Ted, liked Kent and the steady job and the unaccustomed freedom 'to be at the seaside in a matter of minutes'. And Mrs Cox fought her homesickness. "I had a wonderful husband. I was lucky. He made sure I was never short of money. I was a quiet girl and didn't mix very easily and Ted would say every week, 'Well, alright, we will go back: I'll give in my notice and we'll go back!' But we never did, and I'd say, 'Well, I'll give it another try, love…' He was a wonderful husband and a well-respected union man…"

Part of the hostility towards the miners was rooted in envy. Their wages far exceeded the weekly earnings of most agricultural workers.

Molly Ramsden was born in Deal in 1928. Her father

[92] Mrs Cox from Monmouthshire, 2013, Oral History
[93] Ibid

was a stockman on the farm at Cottington Court, and Molly remembers the influx of miners. "I asked my mother who all these men were, going along on bicycles, in one direction. She said they were miners going to work in the colliery, and she explained that they would go down into the mine in a cage and then find their place of work once they got down there, thousands of feet below us, in the deepest mine in Kent. And I remember being concerned about that: would they be safe down there?"

Molly went to the local parochial school; Church of England. Most of the miners' children went to the Catholic school. "We used to call out naughty things to them and they retaliated, of course. They called us 'dirty Protestants, dirty Proddy dogs'. We called them 'dirty Roman Candles'. Horrible, wasn't it?" Did she notice any ongoing hostility as she grew up? "I wasn't aware of it. Maybe I closed my eyes to it. I think people were pleased because it was good for Deal because the mining families were spending their money there."[94] Living near the mines made a deep impression on Molly. "I knew this because when I was 10 years old I moved back, away from the coast, to be with my family in Marden. At school, we were asked to write an essay – in those days they called it a composition – about where we lived. Well, I was now living in the country village of Marden, in mid-Kent – but I chose to write about my life in Deal which I'd left behind; the mine, the miners and their children. My mother reminded me how to spell 'Betteshanger' and the teacher of the day asked me to come out and read the composition to the rest of the class. I wasn't sure if I was pleased or not at the time.

"I didn't like the thought of people having to go down

---

[94] Interview with author, 2017

a mine and yet I realised it was nothing new to them. It was probably something they'd done all their lives. And we couldn't have done without coal, could we? I don't think we could. I think most people, whatever they said to each other, admired these men for what they were doing, and what they were going through every day. And I think a lot of them integrated with the locals very well; we loved their singing and their music."

But violence would scar some Saturday nights, as Jim Davies recalls: "The Scots would fight the Welsh. I remember Billy Marshall telling me that on his first night in Deal he saw two sinkers stripped to the waist, having a bare-knuckle fight in St George's Churchyard. Billy said: 'Now that frightened the death out of me. What would it have done to the natives?' But that's how the Kent people saw these newcomers, thousands of them, hard-drinking, hard-living, black as hell, goodness knows what else – and it was all reported in the newspapers. One headline read: 'Man and miner fighting in the street'. That's how they saw us – but we weren't all like that. Just a few."

Anecdotally, all the stresses raised by immigration are embraced in those stories. The displacement of entire populations is one of the tragedies of the 21st Century. This was a migration as surely as any that has taken place in Britain over the years. It was an experience uncomfortable both for those who lived in East Kent and for those who came to settle there. Yet, current studies of the economic impact of immigration suggest that in most cases the effect is small 'and, on average, benefits the native population'.[95]

Economically, it was good for the county. Socially, it was not easy for either community but the heritage that

---

[95] Journal of European Association, Card, Dustmann and Preston

the incomers brought with them – from Wales and Scotland, the North and North East and the Midlands – was welcomed by the locals to the extent that the Snowdown Male Voice Choir and the Betteshanger

Snowdown Colliery Welfare Male Voice Choir 2016

Colliery Welfare Brass Band still thrive after nearly a century.

Snowdown Male Voice Choir proudly reflects its Welsh roots in that it still includes in its repertoire traditional songs, such as *Calon Lâan* and *Myfanwy*, sung in Welsh – though whisper it, only one or two of the current choir now speak the Welsh language. Both Snowdown and Betteshanger had brass bands; the Gibb family from Scotland[96] worked hard to link together instrumentalists from all over the country. Jack Adams was one of the founders of a Welsh choir, having organised concert parties in Abertillery before moving to Kent. The Betteshanger band was formed in 1931 and Percy Barnacle, a retired Royal Marines bandmaster 'brought a professional touch' to the band.[97]

---

[96] George Gibb's grandfather conducted the Betteshanger band
[97] Terry Harrison, conversation with author, 2019

In 1934, following the Gresford mining disaster, the choir and band raised money for the disaster fund at a concert in The Winter Gardens in Margate; artists included Jessie Matthews, Ruth Naylor and Sonnie Hale. On October 27th 1934, wives and families of 21 of the victims of the disaster arrived in Deal for a three-week stay. Accommodation and the costs of the holiday were provided from within the Kent mining community. Jim Davies is still president of the Betteshanger band.

The Kent Coalfield proved that agriculture and industry can live side-by-side, provided planners are far-sighted enough and politicians have the determination to shed their obsession with short-term thinking and the outcome of the next General Election. Kent was fortunate in having the benefit of the wisdom of town planner Patrick Abercrombie,[98] whose thinking was strategic, energy apparently limitless and relationships with politicians both close and mutually respectful.

Language, differing accents, caused awkwardness and highlighted a difficulty in communication that had its roots in differing cultures. But at least the mining immigrants did not have to learn an entirely new language, as had so many immigrants before them. Interestingly, an 'Aylesham' accent has emerged from the mixture of voices heard in the East Kent coalfield, but the structure of the English language remains undisturbed.[99] Unlike foreign immigrants, the barriers the British miners faced in the movement across the country were neither legal nor political. The men simply had to find a job and somewhere to live and to adopt new cultural norms.

---

[98] See Chapter 4
[99] See Chapter 10

No matter where they came from, they all had one thing in common – their motivation for moving. The disturbance and low morale in the fragmented coal industry was as real in Wales as it was in Scotland. George Gibb's family sped south, drawn by the prospect of a fresh start miles away from the poverty and conflict of a miner's life in Fife in the 1920s. Jim Davies' family moved east from Monmouthshire for exactly the same reason. Just as in Scotland, there had been major strikes and disputes from 1921 to 1926. Men now labelled militants could no longer get a job in their home pit so they trekked to Kent where miners were needed and not too many questions were asked – though many miners still signed on under an assumed name because they were publicly backlisted in their home town.

"It was easier for the men," recalls Jim Davies. "They brought their interests and their skills with them. The women had to start from scratch, building a new life in an unfamiliar place, with unfamiliar and sometimes unfriendly people. It must have been difficult."

Rugby brought the Davieses to Kent. "My father had played for Monmouthshire and was quite a big name in Blackwood. The Chislet/Betteshanger rugby team were very good – all Welshmen and unbeaten in Kent. So Les Magness, who was a trade union leader, was despatched to South Wales with orders to find the good rugby players and tell them there was a job for them in Kent. My father was fed up with the strikes in South Wales. There were various ongoing disputes, and the Ocean Coal Company had tried to import 70 miners from Bargoed to break a strike at Blackwood. There was uproar. About 1000 people had gathered at the pithead. Stones and bricks were thrown, miners and policemen were injured and eight miners were arrested."

As often happens, the children suffered most in these conflicts. At the Blackwood and Cefn Fforest School, attendance dwindled as children of school age were needed to forage for coal from the spoil heaps and to help at home. Schools were used as a place to provide food for needy children. Throughout the summer of 1926, children of distressed families were given a midday meal.[100]

A local historian remarked that since the time of the Chartist uprising in the 1830s 'there never seems to have been a period when employment and employee were both satisfied and worked harmoniously together'.[101] 'Bingo' Davies decided to make the most of his chance of a fresh start in Kent – and he brought his skills and interests in rugby and music with him. When he and Thelma married, it was a morning ceremony, leading into a lunchtime reception. At around 2pm, 'Bingo' disappeared. "My mother saw my father putting his bag together and she said: 'Where are you going?' 'Oh!' he said, 'I've got a game this afternoon', and off he went. So they got married in the morning and he played rugby in the afternoon."[102]

Ten years earlier, rugby and mining had provided 'Bingo' Davies' uncle, Wilfred, with a passport to success in New Zealand. He had left Blackwood at the age of 20 where he had played front row forward for the town's team and worked at the Rock Colliery in Blackwood. He thrived in both Union and League Rugby and in New Zealand he captained South Auckland. He went on to manage the New Zealand Māori Tour of Australia and, in 1950, accompanied

---

[100] Blackwood Yesterday, book 5, p47
[101] Blackwood Yesterday, book 7
[102] Jim Davies, conversation with author, 2017

the New Zealand Rugby League team to the World Cup in France. His mining skills enabled him to become manager of a colliery in Huntley, North Island. Wilfred set a pattern that 'Bingo' would follow.

Like his uncle, 'Bingo' was a community man. In Kent, he helped create the welfare sports ground with which he was involved until he died. Eventually, he was surrounded by echoes of the life he had left behind in Blackwood – the eisteddfodau,[103] the silver bands, the amateur dramatic groups, the Band of Hope at the chapel, the flowers and horticultural shows, the Cooperative shop in the main street which had been set up by the Blackwood society in 1904, supplying local bread and meat and always sympathetic to the community in times of crisis. The wives, newly-arrived in Kent, and without their familiar support system, defiantly clung to their roots. Thelma Davies carried her babies 'the Welsh way', that is, wrapped in a shawl over her shoulder like a papoose. More than most, the Welsh coined work-related nicknames for their friends and acquaintances. It is only in the last 200 years that surnames have been adopted by Welsh society. Before that, children were known as an adjunct of their father – Dafydd ap (son of) Howell and Islwyn ap (son of) Evan or Morfydd ferch (daughter of) William. When surnames became more common, ap David became Davies, ap William became Williams and ap Evan became Evans. And, as elsewhere in Britain, ancestors' trades and interests became embedded in family surnames: Farmer, Cook, Draper, Smith, Butcher; occupations we still have. But many others have disappeared: Clark, a scholar; Fletcher, a maker of arrows. Words ending in 'ster' meant 'a skilled woman', so Spinster meant a female spinner and, as many of these were

---

[103] Music and arts festivals

single, the word came to describe a single woman. Some were based on traits: Cruickshank – crooked legs; Frost (in Welsh Ffrost) – a braggart; Jay – a chatterer; Gilchrist – servant of Christ. Fraser comes from the French for strawberries 'fraises'; Grey or Gray – grey hair or beard; and Nightingale – probably sang well.

In Blackwood, 'Dai Plug' was the local plumber, 'Fuse' was a tall, thin electrician, 'Johnny Fortnight' was an itinerant draper who called every two weeks and 'John Squared's' name was John John.[104]

But Jim Davies still doesn't know why his father Arthur was nicknamed 'Bingo'. "What I *do* know is that my father was far more content in Kent than my mother. He would go back to Wales only for funerals. He would say: 'Why would we want to go back? We've got the sea on the doorstep and beautiful countryside'. When we were back home, the only time we saw the seaside was once a year at Barry Island on the Sunday School outing. Mind you, when my mother was due to have a baby, he insisted she went back to Wales so the baby could be born in Wales. In those days you had to be born in Wales to qualify to play for Wales. And he was taking no chances. After all the upheaval, mam gave birth to a girl anyway; my sister, Olive.

"We always had a houseful at holiday time, when his cousins and old mates used to come and visit. He was happy, you see, because, love it or hate it, he had his job."

And 'The Job' was at the heart of the lives of all the families who came to Kent. It was the reason they were there. The umbilical link with the pit spawned welfare clubs and bowls clubs, rugby and cricket clubs, pigeon and cycling

---

[104] Blackwood Yesterday, Ewart Smith

clubs with workers and management generally working together to create the community initiative. They planted their own churches – six, all different denominations, in the Betteshanger area alone. If the mining communities could be accused of being inward-looking, isolationist, it is because of the initial hostility they felt, and their ability to become self-sufficient in most aspects of their new lives. They didn't need anybody else. Entrepreneurs had drawn them across the country to work for them and bring prosperity to Kent; the entrepreneurial skills of the miners and their wives created a community that used to the full the potential they found in themselves and in their new surroundings.

Jim Davies spent 33 years of his life underground. "Grandfathers on both my mother and father's side were miners. My mother's father, we called him Grancha, died from silicosis and in my family we always say that if you were a racehorse, you'd breed a racehorse. The men all went down the pit at 15 and then emerged 50 years later, if they lived that long. I tried for a job as a miner when I was 15 but failed my medical. So I took a job as a milkman – and I tried again months later, failed again. So I think a trade union friend of my father put in a word and I got a job. I've been lucky. I've been a ripper and a deputy and a safety officer, overman, colliery overman, a surface superintendent and I've been in charge of underground operations at the pit. Only once have I had a tricky time when the roof started sitting down and we ended up in 18 inches of height.

"I really enjoyed the job. You'd go into work every day and sometimes you couldn't even talk to each other because of the noise or because you were too busy, coupling arches, say. And you'd just put out your hand and someone would put a nut and bolt in your hand because everyone knew what we were all doing. It was teamwork. Teamwork at the heart of everything."

When the Betteshanger pit closed in 1989, Jim Davies was the last miner to leave. "It was a pretty emotional moment. The end of the East Kent coalfield…But there was always tomorrow…and tomorrow is another day." Jim Davies has remained at the heart of this community. For 43 years, he continued his work as a trustee on the local Welfare Scheme. He ran a successful business in Dover, engraving and printing. He also started to gather facts and artefacts, evidence that, once, there had been a coalfield behind the beach huts and Victorian seafront terraces. He has painstakingly recorded through film, print and audio tape, the story of Kent's Century of Coal. He was awarded the British Empire Medal, the BEM, for his work, in the New Year's Honours List of 2019.

At its peak in the late 1930s, the Kent Coalfield was employing more than 7500 miners. Jim Davies is determined that their story, their achievements, shall not be forgotten.

CHAPTER EIGHT
Life Underground

*"This world is full of willing people –
some willing to work, the rest willing
to let them."*
Robert Frost, 1970

Malcolm John Pitt lived in a neat, well-ordered suburban street in Broadstairs. The hedges are trimmed and, on most days, the air is full of the sound of children playing in the school just opposite his black and white front gate. Which is appropriate because both Malcolm and his wife, Elizabeth, believed education to be among the most important aspects of Life.

Malcolm was a grammar school boy. He was as bright as a button and after he left Sir Roger Manwood's

Malcolm Pitt at rally (on right)

School, Sandwich, in 1960, he went to Selwyn College, Cambridge, to study political history and PPE. He was the first of the Pitt family ever to go to university and his family were very proud. His mother, Elsie, was a bookkeeper. His father, John, known as Jack, managed a department store, Foster Brothers in Margate, a traditional family business where messages and money were crammed into small cannisters and sucked through a tube system above the heads of the customers, to be deposited with a final gasp in the area where financial reckonings were made. Malcolm was close to his father. When he died, Malcolm wrote on Jack's prayer card a quotation from Shakespeare's *Julius Caesar*:

'His life was gentle and the elements so mixed in him. That nature might stand up and say to all the world this was a Man.'

An imposing 6ft 5in tall, Jack Pitt was one of a family of 11 and a man with radical ideas. There were miners in the Pitt family and politics were seldom off the meal time agenda. Malcolm remembered "a romantic idealism in our conversations…don't dwell on the past: Learn from the past and look to the future. I don't know what I'd have done without him…"

Malcolm met Elizabeth at the Saturday dance. They both liked traditional jazz. She was studying at the Maria Assumptia College in Kensington. Soon after Malcolm gained his degree, he converted to Catholicism. He taught at the Catholic Holy Cross Secondary School in Broadstairs for six years.

Elizabeth, too, became a teacher. Coincidentally, her father, Ken was headmaster at Holy Cross, and it was almost as if everything had been pre-ordained. Church on Sundays. Three daughters, Catherine, Marcella and Rebecca; one, two, three. They grew to share their parents' belief in Christian values. Then Malcolm was off to Oxford University in 1971, to take the equivalent of a Master's degree, the Advanced Certificate of Education. Elizabeth remembers: "We bought a house in Oxford for £5,000. We sold it a year later for £10,000 once Malcolm had his degree and then we moved back to Broadstairs. I remember thinking we'd never be poor. We'd made a 100% profit and we felt secure."

But for Malcolm, capitalism was not the key. University had sharpened his political appetite. He joined the communist party. In November 1974, there was a fascist rally in Ramsgate. He went along to protest. He had also joined the judo club and, when a policeman tried to restrain Malcolm's vigorous protest, Malcolm instinctively threw him to the ground. He went to court charged with using threatening words and behaviour, and the local magistrate fined him £15 with £15 costs. For Malcolm, it was a seminal moment. He was puzzled. It was his first clash with authority. In his statement to the court, he said: "I took part in an anti-fascist demonstration at the St Lawrence Hall, Ramsgate...I was saying, "This is a fascist meeting, don't support it..." He recalled that he was punched by a National Front steward and that he saw a fellow protester "surrounded by National Front stewards...a man in trouble." He said he had drawn the attention of two police constables, both to the fact that he had been assaulted and that his fellow protester was surrounded. "The police did nothing. The crowd moved forward to protect the man. I was with them. A police constable appeared to be about to strike me and I threw up my arms to protect my face. As I retreated…I was grabbed from behind…across the throat…my assailant was carried forward by his own weight and to my surprise, I saw it was a police officer…I was charged with assault. I asked who exactly I was meant to have assaulted…"

Malcolm later wrote that the experience illustrated two aspects of life – injustice, because he felt he was the injured party during the exercise of his legitimate right to protest, and, secondly, disillusionment because he had felt the power of the state as an institution, to behave as it wishes, with little chance of redress.

Throughout his life, Malcolm Pitt, academic, father of three, loved to explore possibilities. He would spend hours discussing what Elizabeth describes as "the meaning of Life." The experience of university seemed to have unsettled him. He questioned everything, his faith, society's morals, attitudes, capitalism and the way we lived. He wanted to help those who couldn't help themselves. He wanted to taste what it was like to be a manual worker.

So he became a miner. He enrolled at the Tilmanstone pit in the Kent Coalfield. His parents who had brought up this bright-eyed youngster and watched him follow the road to academia were, well, surprised. To put it mildly.

Malcolm was a miner for 14 years. For seven of those years he worked at the coal face. He suffered from eczema related to the conditions he worked in every day in his life underground. He once narrowly escaped serious injury and emerged with a damaged hand. He left notes and a manuscript,[105] precise and evocative, recording what it was like to work in Tilmanstone in the 1970s. His strong angular

---

[105] Malcolm Pitt's book, The World on Our Backs, Lawrence & Wishart (1979), also includes his memories of the miners' strike of 1972

writing leans to the left, which is appropriate. The word pictures he draws are both clear and poetic, affectionate, yet bitter. It is one of the best-informed descriptions of the life of a Kent miner. For that reason, I quote from his writing freely. He begins by setting the context of 'Kent's Century of Coal':

Coal and iron attracted the attention of industrialists and financial speculators from Britain, France and Germany. Companies mushroomed, went bankrupt, amalgamated and were bought out. A new colliery was started in Kent in almost every year between 1906 and the outbreak of the Great War: Tilmanstone (1906), Guilford (1907), Snowdown (1908), Wingham (1910), Woodnesborough (1910), Stonehall (1912) and Chislet (1913). Enormous difficulties were encountered from the start – inrushes of water, dangerous geological condition, and financial complications. Out of the pre-war speculation, only the collieries at Tilmanstone, Snowdown and Chislet were to survive. In 1924 the sinking started for

The Brotherhood of Kent miners

a new colliery at Betteshanger, and the quartet of the Kent Coalfield was complete.

The four pits were sunk in the middle of a pre-industrial society. Farming, fishing and the holiday trade were the economic mainstay of the area. East Kent had been missed by the Industrial Revolution, and the industrial worker was almost unknown, except as a day-tripper on a seasonal spree in Margate. Even here, though his money was gratefully received, the industrial worker was thought to lower the tone of the place and to scare away the traditionally upper-middle-class clientele of the South Coast. In the coastal towns, a small middle class of builders, brewers, lawyers and doctors held social sway over a motley crew of boarding house keepers, publicans, shop-keepers, boat-owning fishermen and the small army of casual, seasonal workers who scratched a meagre living from the holiday trade. In the countryside, society was still divided into the social classes established in the 18th Century, the landed gentry, yeoman farmer and agricultural worker. There were no indigenous miners in Kent. The sinkers, timber-men, haulage boys, colliers, winding-men – all the skilled men needed to work the collieries – had to be imported from established coalfields.

They were a special breed of men, with their own language, customs, attitudes and traditions of struggle and organisation created by the harsh nature of pit work and the isolation of the pit villages. Even in the industrial north, the birth-place of the industrial working class, the miners were a race apart. The progressive tendency of industrial capitalism to concentrate labour, machines, materials and credit into industrial cities linked by a network of roads, railways, and telegraph wires, had been brushed aside by the immovability of the coal measures. Capital had to go to the coal, and men, women and children were compelled by necessity to follow.

By 1980, Malcolm, now a member of the Communist Party, was President of the Kent area of the National Union of Mine Workers. He analysed the community he felt he was representing in the class struggle.

Coal was king, and determined the location of the collieries and the working environment of the miners. The extent of the coal seams, their depth, thickness, texture, fractures and the surrounding rock, shaped the underground world in which the miners spent a large number of their working hours. The pit and the village isolated the miners from their fellow industrial workers and turned them inwards, away from the outside world and towards their workmates, wives and families. A community against the cruel consequences of accident, illness and death in the pits. This social solidarity was the foundation of a strong, trade union organisation able to resist the coal mine owners' attacks on the living standards and working conditions of the miners. Every miner who came into Kent was the carrier of this unique complex outlook and attitudes. In the worst physical conditions in British mining and in an alien, hostile social environment, the social, trade union and political traditions of many coalfields merged, cross-fertilised and took root. A living social system was created, totally at odds with its surroundings which only reinforced its insularity and the unbreakable strength of its inner cohesion.

The pit dominates the life of a mining community far more than the factory influences the lives of other sections of the industrial working class. Though the pit villages of Elvington,

Aylesham and Mill Hill are situated some distance from the collieries, the pit-head is never far from sight. The gearheads are permanent reminders of the underground world, which moulds and controls the lives of the miners, their wives and children. They mark the entrance to a totally different world of toil, danger and death. Even for the men who work down the pit, it is completely beyond the powers of the imagination to conceive that 2/3000 feet below the fields, marshes and orchards there are hundreds of men working at the coal. Similarly, when a man is working underground, he finds it equally impossible to relate in any real terms to the world on top. Men often talk in the pit about where they are in relation to the surface and try to pinpoint well-known landmarks.

Malcolm then records what he felt to be working underground at Tilmanstone Colliery in the 1980s, a decade which would be among the most tumultuous in the history of the Kent Coalfield.

Few men can honestly say that they can really imagine that 3000 feet of rock and chalk separate them from cows chewing the grass. The miner underground is somewhere, but nowhere, temporarily imprisoned in a world of unchanging artificial light and working to a routine at complete variance with the natural division of the day. Only when there is a major disaster and everyone is discussing what the chances are of trapped men ever getting out alive, or when there is some trouble with the winding gear, with all the men on pit-bottom waiting to go up, and someone jokes, 'Don't worry, Alf, you can always climb the rope', does a man become acutely conscious of his precise situation in the depths of the earth.

It is this complete difference between the environment of the surface and the mine that makes the act of going to work such an effort for most miners. Going to work on the bus through the Kent countryside for an afternoon shift is a sheer test of will. The bus passes though orchards and fields, past country pubs still serving the dinner-time drinkers. Someone is sure to express the forlorn hope that the bus will break down, or get wedged between two parked cars or, as they pass the Eastry Mental Hospital, voice the opinion that the only mad people in the world are the men in the pits. The ordeal continues until the men are on the cage and down the pit. A team of men will move off from the canteen when someone summons up the will to say, 'Come on, let's get in there, and get it over with'. It is said with the finality of a prison sentence. Miners often say that the worst part of the shift is getting into the pit.

A factory is built of brick and steel on solid foundations and can be left for some time without supervision before it deteriorates in any serious way. But when coal and rock are taken out of the earth and a mine is made, the equilibrium of millions of years is disturbed. Tremendous weights go into motion, explosive and poisonous gasses are released, and water, hitherto confined to the rock strata, flows into man-made channels. The miner's job is not to stop these natural forces, because that is not humanly possible, but continually to control them.

Malcolm's carefully written manuscript addresses the ever-present danger lurking above the miner's heads.

When a roadway is opened up, the weight of the rock above comes down, and the rock at the sides moves inwards, forcing the floor upwards, like a boil being squeezed. Anywhere in the pit where a wall of brick has been built, or a concrete floor laid, great cracks appear as the rigid surfaces are caught in the vice of the moving rocks. A piece of timber dropped in the side will be fast and impossible to get out by the next day. 'Let it go, Kent's got it', a man will be told as he struggles to release it. 'Kent's on the move again', a man will reply to the echoing thud of stone as a steel girder visibly sags under immense weight. Steel props and rings, circular steel girders used to vault the roadways will sink into a soft floor like nails hammered into wood.

Some of the best coal in Kent had to be abandoned in the Millyard Seam in Betteshanger Colliery because the floor was so soft that the roadways could not be kept open. Men, called 'back-rippers', have to be continually employed, like Forth Bridge painters, taking out rock from the roof and setting new supports, while 'dinters' dig out rock from the 'blown' floor. But for the continuous action of pumps, the pit would be flooded out in a short time. At Tilmanstone Colliery, the men work on the Millyard Seam at 3000 feet, 1440 feet below the abandoned workings in the Beresford Seam, which are now a vast lake whose flood waters are kept from plunging down the shaft by the constant attention of pumpmen.

The Kent Coalfield was always wet, from the moment coal deposits were discovered at Shakespeare Cliff in Dover. Malcolm wrote:

In every colliery in Kent, water is an ever-present danger and discomfort, coming through the roof, welling up from the floor and collecting in dips in the roadways and faces. Though gas has never been a major problem in the Kent coalfield, its absence can never be taken for granted. Small pockets of explosive methane, 'fire-damp', can collect in small hollows in the roof, and the open ground behind the advance of the face. In old workings, or man-holes in the side of roadways asphyxiating quantities of carbon dioxide – 'black damp' – can lie close to the ground to catch the unwary miner taking a forbidden nap. Carbon monoxide, 'white-damp', is produced by the action of underground fires, and will poison a man before he is aware of its presence. In every way the earth seems to fight back against the intrusion of men into its depths.

The continually changing environment of the underground world makes the presence of men in the pit for twenty-four hours a day a necessity for safety, which coal mine owners and the National Coal Board have used as an excuse for keeping men in the pit day and night to produce coal. Shift work, as in other industries, has had the effect of cutting the men off socially from other people, centring their lives around the pit and within the narrow confines of the mining community. The hours of pit shift workers and their rotation have vastly strengthened the natural tendency of men doing the same job, and living in the same village, to spend their leisure time in each other's company. Inevitably, the miner finds himself drinking and taking part in activities mainly with other miners. The local darts team will play every week, but the miner will only be able to play one (evening) in two or even three. Local societies and political organisations hold regular meetings which the miner is prevented from attending by the ordinances of pit deployment. The home becomes an appendage of the pit, and its members are forced into gear, letting the man of the house sleep, getting his meals and making his 'snap'[106] according to the dictates of

---

[106] Snap – a meal taken by the miner into the colliery

his shift. To the normal tensions in family life, particularly between fathers and adolescent sons, are added the strains of shift working, and many a boy leaves home as a result of an argument with this father over 'taking his mother for granted' – in reality, (it is a question of) which one of them has the first claim on her time and energies.

Over the period of declining wages in the coalfield, more and more women took up employment in local factories to boost the family exchequer, with the result that husbands and wives became strangers to each other, the husband waking up in an empty bed, going to work from an empty house, and coming home to a wife already asleep. Not a few marriages have floundered amid the shoals of competing shift patterns worked out by time and motion men interested solely in the productivity of the 'Company' or the 'Board'.

Malcolm pursued the disruption that shift work has on the miners' personal lives:

Each shift has its own character, plusses and minuses for the men who work it. The mining day is divided into three sections – days, afternoons and nights. The day shift starts at 6 in the morning when men start going down the pit, and finishes at 1.45pm when the first men are wound up the pit. A miner changes for work, rides up the pit, washes and gets out of his working clothes in his own time. For men living some distance away from the pit, the shift starts much earlier. A miner in Ramsgate gets up about 4.30am to catch the pit bus at about 5. It is a time in the morning when food is unappetising, and most men make do with a very light breakfast, often confined to a cup of tea or coffee. There is generally an air of quiet despondency and surliness about the men at the pit bus stop, exacerbated by the darkness, cold and rain of the winter months. Conversation is intermittent and punctuated by remarks about the absurdity of being awake at such an outlandish hour. 'Getting up in the middle of the night', and 'Not even animals are awake at this hour' are typical, and repeated most mornings, to murmurs of agreement and deprecating comments about politician, broadcasters and Coal Board officials who, now comfortably asleep in bed, are continually slamming the miners for 'irresponsible' wage claims. Making men get up early in the morning is clearly a strong incitement to class hatred. In old miners' minds, it carries the memory of days when the light of the sun was never seen, when a man went down the pit before the sun came up, and came out of the pit after it has gone down. The Monday day-shift is particularly hated. It is the first shift after the weekend holiday, and heralds a week of early mornings and long shifts underground. The miner is continually reminded of the fact at the pit. The canteen

South Wales miners, 1910

is empty. There are none of the night-shift men to greet the oncoming day-shift men, and give them the latest news and gossip from the underground. There are no meat pies baked or sandwiches cut up for the man who wants to snatch a quick breakfast, or take some food down the pit to make up for the snap (miners' food tin) left on the kitchen table. The clean lockers are quiet. There are none of the cheerful remarks from off-going men, washed, dressed and ready to go home, 'I bet you're glad to be here', and 'Are you fit?'. The bath floor is dry as the men walk through to the dirty lockers where their pit clothes, 'pit-black', are dusty, stiff with dried sweat and oil, and their boots seem to be made of cast iron, curled up like pantomime shoes for Aladdin.

After the shift, when the men are out of the pit, and are taking off their lamps and self-rescuers in the lamp-room, the atmosphere is completely different, lighter and chattier, even flippant. 'Best part of the shift', a man says, drying himself off in the clean lockers, or, 'That's done. One down. Four to go'.

At first sight, the day shift appears to be the most humane of the three shifts. It seems roughly to fit into the normal working day and to allow the miner to enjoy a traditionally social evening. But, given variations in age and health, most men are not fit for very much after getting up so early and working a shift in the heat, dust and bad air of the pit. Many men take a nap on the settee when they get home so that they can spend a normal evening, watching television, having a drink. However, the necessity to get to bed early to make the morning shift is always at the back of their minds, and is a continual restraint on activities.

The only shift where sleep presents no problems is the afternoon one which begins at 2pm and finishes at

9.45pm. It is a shift universally acknowledged to be the best for sleep and a happy married life. However, most men are reluctant to go to bed almost immediately after work, and the prospect of staying in bed in the morning does not seem to make up for the total annihilation of the evening. The morning is to most men a short, rather futile interlude before going to work. Men say, 'It's all work on afters.[107] You're either at work, coming home from work or waiting to go to work'. Betteshanger and Snowdown Collieries have introduced an early afternoon shift which tries to obviate the problems of the normal afternoon shift. It has become quite popular with the regular drinkers; it allows a man to have a drink in the evening without having to think about an early rising, and has been widely nicknamed the 'boozers" shift.

The night shift is the most abnormal, routine-disturbing and anti-social of the three. It is a world of its own which is either made (of) a way of life, or is an unnatural intrusion into a man's neural programming. The men on regular nights are a community within a community and have completely developed a pattern of living, to which they become so conditioned that many of them could not change to another shift without seriously disturbing their whole metabolism. Whereas the novice on nights will fall into bed immediately on getting home from work and get up after a fitful sleep at midday, the veteran 'nights man' will eat his dinner, spend the morning at his own pursuits, have a drink with his mates at midday and go to bed in the afternoon. On waking he will have his breakfast and go to work, having followed a normal routine transposed in time. But to the three-shift rotation

---

[107] Afters – afternoon shift

man, nights can present a serious challenge to his system. He may suffer from insomnia brought on by the need to sleep at an unaccustomed time during the morning, from acute digestive upsets caused by meals forced down at abnormal hours, and from a loss of time sense.

The strength of habit of our nervous system, and its resistance to rapid change, can be easily evaluated by the fact that many men on three shift-rotation will assert that on nights the pit seems darker than on days or afternoons. They admit that it's completely irrational, but they are quite definite about the fact of thinking it. These side-effects of shift rotation are the most damaging to the miner. The weekly change of shift never allows the nervous system to adjust to any one set of sleeping, eating, working and social habits. At the end of every week, discussion will centre on the next week's shift, and what shift is the best to work. Every miner has his own particular preference but, after the pros and cons have been gone over, the general consensus us 'none of them are any good'.

Malcolm's manuscript spells out in detail the daily routine of entering the underground world of a coalmine.

Whatever shift the miner is on, he must go through the same routine, near ritual, preparation for his descent below ground. He has to be totally equipped for his sojourn underground before he steps onto the cage. If he forgets anything on pit-top, he will have to do without it for the entire shift, or else try to cadge it from someone down the pit. The latter is not generally a very difficult task unless it becomes routine, when the offender will be told that a man has enough to do to carry his own gear without carrying everybody else's.

The miner's first stop after his arrival at the pit is the Deployment Centre. Here he reports for work, and his place of work is decided. Most men have a permanent job, and, if it is available, they are entitled to claim it. If a man with a regular job is deployed anywhere else in the pit, there will be an inevitable dispute.

Other men, however, are 'on the market', and are available for any work that is going. Every man starts on the market until he joins a team or is given a regular job. The Deployment Centre works out who is present at the pit, where the gaps are in manning and who will fill them. The 'plan' is telephoned down to the pit bottom office where the deputies and overmen direct the men to their place of work. The Deployment Centre is usually manned by ex-miners, injured in the pit or suffering from an industrial disease, and their twisted limbs and limps are a vivid visual aid for the usually unimaginative safety posters which adorn the walls.

Every man tells the deployment clerk his number through a hatch and receives two 'checks' from a numbered board. The checks are metals discs, of different shapes, with the man's number stamped on them. Check systems vary from pit to pit, but the general principle is the same in all, a means whereby managements can keep a check on the whereabouts of the men: if a man has come to work, what time he arrived; if he has been to the lamp-room, what time he went down the pit, where he is in the pit, if he has come out of the pit, and what time he came back through the lamp-room. Despite the Coal Board's insistence that the check system was only introduced in the interests of safety, it met considerable resistance from the men who saw it as merely another means of management surveillance. One pit in Kent celebrated its introduction by chucking the checks down the shaft at the end of the first shift.

One check is kept by the miner all the time he is underground and is normally attached to a clip on his battery. This check will be used to identify him if he is killed during the shift and his body has been rendered unrecognisable, in much the same way as tags are used in the army or Air Force.

The miner will probably go into the canteen and collect snuff, chewing tobacco, boiled sweets or chewing gum, or have a cup of team and a cigarette before undressing at the clean lockers, picking up his washing gear and going through the dirty lockers, picking up his washing gear, going back through to the dirty lockers to put on his pit black. Most miners dress and undress about eight times a day:

> Dress on getting up,
> Undress in clean lockers,
> Dress in dirty lockers,
> Undress underground before working,
> Dress underground after working,
> Undress in dirty lockers,
> Dress in clean lockers,
> Undress before going to bed

If a miner goes out in the evening and likes to be smart add twice more – undress on getting home, dress for going out.

In most cases, pit black is a normal set of clothes with minor adjustments like enlarged pockets for a flask, sandwiches, etc., but made incredibly dirty with coal-dust, grease, oil, pit-water, rust, wood-sap, and sundry other pollutants, and visibly rotting under the impact.

Waistcoats are very popular for the combinations of pocket room and the maximum freedom of movement for the arms. The men have to provide their own working clothes and, as the NBC does not undertake to launder them, articles of pit black are often worn until they become too foul and decayed to merit taking home to be washed, and are dumped in the rubbish baskets which line the walls of the lockers.

Conditions underground may vary dramatically – hot, damp, dry, cold. The miners' 'uniform' varies accordingly.

The amounts of clothing worn by a miner depends entirely on his place of work in the pit, as temperatures can vary between extremes of oppressive, humid heat and intense cold. A man with no regular job will go down the pit muffled up in a donkey jacket, pullover and scarf, but will be prepared to strip down to his underpants if he should be deployed to the dusty heat of a tail-gate heading. The miner leaves the dirty lockers clad in steel-capped boots, a plastic helmet and a heavy belt. He will normally carry a water-bottle, sometimes a round metal can called a Dudley – after a manufacturer – but more than likely a plastic orange or detergent container and a snap tin, a metal box made of two interlocking compartments, rounded at one end, for sandwiches. Leather gauntlets, knee-pads and a dust-mask complete his equipment before he continues his progress to the lamp-room.

The miner passes though the turnstile of the lamp-room, and takes down his third and last check from the hook over his lamp.

The impenetrable blackness of the mine can be disorientating for the newcomer. It is likely that what follows is autobiographical – Malcolm Pitt describing what, as a young miner, happened to him.

It is difficult to imagine how absolute, total and complete is the darkness of the mine. In almost every 'on the surface' situation, total darkness is unknown, and there is always some source of light however weak and diffuse. We often talk about 'his eyes got accustomed to the dark'. But the only light in the pit is man-made, and comes down the shaft through electric cables or the battery on a miner's belt. A Welshman at Tilmanstone tells how his lamp went out when he was alone, deep in the pit. To be so suddenly deprived of sight was a shattering experience. First, he tried to feel his way with his hands outstretched but, stumbling helplessly over formless obstacles and catching himself on sharp rocks in the side, he lost his sense of direction and began to panic in the darkness. He sat down on the firm ground of the roadway and steadied himself to think. He was in the return airway and, as long as he followed the draught of warm air, he thought to himself, he must come to pit-steel rails in the middle of the roadway, and the idea struck him that here was his guideline. With one foot always against the side of the rail, and keeping the warm air on the back of his neck, he made slow progress to pit-bottom.

Even with the lamp alight, the miner's sight is severely restricted, and a good sense of hearing is a great aid to survival. On the surface, the eyes will blink in a reflex action to keep out small particles or insects even before the person is conscious of their proximity. But in the pit, this defensive mechanism is nullified by the scarcity of light, and the miner's eye is vulnerable to flying pieces of grit and metal. Young miners are always told that the worst thing a man can do in the pit is to throw anything at a man's face. When the atmosphere is very dusty after coal and rocks have been cut by machines, or blown out by explosives, the light from a cap-lamp is reflected and dispersed by the moving particles, and the miner is surrounded by a luminous fog, like a diver on the bottom of a muddy river, immobilised until the dust has settled.

From another rack in the lamp-room, the miner takes his self-rescuer, and attaches it to his belt. The self-rescuer is a heavy, cumbersome, sealed metal box, which contains a mask designed to prevent carbon monoxide poisoning in the case of a pit-fire. Thus equipped, *cap*-à-*pie*, the miner can now approach the pit-head.

The miner's entrance to this underground world is crude and sudden.

The shaft is a black hole in which the miner can see a swirling cloud of vapour rising from the depths below. With the hum of the winding gear, the iron thud of the lowered draw-bridge, and the buzz of electric bells, the cage surfaces from the shaft. The banksman removes the iron gates, and the men file on to the empty deck.

The cage is not designed for the transit of men unless, as was once remarked by a Betteshanger miner, the designers were 'under the impression that all miners are five foot nothing'. It is an iron box, with two or three decks specifically built to wind mine-cars in and out of the pit. The men fit uncomfortably into the space available between the rails and jacks of the floor and the girders of the roof, and they slip about in the grease and dirt

Betteshanger miners

and are soaked by the continual drizzle of water down the shaft. In the early days at Betteshanger, a massive skip was attached to the rope to wind coal out of the pit, and the men would crouch in its bottom covered in sacks, swinging and rotating as they were lowered to the workings. After half a century, miners were at last no longer treated as sacks of meat, but given all the respect due to living cattle. As the last men step on to the cage, they are pushed back by the gate-man as he slots in the heavy grill, and the unwary miner may well be caught with his head fast to a girder against the natural inclination of his neck, or with the self-rescuer of the man in-front stuck hard into his groin.

The cage is the lowered slowly in jerks and pulled up to allow the men on to the top deck. For the men on the bottom deck, suspended over a two or three-thousand-foot void by a steel cable, the phrase 'hanging about' is given a new dimension. With a hiss of compressed air, the draw-bridge is raised, the signal bell rings, and the cage is released on its downward journey.

The descent is quite slow at first, but the cage rapidly gathers speed until it is dropping at a speed of about 35 feet per second into the darkness. The air rushes past the falling gate – and through the holes in its iron sides, playing on the faces of the men, and lifting the hair below the rims of their helmets. There is the quick, sudden rush of sound of the other cage passing on its ascent of the shaft, like two express trains passing each other in a tunnel. The continual creaking of the guide ropes which keep the cage on a steady course are a reminder of the dangers of riding the pit.

The risk of death or injury is part of the common currency of conversation in a pit.

The shafts of the Kent pits have always been associated with the death of men. An onsetter at Tilmanstone tells how his grandfather was working on the shaft and, under the impact of a sudden inrush of water, the platform on which the men were working broke loose from its cables and tipped the men down into the sump. It was a night shift, and the grandfather had been having a drink in a local pub before going to work. When one of his mates came in to pick him up from the pub, he said at first that he wasn't going to work that night as he had a funny feeling that something was going to happen. But in the end, he decided to ignore the warning, and he went to work and his precipitous death. These stories are the common tradition of the coalfield. They are told by father to their sons, and by old instructors to their trainees. They become part of the bloody backcloth against which the miner carries on his working life.

Death and injury are rarely discussed without becoming the subject of a grim joke. During one snap time at Tilmanstone, the men were sitting together in the roadway, discussing what it's like to be dead. 'It can't be that bad' said one of the numerous Nobby Clarks. 'Only one bastard has ever come back, and he didn't hang around for long'.

When an injured man is carried out on a stretcher, he will often be asked by his mates where he lives. An address given in reply to the apparently sincere concern of his workmates to inform his wife, will attract the rejoinder: 'Good, we wouldn't like to think she was going to be lonely!'

Pit humour is a continuous, often cruel torrent of words which push back the darkness, and the pressing nearness of danger and death.

It is a generally observed convention for men to turn out their lamps in the cage. The beam will illuminate the walls of the shaft and, quite suddenly, the visual impression of descending at great speed will be inverted, and the cage appears to be going back up the shaft. At full speed, it becomes increasingly difficult to imagine that the cage can ever by brought to a standstill, except by the rock and mud of the pit sump. But there is a jerk of brakes being applied and relaxed, and as it is repeated the cage slows down. The shaft begins to become visible. The shadowy silhouettes of men's heads begin to appear, and the cage lands in the barrel vault of the pit-bottom amid the orange and white glare of electric and neon lights.

As they file off the cage, the air at the pit-bottom is often warm and humid, usually laced with a fetid stench.

The miners place their checks into a rusty tin, held out by a pit-bottom man whose shabby donkey-jacket, dirty boots, hitched-up ragged trousers and grimy hands and face conjure up the picture of a down-and-out with a begging bowl. At Tilmanstone Colliery, the men have to walk in the face of a strong blast of dusty air which makes them lower their heads and hold on to their helmets like city gents trying to save their bowlers from a London gale. At Betteshanger, the current of air is less violent but is heavy with droplets of the icy cold water which continually drizzles from the roof, and makes rippling, oily puddles in the roadway.

On the other side of the pit, the down-cast shaft pit-bottom is swept by a chilling draft of fresh air, drawn straight from the surface. Men walk backwards and forwards rubbing their hands together, wrapped in monstrous ancient overcoats which have been kept permanently in the pit from time immemorial for any unlucky 'market-man' deployed to work in this artificial desert.

Most miners begin and finish their working lives underground on pit-bottom. It is a long, monotonous shift which begins as soon as the man is off the cage, and continues – often under the eye of the officials – until the colliers ride the pit at knock-off.

Men new to the pit, after a preliminary training, will spend their first few months underground uncoupling empty mine-cars as they come off the cage, or pressing the buttons which operate a series of creepers.[108] The creepers draw a journey of mine-carts full of coal into the range of powerful rams which push them individually on to the cage. It is soul-destroying work demanding no special skill beyond a modicum of common-sense, and attracting more than its fair share of abuse from colliers, rippers and ovther workers. 'A young, strong lad like you idling about on pit-bottom. Get in the pit, man!' In the showers, the clean back of a young man on pit-bottom will draw sarcastic remarks from the black

---

[108] Creepers are coal conveyent belts

Welsh miner's wife washing husband, 1931

figures of the other men, 'If all our backs were as clean as yours, we wouldn't have much to worry about!' and 'What do you want your back washed for?'. The pit-bottom man is on the lowest rung of the underground social hierarchy, and getting a dirtier and heavier job on supplies or haulage is considered by most pit-bottom men to be a blessed relief.

Being a miner inevitably takes its toll. For the veteran, coming to the end of his working life through age or infirmity, employment is rare and treasured.

For the old men on pit-bottom, the only other jobs they can hope for are on the surface, with a consequent loss of income. A pit-bottom man has probably worked all his life 'on the coal' in a world of men where physical strength and stamina are not considered merely to be a necessary qualification for a particularly arduous job, but qualities admirable and even praiseworthy in themselves. His skill as a 'pit-man' is his proudest possession, a source of dignity and self-respect against the insult of 'dirty miner' from an ignorant and hostile world. But dust, injury and, above all, age, take away from his strength and agility; his breath becomes short and hard to get. The 'Let's have a minute' becomes longer and more frequent, and the 'Give us a lift with this' is offered by his mates before he even asks. There comes a time when there is a job vacant on pit-bottom, and someone in Deployment asks him if he'd like to give it a try. He takes the job, often consoling himself with the thought that he can always go back on the face, back to the coal. But he never does, and the skills and knowledge of a lifetime become redundant – a mere relic of youth and strength. So he carves out a niche for himself on the bottom, learning and creating the knacks which will make the job go smoothly, and trying to make himself indispensable.

Every day, a veteran Welsh miner sits in the dirty lockers at Betteshanger morosely smoking a cigarette before having a bath. He is a talented compere, singer and raconteur, widely read and with a passion for painting. He is about fifty, and works as a pit deputy. Contract work on the rips had ruined his back beyond repair, and his life is punctuated by recurring bouts of crippling pain. One morning, he summed up the prospects of old age in the pit. 'In other societies, when you grow old, you are respected, venerated for your age and experience. But in our society, you're past it, finished. Put him on a switch, on the scrap heap!'

The business and geographic heart of the pits is the upcast pit-bottom, the base camp for the underground community. The roads of a mine are laid out to enable air to be drawn down the 'downcast' shaft, through the coalfaces and back up the upcast shaft to the surface.

Comparatively well lit, and hollowed out of the pillar of coal which protects the shaft, the upcast pit- bottom has a look of permanency and stability. Here, the coal and rock are hidden behind white washed brickwork and concrete blocks, and held back by huge steel rings and girders. In the pit-bottom are the offices of the under-manager, overmen and deputies, with desks and chairs, notices, telephones and switchboard. Here, a man can take off his lamp and battery, have a cup of tea and read a newspaper in comparative comfort. Nearby, off narrow brick alleys, are fitters' and electricians' workshops. It is the one area of the pit where there is a broom, an implement which anywhere else would have as little function as a mop on the beach.

From the pit-bottom, the major roadways stretch out into the pit, and are the highways of this underground world of tunnels and passages. The roads are named and numbered accordingly to the geography of the pit. The road along which the air passes to the face is called the 'intake'; from the face, the 'return'. In addition, the road or 'gate' in which the conveyor belts take coal from the face to pit-bottom is called the 'main'; that at the other end of the face, the 'tail'. Roads are also numbered according to the district of face which they serve. For example, in Tilmanstone Colliery, there is a major roadway called '2's Return',[109] off which there are several 'tail-gates' to faces, each numbered in order, odds on one side of the road and evens on the other, as they progress into the pit.

One exception to the rule is that there is no '13's Face'.

---

[109] '2's return' refers to No 2 shaft

CHAPTER NINE
The Miner's Road

*"You've never seen 'dark' 'til you've
seen dark in a coalmine."*
Tom Benner, 1960

Most people have a confused notion of the lay-out of a mine, a mental picture of tunnels and walls of coal, connected haphazardly with a shaft, and a general idea that most miners are colliers who work on the coal-face with a pick and shovel. Propaganda of the time describes roomy, level roadways of Roman straightness, leading to spacious, well-ventilated coalfaces, worked almost entirely by machines and manned by overalled technicians.

Neither is a true picture.

In his summary of what it was like to be a miner in Tilmanstone in the 1970s, miner Malcolm Pitt describes the Kent Coalfield thus: the coal seams are depressed into a basin, fractured and disuniform in dimension. They resemble a saucer which has been dropped, broken into pieces and hastily reassembled, with bits overlapping and parts splintered to dust. This geological environment conditions the geography of the pit, its specific physical characteristics and contours, and its climate. The roadways of the pit cling to the seams

Steel prop and bar coalface

like dogs to a hare. They rise and fall with the undulations of the coal and jump up the giant steps where massive sections of the earth have faulted and fallen away. Every such ascent is a memory in the lives of the miners who toiled to drive the road through the solid rock in pursuit of the coal.

In the days of the coal-owners, Pearson and Dorman Long, once the men left the pit-bottom of Snowdown Colliery, they had to run bent double for two-and-a-half miles to the coal faces. The management would maintain the road ways only sufficiently to let tubs in and out, and haulage boys spent most of their time getting the tubs back on to the road after hitting props and bars. The low roadways, often blocked with the debris of roof falls, prevented the proper circulation of air to ventilate the pit. Snowdown Colliery, already incredibly hot from the depth of the workings, became known as 'the Inferno'. Haulage boys of 15 worked naked, wearing nothing but a leather pad over their buttocks to push over the tubs when they came off the road.

The underground railway that sometimes carries the men along the road to their work is called a 'paddy'.

The modern roadways of the pit are often provided with an underground railway, a 'paddy'. Notices announce the set times when the paddy leaves the pit-bottom station, and warn the men not to mount or dismount while it is moving. Like commuters on the way to the office, the miners discuss the affairs of the industry, the results of the darts or cricket match, the latest canine acquisitions, and offer each other a 'pinch' of snuff. The men turn off their cap lamps and, as the paddy moves away from the electric lights of the station, the faces of the men opposite fade into silhouettes against the circular beam of the spotlight on the front. The paddy is pulled along by a steel cable which circulates the drum of a huge traction engine. An engine-driver starts and stops the paddy instructed by the number of rings given by the paddyman on overhead wires. On occasion, the paddy has run away down one of the many steep gradients of the road, and the men have been forced to bail out into the darkness of the side. One paddy road in Tilmanstone was so steep that the paddy had to stop half-way up while the engine driver changed gear. The paddy was literally suspended in the middle of a stone gorge carved out between a nave of steel rings from which hung some strange kind of stalactites formed by the incessantly running water from the roof. At regular intervals, the spotlight picks out the bricked-up entrance to a worked-out face, and the men will swop reminiscences about the time they worked there. Up ahead, the dull orange glow of a grimy lamp in the roof marks the bottom of the road to a face.

A bell rings once, and the paddy comes to a standstill. A team of men dismount and begin the long walk up the road. The air is now quite hot, and there is the smell of stagnant water. The dust lies thick on the floor and, as the men walk on, their boots kick up a cloud of fine particles which make a man spit to clear his throat. As the road begins to climb, the men begin to feel prickly with the heat, and their breathing becomes heavier. A few older men will take a short rest on some bags of stones to get their breath back. It is a customary stop, as they will have to walk another thousand yards before they reach the face. Many of them are getting near to retirement after 50 years underground. They may have bronchitis or a chronic back complaint, and they will all have some dust in their lungs. The rest of the men continue their march, and the side of the road begins to be littered with wooden blocks, steel girders and lengths of bark-covered timber, stacked lattice fashion to stop them toppling into the road. The huge metal mass of the switches and transformers, suspended from the steel girders, announces that the column is nearing its destination. The supplies men and switch boys have already sat down on lengths of timber to have a sandwich for breakfast, and the lights of the colliers and rippers are dancing on the sheer rock face of the heading. Beneath the grey, slaty semi-circle of stone, there is the sparkling, black band of coal.

The coalfaces need a constant supply of materials, mainly timbers for the roof, to keep in production. These supplies are brought into the pit from the pit-bottom by the haulage men.

Before the war,[110] young miners used to start on the haulage before going on to the face as a collier, and today, men of 50 on the haulage are commonly called 'haulage boys' or 'timber lads', while colliers of 25 are referred to as 'the men'.

Haulage systems vary from pit to pit according to the size and layout of the roadways, and the transport available. At Tilmanstone, the materials come down the upcast shaft in mine-cars and on flats, and are taken by an underground locomotive to the top of '2's return.' Three coupled mine-cars are pushed round a sharp turn onto the steep downward gradient, and lowered onto a warrick, a steel girder hanging from the roof which will throw a runaway mine-car off the road. The 'journey' of mine-cars is chained both ends to an endless steel rope, which circles massive wheels at the ends of the roadway. The haulage

Typical stage loader transfers coal

[110] World War Two 1939–1945

team consists of three men, two to see the 'journey' in, and one to drive the haulage engine.

The warrick is raised by a pulley, and two pulls on the signal wire send the mine-cars on their journey into the pit. A variety of accidents can now take place, and a 'journey' rarely reaches its destination without some mishap. A coupling can come adrift, the front chain can break, and two mine-cars will career down the slope smashing everything and everyone in their path. A twisted warrick in the side of the road will mark the end of a 'runner's' course. Manholes are built into the side of the roadway at regular intervals to provide a refuge for men walking the roadways of the pit, though they are sometimes so poorly maintained that the tremendous weight of the surrounding rock has reduced them to inaccessible proportions. An obstacle on the rails can throw the front car into the steel rings of the side, and the 'journey' become stuck fast. If the haulage engine continues to pull the 'journey' forward, the steel rope will break and lash around like a whip, mowing down everyone in its way. Many haulage men have lost fingers trying to correct a twisted chain, or release a hitched-up rope.

When the 'journey' reaches the bottom of '5's Tail Gate', it has to be transferred to another haulage rope. Invariably the manoeuvre is accompanied by one or more mine-cars coming off the road and having to be lifted bodily or levered back on to the rails. Once the 'journey' is successfully round the points into the tail-gate, the men will strip down to their underpants because the heat will become increasingly oppressive as they penetrate deeper into the pit, where merely walking makes a man run with sweat. In several places the men have to paddle ankle deep in slimy, oily water, while freezing cold drops splatter down from the roof. The wooden struts between the ring girders are broken and rotten, covered in hideous fungoid growths, and boulders in the side indicate minor falls of loose rock. Where corrugated-iron sheeting has been used, it is rusty and hangs down, ragged-edged, ready to gash an unwary shoulder. The warm, dank atmosphere adds to the sensation of travelling through an enclosed swampland.

The man in front of the 'journey' keeps close to the signal-wire in case of emergency, and has to dodge the steel haulage rope, flailing about under the moving weight of the mine-cars. He tries to keep some distance between himself and the 'journey' to avoid being crushed against the ring girders. As the 'journey' approaches the rip,[111] the dust becomes thick and heavy, filling the narrow vault of the gate, and the noise of drills and pumps drown the voices of the men.

The 'journey' is stopped about 40 yards from the rip, where it is unloaded. Clambering about in the cramped space between the top of a mine-car and the girdered roof, and heaving around heavy bags of stone dust in the heat and dust of the tail-gate is a gruelling test of a man's stamina. In most cases, the two haulage men will be helped by the two face-supplies men who trolley and carry materials from the end of the haulage road to the face. It is a reciprocal arrangement whereby the haulage men have their job considerably lightened, and the supplies men make sure that the materials are unloaded in accessible areas of the road. Unloading heavy steel grinders is often the recipe for pinched or amputated fingers, while corrugated iron sheets have a tendency to rip and tear a man's body.

---

[111] The rip means the rock above the roadways (tunnels) and the coalface

Once they have unloaded the 'journey', the haulage men can ring away the empty mine-cars. But signal wires stretched over some thousands of yards tend to be very unreliable, and sometimes only two of the three rings will reach the engine driver's car. The 'journey' of empty mine-cars, instead of going out of the gate, will move in towards the face, and end up in the return-wheel of the haulage rope, to the extreme agitation of everyone in the vicinity.

Meanwhile, on the other side of the pit, another haulage team will be battling with the bitterly cold coal dust-laden winds of the main airway. A shift driving the haulage engine in the main airway is like a six-hour sentry duty on the parapets of Dover Castle in mid-winter. Cold and boredom have a demoralising effect, and engine drivers in the main tend to become sullen, resentful creatures, easily moved to anger.

Being a 'haulage man' is, in Malcolm Pitt's opinion, one of the most dangerous jobs in the pit.

For the two men involved in the 'journey', the conveyor belts carrying coal from the faces to pit-bottom are a source of danger and constant nervous strain. The conveyors take up a large part of the roadways, which are constantly being narrowed by the pressure of the rock. The 'journey' is often caught fast in the rings and sometimes knocks them out, exposing the haulage men to the dangers of a fall of rock. If the face is reached without serious mishap, they still face the problem of where to unload the materials, and a lot of time and energy is wasted filling concrete blocks neatly under the belt, and propping lengths of timber precariously against the sides.

The haulage is a dangerous and difficult job, and accounts for many of the fatal accidents and serious injuries in the pit. An experienced haulage man can know every inch of his road and all the dangers of a moving 'journey' of mine-cars, but still lose a finger, a leg, or his life. Every man knows that, however careful he is at his work, there is always going to be the situation where only blind chance will lie between him and serious harm.

Whereas the haulage men travel the major roadways of the pit, the supplies men follow the advance of the coal-face. From the stacks of materials where the mine-cars were unloaded, they bring forward to the rip and face-conveyors the girders, corrugated sheets, concrete blocks, various lengths of timber, wooden blocks and a host of other things which are constantly in demand to keep open sufficient space to take out the coal.

The materials are either pushed manually by the supplies men, or pulled up by an air powered winch called a tugger, on the flat top of an iron or wooden tram. The distance trammed is normally about forty yards, but at Tilmanstone on the Webster Face the road was so low and narrow that mine-cars had to be unloaded at the bottom of the gate. The face was approached through shin-deep water, and beneath girders so low that if they put their hand on top of the tram they were liable to get their fingers wedged in the roof. The last climb to the face was so steep that both men had to edge the tram up, a sleeper at a time, on a drag-bar, an iron bar attached to the back axle, to prevent the tram running backwards. If one of the regular men was out, a market-man deployed on to the Webster supplies would often refuse to do it.

'They've taken the ponies out of the pits', they would inform the official.

At the coalface, the actual capture of the coal is not an individual's job. It is carried out by a team of men with varied skills.

The extraction of coal is the combined work of a team of men, and any stoppage by one section of the team will hold up the advance of the face. A face team is basically made up of colliers, heading-men and rippers, with shearer-men,[112] electricians, fitter and supplies men as essential auxiliaries.

The colliers push forward the hydraulically-powered face supports after the extraction of the coal, and re-set them under the newly exposed roof. The heading-men take out the coal (and often the stone) in advance of the face, and in line with the gate, clearing a space to allow the shearer and the face conveyor to move forward for the next cut of coal. The rippers take out the stone above the heading, and set the girders of the gate as the face advances. On faces which used a 'plough', a kind of coal-cutter, it was usual to have a heading and a rip at both ends of the face, but nowadays, with the introduction of shearers, the normal practice is to have a rip at the tail-gate, flush with the face, and a heading at the main-gate, in which the whole roadway is advanced several yards in front of the face.

The semi-circle of stone, or 'muck', above the coal seam in the roadway (the rip), and getting it down is probably the most dangerous and heavy work in the pit. A sandstone rip will resist the best efforts of a cutting machine, and will have to be bored and fired. Boring the stone with a 'web' of holes entails using a compressed air drill. The noise of the drill,

---

[112] Shearers are mechanical cutters of coal

particularly in the enclosed space of the gate, is so intense that a man's ears will still be ringing after the end of a shift, and over a period of time a ripper can be deafened. Terry Harrison, secretary of Betteshanger branch in 1978, is permanently deaf in one ear after 18 years on the rip, though in the mines this disability is still not recognised as an industrial injury. The drill is fixed on to an extending air-leg, which forces the revolving teeth of the drill to bite into the stone. The air-leg is operated by a none-too-delicate valve, and a false movement can send the operator up into the roof, or fix him against the rings. A jet of water plays through the hollow bit to keep down the dust, and the rippers are splattered with the grey sludge which pours out of the hole. The constant vibrations send an acute pain through the muscles of the operator's arm, and can cause the steel drill rod to snap through metal fatigue. On some such occasions, men have been thrown forward by the machine and transfixed on the end of the broken drill rod. At any time while he is boring the rip, a man is in danger of the stone coming away and crushing him under a mound of rubble.

The holes are charged with explosive, and fired by the shotfirer. Everyone retires down the gate behind a pair of steel mesh curtains to find refuge in the manholes along the side. Pieces of rock will fly like shrapnel several yards down the gate as the 'shots' are detonated with a sudden shudder and a roar is amplified by the round vault of the gate.

After the dust and acrid fumes of the explosives have settled, the rippers begin 'plucking' down the loose stone from the roof with an iron bar or 'rigger'. The ripper will jab at the rock, knowing by experience where it is likely to crack, and which are the key-pieces holding up the larger boulders.

The iron bar will give a clear ring when it strikes the solid rock, and tells the ripper that the ground is safe. The fractured stone he will lift and lever loose, until the pieces drop from the roof. He has to be quick on his feet as big boulders will drop unexpectedly, and bounce with the impetus of their fall, crushing a bone or gashing a man's arm to the bone.

The ripper's body is covered with the telltale blue scars which pick out a miner in a pub or a crowd. Once a miner is cut, the pressure and heat of the pit makes the blood gush out of the wound, which rapidly becomes impregnated with the omnipresent particles of coal dust. Though the nurses in the ambulance room try to scrub the coal out with carbolic, the wound normally heals into a black scab which mellows to a blue scar.

The rippers set the ring in place, using a crown and two legs.[113] The peculiar shape of the leg-grinders and their unevenly distributed weight make them extremely difficult to handle, particularly when they have to be dragged about 30 yards over machinery and timber, liberally covered in oil and water. The rings have to be set with extreme accuracy because they will have to carry the tremendous weight of the strata above, disturbed by the extraction of the coal.

Once the ring is set in place, the sides are packed and the roof timbered. The pack is a four-yard stone wall from the side of the gate into the gob,[114] and it supports the gigantic 'weight arch' which covers the length of the coal-face like the roof of a massive cathedral. The stones of the pack are provided by the debris of the rip, which has to be broken

---

[113] 'Crown and two legs' means the top and two legs of the supports that kept up the tunnels

[114] 'The gob' is an area of waste material after the coal has been removed

up into conveniently-sized pieces by the repeated action of 14-pound sledgehammers.

Some boulders never crack, and the ripper has to chip away tediously at the edges until the stone is reduced to a manageable size.

When rippers are 'on contract' and paid according to the advance of the rip, they will run into the gate and work flat out until they vomit into the side, setting two and three rings a shift. "We were like animals," says Johnny Moyle, Betteshanger chairman in 1978, as he shows the blue scars on his knees from the wounds inflicted by the rapid action of a shovel. The rippers have earned the name of 'big hitters', a title which, in the pit, has much the same connotation as 'berserker' must have had among the Vikings.

Many rips are equipped with 'doscos'. A doscos is a huge tractor armed with a boom which cuts the stone of the rip with revolving picks. The debris falls directly onto the face-conveyor below, and is carried up the face with the coal. If the packers require stones for the pack, they have to clamber on to the conveyor and throw them off after breaking them up in the confined space of the face. Although the doscos have taken a considerable amount of the hard sweat out of the rippers' work, the men are still compelled to work continuously in a dense cloud of deadly stone dust.

Lengths of timber are set in the roof above the rings in a tight lattice-work to prevent falls of rock, loosened when the weight of the strata above comes down on the hollowed arch. Many a blue scar on the face of a ripper testifies to the sharpness of stone flakes which suddenly detach themselves from the apparently smooth surface of the roof as the timber is manoeuvred into position.

In front of the rip, the heading-men hollow out a rectangular chamber in the coal seam to accommodate the advances of the face-conveyor and the shearer. Because the heading is in advance of the face, the ventilation is extremely limited, and heat, dust and noise become concentrated and inescapable. Though the transition to solid headings has allowed the introduction of mechanical loading, much of the work in the coal headings is still done with a pick and shovel. An old miner will shovel coal on his knees even though there is enough room to stand. It is a habit left over from the days when coal was hand got, and the coal-face was only as high as the coal seam.

The old collier will shovel very slowly, apparently without exertion, pushing the shovel forward and pulling it back at a slow rhythmic pace, never stopping, and moving an amazing amount of material. A novice will normally stand to get the maximum use of the knee behind the shovel, and work at a furious pace until the sweat is pouring off his body and he is forced to take periodic breaks. In quite a short time, most men take the advice of the older miners, and 'take it slowly'.

The heading is supported by steel girders set on hydraulic props called 'Dowtys' after the manufacturer, which are pumped into position with a steel key. The props have to be set absolutely vertical to the roof, or the weight of the roof will push them out, and the girder will fly down with enormous force. On one occasion, a man was killed with a broken neck, and another had his jaw crushed.

Where the major roads of the pit are advancing in preparation for the opening of new faces, and increasingly on shearer faces, the coal and the stone are taken out together in a solid heading. Because the solid heading is several yards beyond the face, there is no circulation of air, and fans connected to huge caterpillar-like tubes blow a current of air into the workings. But even then the heat is so bad that men often work completely naked because even a pair of shorts is torture to the skin. The danger of working in unknown ground is increased by the absence of any exit if the roof falls in; only a contained number of men are allowed to work in the development headings, and a constant check is kept of who is there in case they are walled in.

The coalface, or 'wall', is a narrow corridor about 150 yards long which advances into the coal-seam, allowing the roof of the open space behind, the 'gob' or 'waste', to fall in under its own weight. The coal is cut by the rotating picks of the shearer which hauls itself along the wall on a chain stretched between the two gates, and deposits the cut coal on to the face-conveyor underneath. The chain is put under an immense strain as the pick fights to cut the stone of the roof or floor, sometimes breaking and flailing about in the enclosed space of the wall to the extreme hazard of the colliers. An electric cable follows the shearer and is fed into a channel on the edge of the steel pans of the conveyor. On one occasion at Snowdown Colliery, the cable came out of the channel and caught the leg of a collier in a loop which tightened and amputated his foot above the ankle.

Being a collier is the highest paid but probably the least pleasant and the most demanding job in the pit.

When coal was cut by hand and, later, by cutters and ploughs, only the coal was extracted, and the height of the face was determined by the thickness of the seam. The 3ft 6ins minimum cut of the shearer guarantees the miner squatting room, but at the cost of a colossal increase in the amount of air-borne coal – and stone dust. The shearer literally grinds the coal into granules and, in spite of the continual sprays of water, the collier is completely blinded by a cloud of black dust as the machine passes him. Dust-masks are provided, but most men find them suffocating in the close atmosphere of the face, and often impossible to work in. Because of the variations in the thickness of the coal in Kent, the shearer often has to cut into the stone of the roof or floor, and to the dangers of airborne coal dust is added the greater hazard of inhaling minute particles of stone dust. The collier at the end of a shift will be continually bringing up viscous globules of black phlegm, 'black'uns', and his handkerchief is permanently stained black from blowing his nose.

The collier has to suffer the discomfort of bloodshot eyes and a sore throat with the uncomfortable knowledge that the dust is slowly killing him. Some clown of an official will tell him that if he can see the dust there is no need to worry because it is not the large particles that do the damage. This 'argument' was once used on a gang of rippers who were threatening to walk out if nothing was done to quell the dust in the tail-gate. The next day, the official found the team sitting down at the top-end of the gate, and asked them what they were about. 'It's the dust!' they replied. 'But I can't see any dust', the official exploded. 'Ah', came back the men, 'yesterday we were told that if you can see the dust, it's not dangerous. Well, today, we can't see it, so we're not going to work in it!'

Today, most coalfaces have hydraulically-powered roof supports, 'chocs', which consist of four props covered by a metal canopy with two arms, each on a prop, protruding over the pan-line to the coal face. When the shearer has finished cutting the coal, the colliers push over the pan-line with powerful rams, operated from under the canopy of the adjacent support. The powered supports are lowered, pulled in on the rams, and then raised tightly to the roof. The whole operation, which in NCB manuals appears so simple, is considerably complicated by the tendency of the roof, exposed by the extraction of the coal and the lowering of the choc, to fall in onto the face, leaving gaping holes, sometimes several feet high and several yards long, which have to be packed with timber before the support can be tightened to the roof. Some holes are so big that the collier has to climb up over the supports to timber the hole from the inside where he is constantly exposed to a fall of stone, and has to work in incredible heat and a suffocating atmosphere.

The timber is loaded onto the face conveyor at the tail-gate, and normally taken off by the colliers while the chain is still moving so as not to hold up the job. If a length of timber is inadvertently picked up from the front, the face-chain can lift it to the roof, crushing the hand of the collier. Handling nine- and six-foot splits, sometimes heavy with water, in the cramped and low conditions of the face, and impeded by the line of props, can result in pulled muscles and twisted joints. Many miners suffer from a kind of 'housemaid's knee' in the knees and elbows from crawling along the face. Although knee pads prevent cuts and bruises, the straps are liable to cause serious cartilage trouble.

The collier is exposed to the constant dribble of stones from the unstable roof while he places the timber above the supports, and many colliers' backs and arms are covered in a rash of small blue scars. The break-up of the roof can be aggravated by the failure of the gob to fall behind the line of face supports. Several yards of unsupported roof will begin to sag in the middle, and break up the strata above the advance of the face.

The gob is like a massive cavern which can come down at any time, and at any speed. A great mass of stone, the size of a bus, will suddenly come down like a steam hammer, or segments will inch themselves down very slowly to the floor. On faces where girders are still used, the sudden fall of the gob will send the props flying like skittles, and the falling stone will flush into the face, with big boulders running like marbles. Great quantities of gas and foul air collect in the unventilated waste, and the massive fall of stone forces them out, like a pair of bellows, through the face and into the tail-gate.

The threat of ill-health haunts the miners. Pneumoconiosis and silicosis, suffered through inhaling the dust in the pit, are the killers they fear most.

The coalface is swept by a chilly, dust-laden breeze from the main-gate. Streams of icy water often come down from the roof and turn the floor of the face into a muddy morass. As an added discomfort, the colliers have to wear a yellow plastic raincoat and rubber boots. The rapid changes of temperature in the pit, and water and the constant irritation of dust, cause many miners to suffer from recurring colds, chronic bronchitis, emphysema and rheumatism. Once a cold is contracted in the pit, it can last for several weeks, and terminate in a heavy, black nasal catarrh. However, pneumoconiosis is the most horrific disease caused by the dust-laden miasma in which the miner is forced to work.

Every miner's lungs will take in and retain a considerable amount of dust after working for several years underground, but for many miners 'dust retention' becomes a hideous disease whereby the tissues of the lung are destroyed. The miner who suffers from 'pneumo' is condemned to the life of a cripple, incapable of walking up the street without stopping to get back his breath. Every miner has witnessed the lingering, choking death of a relative or friend.

Because the colliers do not actually hew the coal, although they still use a pick and shovel occasionally, many older miners who can remember getting the coal by hand deny that there are any 'colliers' left. They remember 'the good old days' when a man started shovelling as soon as he got into the stall or face, and continued until the end of the shift. The ventilation was so bad that men used to take off their boots or clogs and pour out the sweat, and even suck air out of the compressed air pipes. In Snowdown Colliery, a water-barrel would come round the workings once, or even twice, a shift for the men to refill their water bottles. The working conditions were so bad that men would sign on in the morning, work half a shift and be so exhausted that they would go up the pit and give in their notice. At Chislet Colliery, Dickie Stinton, later a Betteshanger face instructor, recalls the endurance test of his first shifts in Kent:

"I'd never seen anything like it. What kept me going was the thought that, if the other men can do it, so can I."

Men came home so tired that they went to bed at four o'clock in the afternoon and slept through to the next morning. In Aylesham, the mining village for Snowdown Colliery, there was a house where the woman offered lodgings to miners. Behind the table, there were black marks on the wall where the heads of the men would loll back when they fell asleep at their meal.

For most of the shift, the coalface is full of the noise of the face-chain and the shearer, of shouts of 'Watch the chain!' and 'Two dozen lagging for the main-gate!' But there are periods of absolute, oppressive silence, broken only by the sounds of stones falling on the gob and of the coal cracking under the pressure of the roof.

Elizabeth Pitt remembers Malcolm marvelling at the curious stoicism of his colleagues. "Malcolm was a driven man. He never lost sight of the big picture and he built that picture by observing the small things in life. And if he could change things for the better, he did so. He never did things by halves. His motive, was always to improve the life of his colleagues. He, literally, fought for them."

The miner has to live for over seven hours underground every working day. He must adapt himself to a totally alien environment, and abandon many of the standards of safety, comfort and hygiene which most workers have come to take for granted at their place of work. Miners say that when a man goes down the pit he leaves the 'human bit' behind on the surface.

Over the generations, miners have had to learn to make the best of the worst conditions. It has become so much of an ingrained habit for many men that they will not make an issue of deplorable conditions which a little thought and investment could easily remedy. But beneath this grim outer shield of the miners' resignation to exploitation and bad conditions, there runs a continual, nagging resentment which will, quite suddenly, break out and manifest itself in long and bitter industrial struggle, when a whole period of acceptance and retreat is challenged. Such periodic eruptions are marked by a determination and solidarity which are a product of the unique milieu of the mine.

The dirt and danger underground gives birth to a human comradeship which miners who leave the pit never find, and continually miss, in other walks of life.

The contradiction between the terrible physical environment and the close companionship of the pit creates a near schizophrenic state of mind. The pit is always the 'bastard hole', hated by the miner with the bitter venom normally reserved for a personal enemy. The latest threat of closure is greeted with the resentful retort, exasperated by the monotony of similar NCB pronouncements, 'Let them put the bloody lid on the hole!' The first advice gratuitously given to a new entrant is, 'Get out while you've still got the chance'. Young miners are continually being asked by the older men, 'Are you going to make mining your career, then?' The question is asked with such irony, and so full of bitter experience, that anyone who answered a straight 'yes' would call into question his own sanity. Every day, a fitter comes down the Training Face at Betteshanger and, as he crawls over the legs of the instructor and trainees inquires, 'Glad you're here? There's plenty of men who'd like to be where you are, but they're all up the cemetery'.

It is commonplace that many miners fight tooth-and-nail to stop their sons from going down the pit.

After several years underground, some miners experience a sudden revulsion at the idea of working another day in the pit, and an irresistible compulsion to give in their notice to find work elsewhere. But many return, sometimes because of the limited opportunities for other employment in East Kent, but often because working in a factory away from their mates they are like fish out of water. Back in the pit, every so often the feeling of desperation wells up afresh inside them, but they learn to push it aside with: 'What a bloody place to come to!'

The miner develops another self which is continually learning how to survive underground. Because the coalface is continually advancing into new ground, the miner is confronted every day with new and unknown dangers. He is like an explorer, or deep-sea diver, who uses his past experience to understand the signs which tell him the nature of the ground he is going into. He has to employ his senses of sight, hearing, touch and smell to divine the hidden hazards of the disturbed strata. The line of a crack or the ring of the stone can tell the experienced workman a whole story of what lies behind the wall of coal and stone. Before shifting a prop or setting a ring, a miner will take his time to look at, and test, his ground, interpreting the surface indications and carefully considering the next move. Often he will discuss the problems with his mates, and bring to bear the collective experience of the team. At all times he is aware that a wrong decision and a mistaken action can cost him and his mates their lives, or the use of their limbs.

Over the years, the miner develops 'pit sense'. Pit sense is not a skill like carpentry or bricklaying, but a continuous adaptation of a man's whole psychology, his senses, intuition, reflexes and emotions, to an alien and hostile element. Pit sense is the essential characteristic of the 'pitman'. In everyday usage, the word 'pitman' is normally considered to be the rather archaic synonym for miner. But, in the pit, it has an altogether different connotation of qualities and attributes which differentiate the true miner from the man who only works in the mine. A man can work all his life in the pit, and still not qualify for the name of pitman.

A miner's wife in Mill Hill, the mining suburb of Deal, said, 'Not everyone can work in a mine. It takes a special breed of men'. 'That's right,' her husband replied, 'I remember the Bevin Boys.[115] You could tell they'd never make it'. There is a strong idea among miners that the pitman is born, not made and – like the yeoman archers of England – it takes at least three generations to train for the work.

Once it was a general rule that miners came solely from mining families, grew up and went to school with their future workmates in the same mining village. They were weaned on the still incessant talk amongst miners about mines and mining. When they went down the pit immediately on leaving school, they already knew the rudiments of the job and the peculiarities of pit terminology. Before the war (World War Two) they would be trained by their fathers and work in a team composed of cousins, uncles and brothers. The pit was 'all Brother and Bob'. In later, more formal days, after nationalisation, 'green' labour was trained by special instructors, and young miners, perhaps pitmen's sons, would challenge the way they were shown to turn a pan, or set a girder. 'That's not the way my father does it!' the trainee would tell his instructor.

In spite of the social disruption of the period of mine closures and the drift away from the pits, the miner still

---

[115] Bevin Boys – in World War Two when more labour had to be recruited to meet Britain's need for coal, some National Servicemen were drafted into the mines rather than the Armed Forces. They were called Bevin Boys

usually begins his mining career on leaving school. He grows into adult life in the pit, and the underground world becomes a second element. The comradeship of the common experience of the 'shift and dirt' is therefore lifted to a higher plane, a confraternity of a special type of man, the pitman. It is a bond cemented and reinforced by blood, marriage, community tradition and culture. A miner is always a miner. After years away from the pit, he remains a 'Chislet man', or 'he's pit'.

The hard core of Kent miners can trace their descent through generations of pitmen, and many men have brothers and cousins elsewhere in the British coalfield whom they have down for a holiday at the seaside, or go and visit for a wedding or a funeral. Men who come into mining from other walks of life are never quite 'in the family', however many years they spend underground. Miners who are native to Kent are labelled 'cherry pickers' and 'swede gnawers' by their comrades of impeccable mining pedigree.

The relationship between the miner and the mining official is prickly; when a miner becomes 'management', he is crossing a frontier into another camp.

The exclusive circle of pitmen is extremely strict on its rules of membership, and underground management is quite definitely outside its limits. Underground management is recruited exclusively from the 'shopfloor', and men will say of an under-manager or deputy, 'I worked with him on the rip at Chislet', or 'We worked together on 42's'. They were 'one of the men', but once they joined the ranks of management they become exiles. They know the men, often live in the same village and have relatives in the pit. They work underground

Typical colliery pit shaft bottom

and think of themselves as miners. But to most men they are objects of distrust, suspicion and even hatred. Many men will avoid sitting next to a deputy on the pit-bus, or having a drink with him in the local pub. An official's status of pitman is systematically destroyed by a constant disparagement of his mining ability. 'He was never any good when he was on the coal', and 'He was always an idle bastard' erode his past record as a miner.

This ostracism of officials by the men stems from their function as the 'eyes' of the National Coal Board (NCB). Though the deputy's official responsibility is the safety of the working area, testing for gas, inspecting the supports, etc., they have become primarily supervisors of the men. In addition, their numbers have dramatically increased over the last few years, and the image of the 'bosses' nark' has grown in proportion. No man likes to work under the eye of the master but in the pit, where every man evolves his own particular personal way of doing the job, the interference of a deputy or overman is quickly resented, especially when an official is known to have never done the job himself.

The very geography of the pit makes constant supervision impossible, and the advance of the face depends entirely on the cooperation and self-discipline of the men. In spite of the gross press misrepresentation of the miner as a latter-day Luddite, he is extremely conscientious about his work, and makes it a matter of pride to do his 'stint' properly. 'I've got to work under it,' a man will say to anyone who tries to make him hurry a job and cut corners.

Many men phone the surface during the shift to find out how many mine-cars of coal have been wound up the pit. In the dangerous conditions underground, self-discipline is absolutely essential if a man is going to come up the pit in one piece, and the men themselves will keep an unruly member of the team in line.

The supervision by the officials is considered both insulting and irrelevant, a reminder of the hated master-and-man relationship which miners had fondly expected would disappear with nationalisation. The situation is aggravated by the Board's guarantee of a 10 per cent differential between the pay of an official and the highest-paid coalface worker. Separate bathing facilities, early rides up the pit, fully-paid sick-leave and a host of other benefits serve to increase the divisions between the officials and the men underground. In addition, pit officials have inherited the lasting hatred of the past when a deputy would take his belt or stick to a young miner, or take bribes when, notebook in hand, he measured the advance of the face on which depended the size of the docket (earnings).

Words like 'comradeship', 'solidarity' and 'companionship' may suggest that an aura of sentimental affection permeates the pit, and that miners are continually exchanging kind words and deeds. In many ways, the complete opposite is true. The terrible physical conditions underground and the continual frustrations of coal-getting combine to bring out the most irascible traits in the human personality. Miners rarely converse underground without exchanging a series of highly imaginative epithets which often become a set routine between a pair or individuals. Physical peculiarities are enlarged upon to an extent that, if true, the miners would be a race of grotesque deformities. Nicknames, like Hogger Dog, Gargoyle, the Chocolate Toad and Jimmy No-legs, conjure up the most bizarre inventions of a medieval bestiary. The first and soundest advice to a new member is 'Don't bite!' A continuous stream of insults and epithets, remarkable in their ability to wound, is the common mode of address in the pit, and a swift rejoinder is the only effective defence. Putting crickets into a man's sandwiches, or rust into a tin of snuff, or telling a trainee to swallow his first chew of tobacco help to make the hours pass more quickly.

Malcolm Pitt reflects on a society where the humour is often cruel, divisions very clear, and conditions of work testing in the extreme.

Only in a situation of complete intimacy could men vent their feelings of frustration and resentment on each other without constantly coming to blows. Violence underground is an extremely rare and transitory occurrence. Men underground are confined for long periods of time in a closed space and in a situation of extreme danger and, of necessity, soon get to know each other extremely well. Every man has to rely on his workmate's ability and skill to ensure that the job is kept safe, and to get him out if anything goes wrong. A man is soon discovered if he does shoddy work, or is liable to panic in moments of danger.

On every shift, there are meal breaks. Miners take with them their food, called 'snap'.

Miners are only allowed one break of 20 minutes a shift. 'Snaptime' is spent normally where a man is working because there are no special facilities provided in British pits for men to eat their food. Getting comfortable in the pit is an art practised by miners with great verve and imagination. It can be extremely painful to sit down in the pit without some form of seat. The stones of the floor and the curvature of the rings necessitate a constant movement of the body to avoid cramp and bruising. The simplest form of seat is made up of two lengths of green timber, one horizontal to sit on, and one at an incline to the side to form a back rest. This construction is not as simple as it looks, and many new miners spend a considerable time in overcoming the problems of sliding back rests and cocked seats. More elaborate forms of seat proliferate around the pit, employing wooden blocks, planks, conveyor-belting, stone dust bags and a variety of other materials. In the main airways, brattice sheeting is used to erect covered pavilions to protect the occupant from the cold, driving winds. In odd corners of the pit, an occasional discarded car-seat provides a little comfort for the man condemned to operate a belt-switch.

Most men have sandwiches in their snap, and maybe an apple or orange. Choice of food is important because not everything can be eaten without severe digestive repercussions. Meat is normally avoided as being too 'heavy' to manage in an atmosphere which does not encourage the appetite. Cheese will sweat in the heat of the tail-gate; it is also difficult to eat after a man has swallowed a large quantity of dust and is dehydrated with sweating. Some men lose their appetite completely when underground. Fresh fruit is popular because the juice will moisten the mouth and the acidic sharpness pierce the film of dust which smothers any taste. At the end of the shift, the gate is often filled with scent of an orange as a man passes round the segments to his mates.

Eating is made difficult by the total absence of washing facilities and the constant presence of airborne dust. Peeling an orange or eating a sandwich without making them black from the coal dust and oil on his hands is one of the subsidiary skills a miner picks up during his pit career. Before a sandwich is eaten, it begins to take on the grey hue of its surroundings and, if found on the surface in that condition, would certainly be thrown away. Some men drink tea and coffee from thermos flasks which have such an extraordinarily short life underground that many men have given up replacing them in despair. Water is drunk universally from a variety of containers, the condition of which would qualify them on the surface for the refuse tip. It is remarkable how sweet stale and tepid water from a rusty Dudley can taste after half a shift in a tail-gate.

And, thousands of yards underground, there are a surprising number of creatures ready to share the 'snap'...

At Betteshanger Colliery, if a man does not use a snap tin, he will invariably hang his sandwiches by a piece of string or shot firing wire from a ring to keep them out of range of the mice. These mice originally came down the pit with the timber and materials, but they are not native. They are totally blind and, in their long struggle against the endeavours of miners to exterminate them by a variety of horrific and often sadistic methods, they have become extremely cunning and difficult to catch.

At Tilmanstone, crickets provide a background chorus of chirping, and a host of these grey, locust-like creatures will immediately cover any food thrown away. They can jump to a considerable height, and often a seated miner will suddenly frantically dance about trying to get one out of his hair or clothing. Pit crickets are cannibals, and if one of their number is killed by a stone thrown by a miner – a pit pastime – it will be instantly devoured by its fellows. The occasional wood hornet comes into the pit in the bark of the timber. At one time at Chislet Colliery, wood hornets were so numerous that the men threatened to go on strike if they were not dealt with. The sting produced a big painful lump, and so many men were constantly bitten that management finally had the bark treated with poison to kill the grubs.

Some of the older men can remember when they had to put up with huge brown rats which came down the pit in the hay for the ponies. The ponies have long since disappeared from the Kent pits, but are often the symbol of the hypocrisy of the people who agitated against the terrible crime of allowing animals to live and work in the pits, but calmly accepted the fact that men were condemned to labour out their lives in the same subhuman conditions. A bird regularly came down the shaft of Snowdown Colliery and used to live on the pit-bottom. The men used to feed it regularly, and even made it a nesting box.

In these dark, hostile conditions, hygiene is reduced to it crudest standards.

The total absence of eating and washing facilities underground is matched by the inadequacy of the toilet arrangements. Chemical toilets are provided by law, but they are placed at such inordinate distances from the coalfaces that few men can make use of them. Deposited in the unventilated confines of a manhole, draped with a filthy brattice sheet and often provided with a few grimy pages of *Coal News*, these foul privies are surrounded by a vile odour which will deter all but those with the strongest stomach. Every day, the 'shit bucket man' tours to remove the human waste to the surface. He is the nearest the pit has to an 'untouchable', and is rewarded for the physical and social disadvantages of his work with the shortest shift in the pits. Most men are forced to improvise near their place of work, and the remains of a stone-dust bag on the end of a shovel are the best that 'modern mining' can offer. But to be caught in a spotlight with his trousers round his ankles, squatting on a shovel end, is surely the ultimate in the destruction of a man's dignity.

The disposal of human waste in the closed circuit of the pit is a serious social problem, and anyone who insists on performing his natural functions upwind of the men, or in the unventilated confines of a heading, is liable to be branded as a public enemy for the rest of his working life. A Betteshanger miner still carried the nickname of 'Basher' from his days as a ripper in Chislet when he dealt out summary justice to one such persistent offender. Trainees are seriously warned not to pick up any paper in the pit, because 'You never know what you might find in it!' But, despite the limitless fund of pit humour on the subject, miners deeply resent the fact that they are expected to suffer the abnegation of the minimum requirements of civilised living.

Relaxation in this environment is both difficult and rare. Most everyday habits are left at the top of the pit shaft.

Most men claim that they don't miss cigarettes while they are underground, but the majority use some form of substitute. Chewing tobacco is the traditional vice of the inbye[116] worker, and is generally condemned as a 'filthy habit'. The chewer bites, or cuts off, about an inch from a half ounce of tobacco leaf rolled into a rope-like strip. He proceeds to champ away like a cow chewing the cud, until he has extracted all the juice, and spits out a soggy, bleached-brown ball. The practical reason claimed for chewing is that it keeps a miner's mouth shut and prevents him swallowing large quantities of dust. Also, the tobacco draws saliva into the mouth and, as the man spits out the juice and loose shreds, he cleans his mouth of the inevitable film of dust which forms on his teeth and palate. The price of tobacco-chewing is stained and rotten teeth, heartburn and even stomach cancer. It is extremely addictive and, for many men, making sure that they are well supplied with tobacco is a top priority before a shift. Men are constantly 'giving it up' or 'begging a chew' if they find themselves without tobacco underground. Chewing tobacco is the common currency of the pit, and a 'half ounce' the normal stake for a bet. Chewers take great pride in introducing trainees to the habit, and several innocents underground have been

---

[116] 'Inbye', going towards the mine and coalface; 'outbye', going away from it. This would apply if you were, say, travelling from Canterbury to the mine just as much as when you were approaching, or leaving, the coalface

carried out of the pit on a stretcher after swallowing their first chew.

It is recommended as a sovereign remedy for constipation in humans – and for worms in dogs.

Taking snuff is the most common social habit in the pit, and a group of miners will often stop to pass round the snuff tin, and 'take a pinch'. Like chewing tobacco, snuff is praised for its medicinal qualities of cleansing the nose of dust. On the paddy out to pit-bottom, the air is heavy with the scented smell, and the chatter is broken by the sound of men expelling the clotted coal-dust and snuff from their nostrils. Boiled sweets are handed round, and the sharp sweetness takes away the sour, clammy taste of stale tobacco. Men gargle with water from their bottles to wash away the taste of the shift, and empty them into the side of the road.

As with all aspects of a miner's life, the end of the shift and leaving the pit – known as 'knock off' – is subject to a routine.

Riding the pit at 'knock-off' is a source of continual warfare between management and men, and riding times are a good index of the state of battle. There is a tendency for riding times to get earlier and earlier, until bottom becomes the scene of an angry mêlée. The fixed aim of every miner at the end of the shift is to get out to the 'hole' as soon as possible. When there are over 400 men with the same fixed aim, and only fifty can ride the pit at any one time, there is bound to be trouble. The pressure of men towards the cage was so strong at Chislet Colliery that one man was pushed down the sump and only a ledge ten feet below the pit-bottom saved him from a muddy death.

Pit-bottom is equipped with wire-mesh gates, and at knock-off resembles a fortified prison compound. The men either queue up, or sometimes mass outside the gates and are only allowed through when they have collected their checks. The trouble begins when the deputies and pit technicians are allowed to bypass the men and ride the pit first. The mood of the men, exhausted and dirty after the shift, becomes irritable and downright ugly when a clean-faced official strides nonchalantly through the gates in front of them. Derogatory remarks and catcalls fill the air, and tempers rise when a smiling official throws back a provocative reply.

The next complication is the 'wet ride'[117] and the thorny subject of who qualifies to be on it. Naturally enough, men who are subjected to working up to their knees in water, or under a freezing cascade from the roof, are allowed to ride the pit before the other men, but officials will often ring out the numbers of men who have done them a favour by carrying some item into the pit, or doing something not strictly part of their jobs. As the numbers qualifying for the wet ride swell, the waiting men begin to challenge the credentials of the wet rides. 'I don't see any water on your boots!' and 'What have you done? Emptied your water bottle over your boots?' are thrown at the passing men. The remarks are generally good-natured and jocular, but there is a constant undercurrent of the exasperation of fatigued men, kept hanging about and knowing that they can't do anything about it because the shaft is the only way out.

The ride up the pit is far more uncomfortable than when the men came down before the shift. The cage is packed to capacity with men covered in sweat, oil and dust. Often a man will have to endure the ride with a piece of wood,

---

[117] Wet ride: men in wet clothing are meant to be given priority in the queue to leave the mine

carried by the man behind, stuck into his ribs. Most miners take a short length of timber, called 'cock wood', up the pit for kindling. 'Cock wood' is a traditional practice in the pits, and its name derives from the old days when kindling wood was a valuable addition to a needy household and was thought to ensure the favours of a wife, or a landlady.

Towards the end of the ride, the eyes of the men are raised to catch the first glimmer of light from the surface. The men are impatient as the gate-man removes the grid of the cage and, once off the deck, they run to make the air doors. Their haste comes partly from a strong desire to discard their pit-black and have a bath, but also from a suspicion that some practical joker will shut the inner door and, by leaving the outer door open, make it impossible to get out through the airlock.

Once the miners have crossed the pit-yard, they may discard their lamps and self-rescuers in the lamp cabin, and have officially finished their shift. They are covered from head to foot in thick black grime, their hair is thick with dust and their clothes sodden with sweat, oil and water. 'What are you looking so black in the face about?' quips a mate.

Before the construction of the baths in the late 1930s, the men had to go home in this foul, uncomfortable condition. Miners at Betteshanger can remember being dropped from the pit lorry in the middle of Deal, and walking up the High Street in their pit-black with people crossing over to the other side of the road to avoid contamination. In these more civilised days, miners are allowed the luxury of a shower on NCB premises – but in their own time.

Pit showers are equipped with a lever marked 'Hot-Tepid-Cold', but the miner's choice is mostly limited to scalding hot or icy cold. Many miners wear Roman sandals to avoid contracting 'athlete's foot', a fungoid ailment of the feet, known to the miners as 'Kent Rot'. The fungus attacks the crevices between and under the toes, turning them into soggy, oozing pads of raw flesh which can itch so badly that it will wake a man from a deep sleep.

A miner can wash every part of his body but his back, and washing each others' backs is an established and necessary custom of the pit. Sometimes, three or four miners will line up in a lathery column and wash the back of the man in front. Some men, instead of using a sponge or flannel, procure a cut-off section of an abrasive, sponge-like material used in the cleaning of water pipes underground, and scour, rather than wash, the dirt off their bodies.

After drying himself off, the miner can dress at the clean lockers and regain the appearance of the ordinary run of humankind, except for a telltale ring of black coal dust around the eyes. A Tilmanstone miner was once accosted by a woman in a pub, and asked how he managed to apply his mascara so finely. He replied politely that it has its problems, but if she would like to help…

Many men rub Vaseline round the rims of their eyes before the start of the shift to provide a protective film of grease against the fine dust.

The miner makes a final stop in the canteen for a cup of tea or a bottle of milk and a meat pie, or a quick visit to the Welfare Club for a pint of beer 'to wash away the dust' before he catches the pit bus. The men have a few words with their cross-mates[118] to inform them of the state of the face, or of any problems or disputes. Before the bus leaves the colliery,

---

[118] The next shift

everybody is counted to avoid leaving anyone stranded in the middle of the Kent countryside. There are constant delays as men find out whether 'Tied is stopping on' or whether 'Bryn's got a lift'.

Eventually, the bus sets off at incredible speed through the barley fields and coppices, and another shift has been completed. But, as a miner once said:

'I don't know why we get so worked up about getting to the end of the week. There's always one more shift to do!'

Towards the end of his life, Malcolm Pitt became disillusioned with the Communist Party. He wrote that 'living tradition becomes replaced by doctrine and dogma that legitimises the exercise of absolute power by a minority, or even by one man or woman, sometimes with the full coercive power of the state'. He turned again to Christianity and to study.

In that time, says Elizabeth Pitt, "he began to assess his own life and picked over what he had done and what he hadn't done." In 1990, an old Catholic friend, Bishop John Jukes, offered him a part-time job, to run a Catholic initiative, the World of Work. He explored his Christian faith again and eventually became Principal of the Franciscan International Study Centre at the University of Kent.

Malcolm was 65 years old. He was still smoking heavily. "I think he knew he was dying. He began a Master of Arts degree and thought of little else. When he felt well enough, he would wake early and work at it all day. As I say, he was a driven man…"

The subject Malcolm chose was – The Teachings of Pope John Paul II and Karl Marx. God and Mammon. The tug of war, or love, that was the basis of everything Malcolm Pitt ever achieved. On the last day of his life, Malcolm awoke and asked Elizabeth: "Please get it for me, my manuscript…"

"That's my last memory of him," says Elizabeth. It was typical.

Malcolm was awarded his MA on the basis of the unfinished paper, which he had titled: Contradictions. He was 66 when he died. His 10-year-old grandson, Aedan Pitt-Davies, received the degree on Grandpa's behalf, watched and applauded by a full congregation in Canterbury Cathedral.

CHAPTER TEN
The Plumptres and Snowdown

*"I have never found a place with
such warmth and community spirit
as Aylesham."*
Dr David Hornsby, 2019

A large and ancient oak tree grows tall in the garden of John Plumptre. Actually, its home is less of a garden, more of an estate, as the 2,600 acres of land John Plumptre owns stretches from

John and Julia Plumptre today

Nonington in the north, to Barfreston in the east and on to Woolage in the south-west – some of the richest farmland in East Kent. At the northern end of this estate stands a group of buildings, the remains of the Snowdown Colliery, the most distinct physical evidence that a Kent Coalfield ever existed.

Fredville House with trees

And these buildings have survived because of the sheer pig-headedness and foresight of John Plumptre.

The blood of some of England's most powerful and aristocratic families runs in Plumptre veins – the FitzWalters and the Haywardens, the Northbournes and the Mildmays. The Plumptres have always taken pride in their trees. The original mansion, once large enough to accommodate 12 children in the nursery wing, was surrounded by trees "of the most extraordinary height and size in the kingdom…distinguished by appropriate names…Majesty, Stately and Beauty."

The greatest of the trees was Majesty, more than 500 years old and, according to the Guinness Book of Records, the largest oak tree in Britain. In the 1750s, an earlier John Plumptre planted a false avenue of sweet chestnut trees which are still there in Fredville's parkland, though the original mansion has now gone.

Fredville mansion had 'a handsome brick front supported by six Corinthian columns'.[119] In the 1800s, Jane Austen was

---

[119] The Juvenil Tourist, John Evans

Plumptre family, 1920s

a frequent visitor but the mansion became too large for the family, who decided to move to a smaller house. The mansion became a girls' school in the 1920s and was requisitioned by the War Office to accommodate Canadian troops in World War Two. It burned down in 1940 and John Huntingdon Plumptre demolished it in 1945, preferring to bring up his family in the smaller and quaintly-named Little Fredville.

The current oak tree is significant in John Plumptre's life. According to folklore, as long as it thrives, so the Plumptres will survive. It is already more than 500 years old. John and his wife, Julia, still live in Little Fredville and they enjoy the country life, particularly shooting. John is an excellent shot. So is Julia; 'one of the best', they say. John qualifies that: "One of the best *women*," he says.

The conservation of Britain's wildlife is a concern for John Plumptre. He owns the Chetney Marsh, a three-mile peninsula jutting out into the estuary of the River Medway. He has turned it into a wetland reservation, on which rare breeds of bird may nest and thrive. Chetney Marsh is home for avocet and green plover, bar-tailed godwit and ringed plover, redshank and oystercatcher. A single footpath crosses the mile-wide promontory and the ground-nesting birds rest undisturbed except by grazing horses and cattle, and by the Plumptres and their friends who, with warden Chris Henden, keep a keen eye on the depth of the fresh water on this sanctuary which is four feet below the level of the mighty Medway. Natural fleets[120] and ditches collect the rainwater which, through pumping, will neutralise any salty influx from the sea.

Julia Plumptre is on the parish council and involved in a number of charities. John's daily concerns are the estate and the Snowdown Colliery. Yes, the Snowdown Colliery. Although it is decades since the Kent Coalfield produced its last hobbit of coal in 1989, John Plumptre still has hopes for the site of the Snowdown pit. And this is why…

Like so many people associated with Kent coal, the Plumptre family are 'immigrants'. They were wool merchants in Nottingham and, in 1750, one of the young Plumptres married an heiress from Kent. Part of her dowry was a small estate called Fredville, so they moved to Fredville and the family, as we know, have been there ever since, although this was not part of the family plan. Young Plumptre was going to run the family wool merchants business and return to Nottingham, using Fredville as a weekend retreat. But he died young and the couple had no children so the second and then the third sons moved to Fredville and chose to make it their home.

In 1924, Pearson and Dorman Long, the northern steel manufacturers, decided to consolidate their interest in the Kent Coalfield. They had just opened the

---

[120] Fleet – a wide drainage ditch

Fredville Park boring site derrick, 1907

Snowdown Colliery, 1930

Betteshanger Colliery and, having surveyed the results of the comprehensive pattern of boreholes across the county, they were convinced that there was coal under Fredville and that the nearby Snowdown shaft would be worth investment. This was a gamble. Snowdown had a chequered history. Its sole advantage appeared to be that it was close to the main railway line between Dover and Canterbury, which made it easy to transport the coal. Other than that, although the Fredville coal had been discovered in 1896, the development of the mine became a catalogue of difficulty. It was very wet. It was very hot. Among miners it was known as 'Dante's Inferno'. In 1909, shaft number 1 had to be abandoned when the dig broke into a huge natural cavern. A torrent of water rushed through the cavern and 22 men were drowned. Shafts 2 and 3 were worked but a million gallons of water were pumped out every day into the River Stour nearby. The conditions in Snowdown were said to be as bad as anywhere in Britain.

And the workforce were not happy. There were frequent strikes over wages. There were violent clashes, with up to 300 pickets barring the way to those miners wishing to work.[121]

The Plumptre family owned the land where all the turmoil was taking place, "and," says John Plumptre, "I think my grandfather, Henry Weston Plumptre, was only too pleased when Pearson and Dorman Long signed a 60-year lease for the colliery and its land in 1924.

"Mind you, we hung on to the shooting rights, which in the years ahead, irritated the Coal Board enormously because we have been able to continue our shoots on the land ever since."

The new mine owners immediately began modernising Snowdown. The steam-powered winding plant was scrapped and replaced by one powered by electricity. Conditions below ground were improved. But in the General Strike of 1926 and into the 1930s there was further industrial action over attempts to lower the miners' wages. The situation was endemic in the industry. It was also confused by fragmentation. In

Snowdown Colliery first hobbit of coal raised, 1912

[121] Those Dirty Miners, JP Hollingsworth, p50

any negotiation, the mine owners still did not speak with a single voice, so different and separate agreements were being reached all over the country, peculiar to that colliery or group of collieries. In addition, Kent was the only coalfield which didn't have a distinct or regional arrangement on pay, the Kent Conciliation Board having failed to reach an agreement with the Kent Miners' Association.[122] There was a third irritant. Until 1932, when union pressure forced a change in the wage structure, most miners received their pay by what was known as 'the butty system'. It was meant to streamline the wage distribution. In fact it caused considerable resentment. The 'butty man' would collect a lump sum of wages for a group of miners he represented and would then distribute the money to the individuals in his group. If a miner were due, say 9 shillings and 11 pence, the 'butty man' would often keep the odd 11 pence. Management turned a blind eye to the practice and, if a miner complained, he would be 'moved to a less profitable working area'.[123]

John Plumptre says: "The Kent miners have always had a reputation for militancy and when, in 1956, my father was appointed General Manager for the Coal Board in the South East, he knew this. For the Plumptre family, coming to Kent was like coming home. I had been born in Bromley when my father worked for the Coal Board in London so I was seven when we moved to Fredville – and, from then on, Snowdown has been ever present in my life. We could have unloaded it in 1980 just before the lease expired but the Coal Board, who by this time had inherited the lease after the nationalisation of the coal industry, were optimistic about the future of the

[122] Ibid, p50
[123] Ibid, p52

Snowdown Colliery in the 1980s

Kent field. They said there was enough coal underground in Kent to last generations; and they wanted to renew for 20 years. I said to them[124] that they could have it for 60 years and they jumped at it. I wish I'd said 99 years, because they're still paying us rent today. Anyway, they were delighted.

"There's hardly a month goes past without someone approaching me to regenerate the Snowdown site, or part of it; solar panels or a wind farm. I consider what they say, and then pass on the good suggestions to the Coal Authority. They never agree and each idea dribbles away like sand through your fingers. But, in the future, you never know..."

Given his father's involvement, and his own career as a surveyor, Kent coal has played an important role in John Plumptre's life. He was 13 when he was first taken down to the coalface by Peter Rosser, a miner and one of the tenants on the Fredville estate. It was hot and dusty at the pit-bottom.

---

[124] John Plumptre is a qualified surveyor

It was "fairly shocking the way that the tunnels and supports were allowed to cave in and buckle." He crawled on hands and knees to the coal face which was 3 foot high. He imagined working in those conditions for six hours. He noticed the board indicating how many consecutive days had passed since a miner was injured or killed. It was, he says, "an eye-opener."

When John Plumptre went to university, his friends would come to stay at Fredville for the weekend. John took pleasure in showing them the pit. "My university chums were fascinated. It did them good to see the conditions under which coal was produced. They were, I suspect, slightly horrified at how harsh and difficult the working conditions were. Acrid water drips off the ceiling of the mine all the time and our faces were completely black when we got back to the surface. Yes, I know they were slightly shocked."

John Plumptre's father worked in the coal industry all his life. He was one of the first students at Birmingham University to take a degree in mining engineering. It was coincidental that he also happened to own the land on which a coal mine, Snowdown, existed. "He loved being part of a coalmining community, yet he never went to the mining villages, to my knowledge, except on business. The family gave land to the miners for their Welfare Club, and we later sold the freehold of the whole village of Snowdown so that the miners could own their homes. His attitude to the mining community could be described as 'caring and paternalistic', though he never expressed it in my hearing. But, then, he never expressed a paternalistic attitude to his own children, either."

John's father, JH Plumptre, represented the National Coal Board in Kent throughout some of its most turbulent

years. He was painstaking and meticulous and brought
to the job engineering skills that earned the respect of the
mining unions. He lived beside the Snowdown pit and
he presided over all four Kent pits. Consistently, he had a
difficult message to deliver – productivity had to increase
to enable the Kent Coalfield to survive. Between 1959 and
1961, he was meeting the unions regularly to explain 'how
tragic the position of the Betteshanger Colliery really was'.[125]
He quoted productivity figures comparing 1961 with 1959,
indicating that Betteshanger's face output had increased by
1 cwt per man-shaft, compared to 8.1 cwt per man-shaft
in the rest of the Division. The figures were challenged by
the unions and there followed a constructive conversation
involving the use of No6 seam, the relationship between
output and investment, and a possible adaptation of custom
and practice, all of which could help secure the future of the
pit. The outcome of the talks was positive and an agreement
was reached. Betteshanger would prove to be the Kent pit
that survived the longest.

Snowdown Colliery, which once employed 3500 men,
closed in 1987. It had been under threat of closure for some
years and its future lay at the heart of the bitter, year-long strike
against the Thatcher government in 1984.[126] The Government
won and embarked on a programme of razing Britain's pits
to the ground. John Plumptre opposed the idea. He took out
an injunction in the High Court to prevent the National Coal
Board demolishing the buildings and closing the shaft that
together made up the Snowdown Colliery. Firstly, they were
sound buildings and, if the shaft could be kept open, there was

---

[125] NCB SE Division minutes, June 12th 1961
[126] See Chapter 14

always a chance that political and environmental minds would change and coal might once more be mined in Kent. Secondly, the well-constructed buildings on the site could have a future that was not associated with the coal industry in any way. Plumptre's battle with the National Coal Board was brutish and short. "I had warning that the Coal Board wanted to fill in the shaft and they then wrote to me, seeking permission to do so. I wrote back and said 'no'. Then I watched as they brought in some special flints and stored them on-site. I had this action going through the High Court but in the end I was helpless. They filled the first 100 feet of the shaft with these flints and then they bulldozed colliery shale to fill up the rest of the shaft. And then they capped both shafts. They did all this without my permission. I was hopping mad. All I could do, as landlord, was to claim damages against the Coal Board and that wasn't worth doing, nor would it rectify the damage done. My idea was to retain the whole colliery site so that it could be reopened in the future. I fully accept that's impossible now."

But Plumptre takes some comfort in the fact that he prevented the demolition of all the buildings. "Hopefully, one day, they will be redeveloped…"

* * * * * * * *

The new town of Aylesham was planned specifically to accommodate miners who came to work in the Snowdown pit. Building started on the first 400 houses at the height of the General Strike, in 1926. It was 'a very grand scheme and the housing it provided was way in advance of its time.' When, much later, the opportunity came for miners to buy the freehold of their houses, virtually every tenant took up that right.[127] Abercrombie's plans may not have been fulfilled[128] but enough of his vision had survived to ensure, for the miners who came to Aylesham, a much-improved standard of housing.

Most of them travelled light. But one thing they all brought with them, as part of their heritage, was an accent. Today, Aylesham has an accent of its own and because this is a unique village, it has intrigued academics as well as those who have been Aylesham's neighbours for close on a century. In a well lit lecture room at the University of Kent, David Hornsby leads a group of language students, from the UK and Europe, through the complexities of the Aylesham accent. Hornsby added this course to the University of Kent's offer after visiting the town:

"It was like walking into an industrial, working-class town in the north of England but slap-bang in the middle of the Kent countryside. Culturally, it's different from other towns and villages in Kent; it looks different, it feels different and, from my point of view as a linguist, the 'talk' sounds different. For the people

Aylesham New Town (Kings Road)

---

[127] John Plumptre, conversation with the author
[128] See Chapter 4

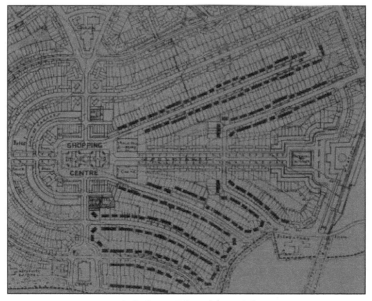

Aylesham Plan (1925/6)

who came here, from all over the country, it was really like moving to the colonies. These people were pioneers and they created a melting pot of sound." Hornsby's interest in Aylesham was fuelled by his French degree as a student, working as a language assistant in the coal town of Avion in France. "Mining towns are very community-orientated, very solid, very together – at least, that's my experience. And Aylesham is unique because of its history and, if you like, the forced march of labour over huge distances to come together in Kent."

Hornsby talks to his students about the phenomenon he calls 'koinéization'.[129] It happens to language, he says, "when a lot of very different dialects come into contact and something emerges from the mix that is different from, and

---

[129] Hornsby, DC, 2016. Welcome to the North! New Dialect Formation in Kent's 'Sunshine Corner' Transactions of the Yorkshire Dialect Society, part CXV1, Volume 23 44–56

greater than, the sum of the parts. One theory suggests that majority features in the dialect mix will win. To a degree, that's the case in Aylesham. Kentish folk, like southern England more generally, have something called the TRAP-BATH split, i.e. they distinguish the 'a' sounds in the words 'trap' and 'bath'. Ayleshamers don't. It's a short 'a' in 'trap' and 'bath' and 'path', almost certainly because miners coming from a variety of places in the north of England did not have the split, and made up a majority in the new village." Other Aylesham features are less easy to pin down. He gives, as an example, the word 'so'. "Lots of people came here from the North. People from Yorkshire, Lancashire, and the North-East all say 'so' slightly differently; many had monophthongal pronunciations (like in 'saw') while others had a range of diphthongs, in which the sound changes as the tongue moves. In Aylesham, the pronunciation is similar but not identical to the vowel in 'cow'. Very different from how the rest of Kent says the word. It's certainly not Estuary English. I suspect it's closest to Nottinghamshire or South Yorkshire, but I can't be sure quite yet…" But why did this pronunciation win out over all the many others one would have heard in the early days? It is mysteries like these that led Hornsby to describe Aylesham as 'a socio-linguist's dream'. There were, for instance, many words for 'alleyway' in the original dialect mix. But an alleyway in Aylesham is a 'jitty', which appears to have originated in Derbyshire and Nottinghamshire. Some families have also retained words that echo their heritage: the Welsh and the Scots and the Geordies have kept on saying certain words, just as they would have done if they hadn't left their home pits maybe three generations ago.

One of the mysteries, then, is why certain language traits have survived, and others haven't. "There are plenty of folk from Scottish families in Aylesham – but I haven't yet found anyone who merges 'cot' as in 'the baby is in the cot', and 'cot' as in 'I have cot (caught) my sleeve on a nail'. Now, why has that form died out while others survived? It's a beautiful puzzle to have.

"And if you examine language, you learn about people. Aylesham was quite a tribal place for the first couple of decades. The Derbyshire miners mixed with the Derbyshire miners, the Welsh with the Welsh and so on. But as people intermarried, they realised they had so much in common. Their kids were native Ayleshamers and a real sense of community has emerged over the years. People are aware of their heritage but it doesn't dominate their lives. I have never found a place that has as much warmth and community spirit as Aylesham."

Aylesham lies in the rural district of Dover, which is 12 miles away and about 10 miles south-east of Canterbury. Today, it has a population of around 4,000. Every Wednesday morning, at the White House in Dorman Road, there's a gathering of men wearing green t-shirts. The shirt is a badge of honour in this unique town. It marks out a man as a former miner. Keith Owen and Eric Norton are friends.[130] They both wear the green shirt and they've been friends ever since they played together in the Aylesham Youth Club football team in the 1960s. It was a fine team. Played 16, won 16. Keith's family came to Aylesham from Blackwood in South Wales in 1927. Eric's from Yorkshire in 1933. Keith's granddad had owned a pig farm and worked at a slate quarry in North Wales, but

---

[130] Interview with author, 2019

Aylesham Boys' Football Team

Back row - Derick Robson, Phillip Bell, Alan Watson, Peter Sutcliffe, George Devine

Front row - Barry Robertson, Eric Norton, Keith Owen, Harry Roycroft, Alan Curtis

Ralph Norton (Ball)

moved to Oakdale in South Wales to mine coal instead. His grandfather wasn't too keen on Kent and moved back to Wales in 1927, but Keith's mother and father, Gertrude and Henry Glyn, stayed on and lived at 22 Clarendon Road, Aylesham, from where Keith's father went to work at Snowdown.

The Norton family, according to Eric, came to Kent from Castleford "because it was a bit overcrowded in Yorkshire." Eric was one of 13 children; seven sisters and five brothers. His father Tom was a miner, like his father before him, and the Nortons, Tom and Marjorie, moved into one of the new houses in Queen's Road, Aylesham. Tom Norton worked in the pit for 51 years; four of the brothers also became miners. Eric says: "Following the General Strike of 1926 they started on the

Aylesham today

construction of Aylesham and, even before the Kent miners officially returned to work in 1926, some were beginning to move into their new houses in their new town.

"Back in Yorkshire, the coal would be chucked on the ground outside the house and you'd have to get it in yourself and boil the water for the tin bath in the kitchen. But when we came to Kent, they had showers and baths at the pit. And the families couldn't believe what they found in their new homes. They had what they called a back boiler behind the coal-fire in the living room and that heated the water as well as the house. When he (his father) turned on the tap, he couldn't believe hot water was coming out. And the electric light; people used to switch them on and off all the time, like a disco. It had never been like that up north."

Keith Owen remembers: "My dad still used to bath us all in front of the fire rather than in the bathroom upstairs. There were five of us. And we'd have a rare old time taking turns in this tin bath. My dad used to say: 'I'm sure I've bathed three of the neighbour's kids from next door.'"

The Owens had nine children – Glyn, Keith, Jean, Sheila, Colin, the twins Rosie and Ron, Elaine, who won a place at grammar school, and Jennifer. Bath night was part of the routine in the Owen household. "It was Mam's rehearsal night with the local choir and, later, after the bath routine, Dad would announce he was 'just going up the club for a box of matches'; he always smoked a pipe. He'd be back soon, after he'd had his regular two pints. Then he'd sit in front of the big log fire in his chair and the sweat would be pouring off him." Keith says:

"When I look at the early photographs of my parents now, they look as if they have just walked out of Downton Abbey. When they first came down here, they were young and they had no children for seven years. Everything was good for them and they look so happy. Dad would see that Mam went into Canterbury to have a cup of coffee on a Saturday, and she enjoyed her outside life, all her life. Dad was a pretty good bloke. He was in the male voice choir and on the Parish Council! People respected him. He and my uncle Ken used to do a bit of boxing in the booths to get some extra money. You could come up against some hard, big men and professional fighters but I think he quite enjoyed it. He never complained about it, anyway."

Henry Glyn Owen died in 1969 from silicosis. He was 69. "He had a job to walk ten yards without a stop. I just remember him gasping for breath. He ended up with oxygen bottles all 'round his bed. My mam went through a bit of distress and hardship because he was a long time dying. It's hard to see a man go through that, but he did. He did."

Keith pauses for a long moment. "I've seen a lot of men like my dad. He was stern but I don't remember him ever hitting me. My mum used to give me a clip but I don't remember my dad… He was very quiet. He was only a little man but he was very strong. In everything."

Soon after he had watched his father die, Keith Owen left the coal mines. He took a job on a building site. "I decided that my days as a miner were over. That was it for me. I thought 'That's not any way to live your life, that's not the way to go'." He worked at a local brewery in the distribution depot. But, after 12 years, he was back at the pit, not Snowdown this time, but Tilmanstone, and later Betteshanger, where he was promoted to materials officer. "I'm not sure, from choice, that I'd have gone down the pit at all, as a young man. But my elder brother had just gone into the army and my mam said: 'Well, you'll have to get a job to help keep the family'. So I did – and, I guess: once a miner always a miner."

His friend, Eric Norton, was always going to be a miner. He was brought up in Burgess Road, Aylesham, and when the Careers Officer came to Aylesham School, the interview was short and sharp:

"I was 14 ½ and I was tiny.
He said: 'Where does your dad work?'
I said: 'Down Snowdown Colliery'.
He said: 'Oh, okay, Snowdown Colliery'.
And he made a note. Next minute, I'm going down Snowdown Colliery."

Eric's ambition had been to become a physical training instructor. His father was good at sport, particularly Rugby League and, back in Castleford, he had been a champion snooker player. But Eric's passion was football. "All our lives we played football. I even went to bed with a football. At Christmastime, if we were lucky, we got a pair of football boots, a pair of shorts, a football shirt and a ball. That's all we did, play football."

The success of the Aylesham Youth Club – unbeaten for a season – attracted the attention of professional clubs. Seven of the boys, including Keith and Eric, went to play at the Football League club, Gillingham. It was a semi-professional club, which means that a few pound notes would be shoved into the boys' football boots at the end of the game. Eric was offered the chance to join Gillingham as a professional footballer. But he had started at the pit, on a steady wage of £6 or £7 a week, and "I was frightened that, if I failed to make it as a footballer, I'd be out of a job… sometimes I wish I'd said yes." Eric's brother, Ralph, did say 'yes' when Reading knocked on his door. He played for Reading until he was 27. And, Terence, Eric's younger brother, played for Brian Clough and Peter Taylor at Brighton.

For Eric, growing up in Aylesham was 'brilliant'. "Everyone helped each other. As boys, we used to go out in the morning with a bottle of water and a couple of sandwiches and play in the field and down the woods. Everybody seemed to bind together."

He was happy at school. "'Taffy' Thorn was my teacher and he started me playing rugby. I was tiny and a scrum half. We went for Kent trials and there were some lads six feet tall. And a bloke came up to Mr Thorn and said, pointing at me: 'He's not playing, is he? He'll get hurt, he's not big enough'. And Mr Thorn said: 'Wait till he gets out there', and I won a place in the Kent team. I was fast, you see, and they couldn't catch me."

Eric met his wife Hazel at Aylesham Secondary School. They married when he was 19 and she was 17. They had two boys and a girl. When England play Wales, Eric "shouts for England, and she shouts for Wales." Keith Owen married Pat Hadfield at Aylesham Baptist church in 1959. They'd known each other for years because Pat's auntie lived across the road from the Owens. It was a white wedding "with bridesmaids

Keith And Pat Owen today

and all that. We had the reception in the back hall of the church and, because it was Baptist, there wasn't any drinking. It was a great day – but when my grandkids and my family ask me: 'Where did you go for your honeymoon?' and I say 'Peckham', they roll about laughing. I say: 'Yeah'. We went to stay with Pat's auntie and uncle and they lived in Peckham. It was brilliant for us because it was only a tube ride to the West End and we went to see all the shows. But, today, they think it's hilarious to go to Peckham for your honeymoon."

But, decades ago, the world was a different place. Aylesham was self-contained and confident. It offered brass bands, polished choirs, community celebrations and street parties, dances in the church hall and a steady, if dangerous, living if your man was a miner. Keith Owen sums it up: "Our first house was a prefab. We had a fridge when almost no one else had a fridge. We knew we had a dangerous job – but it *was* a job and, because we both came from mining families, we accepted that. Some Kent people didn't like the people of Aylesham and we were aware of that isolation. You know when you're growing up, you hear it from friends and neighbours. But everything we wanted was within our community or within reach. We didn't have to go outside Aylesham. I know it's not the best way to live, we should have had a broader view, but that's how it was."

Eric remembers this isolation even as a schoolboy. "We knew we were 'Aylesham'. We knew we were different. We knew they were ready for us."

"It was something we grew up with," adds Keith. "When we played Dover Grammar School, for instance, we'd say 'We'll thrash those toffee-nosed boys' – and then we'd come away with a hammering because they were well trained and we were just learning. We were novices really – but our teacher, 'Taffy' Thorn, was brilliant and we got better and better. If we were isolated, it was as much our choice as the world outside Aylesham."

Both men recall the financial pressures in an industry which seemed perpetually in a state of negotiation or conflict. To them, the recurring pattern was this: The price of coal dropped and the miners were asked to work harder and/or to accept reduced wages, or to work less than full-time, with a resultant drop in wages. Keith Owen says: "There was a lot of people living below the poverty line in the early days. My mother remembers a couple who moved down here from the North East and they had two children. They lived in a pit house and then one of the children died. There was no cemetery in Aylesham, and they didn't have a lot of money, and Mam said: 'I can still see it now: They had this wooden trolley thing with a coffin on it and they were crying and pushing it through the streets, all the way to the cemetery at Nonington. A wooden trolley with just the mother and father walking behind it. It was heart-breaking."

The council or the mine owners owned the pit houses in which the miners lived. The rules were simple: "If the miner died, either at the pit or anywhere else," says Keith Owen, "you had to get out. Now this was not popular, as you can guess. We had our leaders in the community and Ianto Hill[131] was exceptional. I think he was chair of the Parish Council and he recognised injustice when he saw it; anyway, he took matters into his own hands on this day. A family had come from Wales and the husband had fallen sick and couldn't work. So they were going to be evicted from a house in King's Road. All their furniture was taken out and dumped on the pavement. Ianto let the eviction take place and then got a ladder, climbed up the back of the house, opened a window, went inside and opened the front door. Moved all the furniture back in, and he went to the mine manager on the Monday and said: 'I don't want to see that happen again in our village'. And I don't think he ever did."

As a boy, Keith used to earn extra money doing a paper round for Ianto's father. "In those days, if you were interested in horse-racing, you had to wait for the evening newspaper, for the results, which were printed in the *Stop Press*.[132] I did Queen's Road and Hythe Place, and the men would often be waiting for me, and some who had placed a bet but didn't have a regular newspaper order would say: 'Have you got a spare one, son?' Well, I'd find a 'spare one' and pocket the cash. When I got back to the shop, I'd say I was a few short. Ianto would say: 'I'm sure I gave you the right number'. And he'd look at me – but he used to turn a blind eye.

"Some people resented him but in the early days he took Aylesham by the scruff of the neck and made it work. He took on the Establishment. He didn't have a fine education but he was well-respected. He was at his best when times were hard."

---

[131] See Chapter 15
[132] Stop Press – a section of late news

If men can't earn money, they will find it somehow. In the 1930s, one Aylesham family sent their three children, house to house, to the nearby village of Adisham, carrying a letter signed by their mother, saying there was no food in the house and that their father was sick. The village policeman noted that, when he had spotted them, their baskets contained bread, tea, cheese and a pair of boy's boots. The policeman took them back home to Aylesham, where the family admitted sending them out begging. In court, later, a doctor testified that the husband was fit for work but had turned up for only one and a half shifts at Snowdown in the past month. He was gaoled for a month. Petty crime reported in the *Dover Express* at the time included a refreshment hut in Aylesham being broken into, the thieves taking food and money, and the stationmaster's office at Aylesham Halt being burgled, with two pounds, one shilling and three pence being stolen.[133] For some, this petty crime created an atmosphere of fear and some miners wives never settled. Mrs Watkins, who came to Aylesham in 1934, didn't stay long. She had been in service in Surrey; her husband came from Wales.

"I hated Aylesham. I wouldn't put the baby outside because the kids didn't care if they tipped the pram up. I was scared stiff with her outside – it was so rough and I wasn't used to that. After they'd been down the clubs they'd be fighting. It used to be terrible. I wouldn't go out on my own at night. I said 'If we don't move from here soon I'm either going back to Surrey or back to Wales'. Which she did after a year.[134]

---

[133] Those Dirty Miners, JP Hollingsworth
[134] Those Dirty Miners, JP Hollingsworth

Keith Owen reflects far more the majority view. "Despite the fact I wanted to get out of the coal industry for a short time, I've no regrets at what I've done. Living in a mining community, everybody knows everybody and it's the best upbringing you could have had, really. I've been back to South Wales and to Durham, visiting mining areas, and some of them have stood still. We in Aylesham have been given a chance to settle and move on:

'To build a new life for ourselves, if you like."

The end of a shift. Miners changing in the pit head baths

Yorkshire miners experienced their share of tragic accidents.
This marks a disaster at Barrow Colliery

Peter Wentworth Fitzwilliam - who fought hard to save his home

Terry French, one of the leaders of Kent miners in 1984

CHAPTER ELEVEN
Chislet and Tilmanstone

"A single death is a tragedy; a million deaths is a statistic."
Josef Stalin, 1943

The miners drawn to Kent to work on the pits at Chislet and Tilmanstone did not have a special town created

Chislet Colliery, 1920

for them. At Chislet, they built a few houses at the local village and the coal company took leases on several hundred houses in Thanet, both at Ramsgate and Margate. At Tilmanstone, the first Kent mine to produce coal commercially, Arthur Burr's companies set up dormitories for the men at Elvington Court and created small estates of pit houses nearby, as well as in the villages of Woolage, Stonehall and Snowdown.[135]

---

[135] Chapter 3, see Tilden Smith

World War One had a special significance in the development of Chislet. The Anglo-Westphalian Coal Syndicate had leased land in the area in 1911 and, through boreholes, had prospected for coal at Rushbourne, Sturry, Herne Bay, Reculver and Chislet Park. The local director was Herr Willi Perits. Three years on, in May 1914, the company started work on a shaft near Westbere Court. Three months later, in August, war broke out. All the German personnel hurried off to Germany and the company was rapidly re-named The Chislet Colliery Company Ltd. Questions were asked in Parliament about the German involvement and fears were expressed that 'somehow the tunnels at Chislet could be used by the German army'.[136] Mining was halted. A parliamentary delegation visited the site, realistically to consider the threat of invasion, which was nil – and work on the shaft was allowed to resume.

Abercrombie's 1925 Regional Planning Scheme envisaged new towns at both Chislet and Elvington. Neither became reality, though Abercrombie's plans for Chislet were particularly ambitious with a central boulevard and a village green, embracing a church with a rectory, a village institute, shops and an inn. One thousand houses would

Chislet Colliery, Hersden

[136] Hersden by Ross Llewellyn, 2003

be built. Ross Llewellyn, a miner since he was 15, describes it today as 'a romantic idea to build a typical English village but finance dictated that the village went up in bits and pieces'.[137]

By 1928, a rail track was running from the colliery across the main Canterbury-to-Thanet road and up The Avenue and this delivered materials to the builders as the Chislet Colliery village expanded. The houses were, in fact, some distance from the village of Chislet and, as Ross Llewellyn's comprehensive book *Hersden*[138] records, there was some confusion over how to describe this increasingly separate community.

A new name was needed – and the story goes that Griff Davies, then secretary to the Chislet Colliery, is credited with creating it.

In JK Wallenberg's *Place Names of Kent*, he is said to have found the ancient name 'Haseden'. Among the Manors of Chislet, he discovered the 'Manor of Hersing'. He took the first syllable of Hersing and the second syllable of Haseden, and produced 'Hersden'. And so it has been ever since, so much so that in 2019, a move to change the name of the village school from Hersden Village Primary School caused uproar among Hersden residents.[139]

The Chislet pit was initially highly successful. It is the most northerly of the Kent pits and only five miles from Canterbury, with its cathedral, its graceful society and patterns of entertainment. Most of the miners initially came from Wales, partly because some Welsh coal companies had a financial interest in the Chislet Colliery. Because so many

---

[137] Ibid, p9

[138] Ibid

[139] It is also possible, though less romantic, that Griff Davies took the name from Hersden Farm, on the Ordnance Survey map of 1896

miners lived in Thanet, special 'miners' trains' ran every day stopping at Grove Ferry and Chislet Colliery Halt, a station designed specifically for the mining traffic.[140] Chislet had five good years from 1919, production rising year on year: 22,228 tons (1919), 93,468 tons (1920), 104,992 tons (1921), 210,652 tons (1922), and a staggering 223,733 tons (1923). Then, the recession and a series of strikes brought Chislet to its knees until, in 1929, the company was in deep financial trouble. Only the appointment of a new chairman and managing director, EO Forster Brown staved off bankruptcy.

Kent miner at work - with extra lighting for the benefit of the official photographer

Forster Brown was a skilled mining engineer. He was, like Tilden Smith at Tilmanstone, aware of the needs of his workforce. Co-operating with the Mineworkers' Welfare Committee, Forster Brown helped finance Britain's first pit bathhouse, with room for 600 men. They still had to queue for a bath and pay a levy towards running costs but, if they chose to, they need no longer go home in their working black.[141]

---

[140] Those Dirty Miners, JP Hollingsworth, p71
[141] In 1937, Forster Brown opened an extension to the pit baths with facilities for the entire workforce of 1,500

The miners cared for their own. A Chislet Colliery Workers' Medical Aid and Benevolent Society was set up in the 1920s through which, at a cost of three pence a week, a family could receive treatment and medicine from the local doctor. At the same time, across the country in South Wales, a young man named Aneurin Bevan was addressing the same problem of medical care for his community; 20 years later, his ruminations would lead to the launch in Britain of the world's first National Health Service.

Ross Llewellyn's family came to the Chislet pit in the 1930s. His father had been working in the Six Bells pit in Abertillery, but there was no longer a job for him. Unemployment was high – but, unlike many of the immigrant miners, Ross' father travelled to Kent in style. "The Chislet mine under manager, Arthur Sutton, was a rugby fanatic. And my dad could play a bit. So Mr Sutton paid his train fare from South Wales. When my father arrived at Chislet Halt and got off the train, it was an awful day. All misty and damp. He said: 'I'm not stopping here'. But he never went back to Wales."

Unlike his father, young Ross *did* go back to Wales. When war broke out in 1939, Ross was evacuated there accompanied by his mother until June 1942, when the threat of a German invasion had passed. His father stayed on in lodgings in Kent and continued to dig coal. The family eventually arrived back in Hersden with their furniture piled up in the back of a lorry. The war was still at its height and young Ross spent his nights in the air raid community shelters. "The best part was that they all had shaded electric lights so everyone would be chattering or singing and it was a waste of time my mother trying to make us go to sleep. It was much better than crouching in our own Anderson shelter in the back garden, which used to flood when it rained."

As with most youngsters, the war was an adventure. "I can never remember being afraid. We spent our time on the rock tips, sliding down on tins and playing in the gun sites on either side." They popped into the blacksmiths shop where Bill Kelly and Harry Lowther would toast them a piece of bread by passing a red hot iron over it. They learned to swim in the rivers and marshes. "We were nude, of course, and our party trick was to jump up and down as the trains went past. I think we shocked a few old ladies." They fished in the rivers and watched the cormorants nesting on the dead, waterlogged trees in the middle of the marsh. At school, they learned to read from 'Janet and John' books and sometimes their teacher, Mrs Brown, "would send us out to fetch her a packet of Craven A cigarettes and a jar of pickled walnuts, which she loved. The jar would be on her table at lunchtimes no matter what the meal of the day was. Was it medicine, we wondered, or simply something to disguise the food?"

Llewellyn is proud of the way families from all over the country have mixed and lived together. Their skills and interests have enriched the community: "Dave Leitch from Scotland set up the amateur boxing club, Jackie Robinson from Wallsend started the Silver Band and John Jones and Arthur Sutton from Wales brought their enthusiasm for rugby football. Our pavilion at Chislet was the envy of visiting rugby and football clubs."

At the heart of the village for half a century was the Black Hut, near Westbere Court. In the beginning, all the business of the pit was run from this wood and corrugated iron structure. Sacks of coal were weighed and sold and, at the end of the week, the miners queued there to get their wages. In the 1920s, however, Chislet Colliery built its own on-site offices and the chequered career of the Black Hut began – as a timber store; changing rooms for the village football team; a haven for impoverished families during the 1926 General Strike when, for 26 weeks, breakfasts were provided for the village children; a soup kitchen for the adults; a Sunday School; birthplace of the Chislet Colliery Silver Band; headquarters of the Women's Institute, home for the women's choir and a spare classroom for the primary school. The Black Hut was used every night of the week, often for a community concert, with music provided by 'a splendid piano' that cost £100 – money raised through voluntary contributions of a penny a week from the villagers. Sadly, the Black Hut was demolished in the 1960s. In its place: a bicycle shed.[142]

Chislet's Silver Band had its roots in Durham. Jackie Robinson was appointed agent and manager of the colliery in 1927. He then recruited a number of miners from the Durham pits who were also musicians and, in 1929, a set of 'Class A silver-plated and engraved instruments, made to order by Besson and Co Ltd were presented to the newly-formed band, at a cost of £556 and 10 shillings'. The band advertised itself as 'Any time, anywhere: full band of 25' and were very much in demand at fetes, flower shows and events at local seaside resorts. So popular were they in Canterbury, and so huge the crowds as they paraded through the narrow streets, that the Chief Constable banned a repetition of their visit to the cathedral city. 'Band banned' as the local newspaper might have put it.

---

[142] Kinn H McIntosh, Hersden, p16

The band's ambition was to compete in the National Brass Band championships. In 1958, they did so, playing *The Devon Fantasy* by Eric Ball in competition with eight other bands from all over the country. They did not win. But for the stalwarts of the band, the prize was in taking part, particularly for the Hodgson and the Heckley families, who played in the band from 1927 until it disbanded in the 1970s.

"There was always something going on in Hersden," says Ross Llewellyn, "and, if not, there was always the bright lights of Canterbury or Margate to tempt you." Ross met his wife, Esther Virginia (Ginny), at St Mildred's dance hall in Margate and they married six months later. Ginny's father worked in Baxter's sausage factory in Sarre, her mother in Dreamland, on the glittering Margate seafront. Ginny worked in the fields and the pack houses, harvesting cabbages, cauliflowers and mushrooms. Ross' working day began at 4.30am to catch the bus at the end of the road at 4.45am and arrive at the pit at 6am. He slept on the bus to work, and again on the way home. He'd have a nap in the afternoon – "and then round to the Black Horse for a pint." By 1951, annual output at Chislet had reached 400,000 tons and that level was sustained throughout the decade.

Pit ponies, which had been introduced at Chislet in 1945, were being used for hauling timber to the coalface and for other heavy work, releasing men to train for other work at the coalface.[143] John Finn, a carpenter at Chislet, remembers their arrival: "These 10 wild ponies, straight off the moors, were due to be picked up at Grove Ferry, and we had to make a paddock for them in the field behind the offices. We got that done in time and then we had the job of building stables for

---

[143] Hersden, by Ross Llewellyn, pp76/77

them, underground." The ponies were kept there in excellent condition. "Each stall was whitewashed and supplied with electric light. Over each stall hung the pony's name – each beginning with the letter 'A' which I thought rather odd."[144] The last pony, Alex, was withdrawn in the 1950s. Attractive though the idea had been, "they were not a great help because Chislet had a fairly well-organised haulage system anyway."[145]

By 1957, Chislet had been profitable for 12 years but there had been little investment and conditions in the crowded pit had suffered. By this time, the number of miners working in the pit had risen to 1,681. Socially, too, the 1950s were the busiest in Hersden's history. There were 13 sections in the Chislet Colliery Welfare Association – athletics, bowls, boxing, brass band, cricket, choral society, darts, football (soccer), First Aid Brigade, gardening, homing pigeons, tennis and table tennis. The story was the same, or very similar, in every other mining village. The pits competed against each other over coal output and the quality of the coal that was produced. They even vied with each other over the quality of the pies and pasties baked in the pit canteens.

Each pit had its own favourites; 'Lill's sinkers' at Tilmanstone, the Betteshanger pie and the Snowdown pasty, to name but three. Lynn Devine and Sandra Dymond still make their pasties (Lynn) and the pies (Sandra) for special occasions and the ingredients in their recipes are very similar – mincemeat, potatoes, carrots and onions.[146] But the difference, of course, lies in the cooking... and neither is giving away her secret. Lynn says: "Some of the canteen

---

[144] Bevin Boys, by Derek Agnen
[145] Ross Llewellyn, conversation with author, 2018
[146] For recipe, see Appendix

ladies would go in at 6am to start preparing the ingredients and rolling out the pastry and they would be doing that until three o'clock in the afternoon. Just making pasties." The pasties were there for the men who had forgotten their 'snap'.[147] They were also used as a reward, as a boost to morale, if men were required to work over-long shifts. "They used to get a couple of pies and a bottle of milk sent down to them," says Sandra. The men in each pit vociferously championed their own pie or pasty. Only George Gibb broke the mould. "I think," he confided, "that they all came from the same small factory tucked out of sight, somewhere in Kent."

There was always a big demand for pasties when there'd been an incident and men were incarcerated underground.

The Chislet pit closed on July 26th 1969. On Monday August 29th 2016, Ross Llewellyn stood outside the Miners' Institute in Hersden to remind an audience of several hundred of their heritage as a mining village and of the price men paid to bring coal to industry and the hearth. He unveiled a plaque which named every man who had died in the Chislet Colliery. There were 53 names on the plaque.[148]

Chislet Memorial

---

[147] Ibid
[148] The 53 names are listed in the Appendix

A coal mine can kill you in a variety of ways. In a decade at Chislet, 22 men died:

February 1931: John Clunie Williams, aged 15, had been working at Chislet Colliery for only eight days. He was learning to drive an engine used for hauling truckloads of coal from the coalface and had been told to sit inside the engine with the driver and not to leave the engine. The man in charge of the level had, just previous to the accident, told two other youths to 'get a move on' as he wanted to land this journey 'before knock off'. Young Williams, hearing this remark, left the engine to board the back of the load of trucks; he was knocked off and crushed to death.

June 1931: Granville Glover (46) a married man of Cecil Cottages, Westbere, was pulling a tub back on the rails and, in doing so, caught his hip against a stationary tub. He died in Kent and Canterbury Hospital the next day.

January 1932: There were three deaths at Chislet Colliery that month. One casualty, Samuel Merritt, aged 43 of 16 Poplars was struck by a fall of roof and died of his injuries. At the time, he was working with his brother William. They were both single men and had been inseparable. William was wheeling an empty tub just ahead of his brother. He heard his brother shout 'I am fast, Bill!' When he reached his brother he found a stone had fallen from the roof on top of him; it blocked the whole passage and no one could get over it or around it. Other colliers came and the stone was eventually lifted up. The lower part of Sam's body was appallingly injured and he died from his injuries.

March 1932: George Albert James Whitehead, aged 49, of 69 Odo Road Dover was killed by a fall of roof. George Clarkstone of 124 Clarenden Place, Dover, a miner, said at the inquest that he was working with Mr Whitehead and on a previous shift there had been a fall in this place. "We started to shift the dirt. I was packing on the right hand side until we got within about four feet of the gate side then I decided to put the footings in on the gate side. I had just cleaned out to put the fountain in when the whole thing collapsed and I found myself three parts buried up to my waist in a sitting position. Then Mr Whitehead asked 'How are you?' and I replied 'I am fast' and then he said 'So am I, goodbye,' and that was the last I heard from him."

November 1932: Frederick Deverson, aged 26, of 19 King Street, Canterbury, died in hospital as a result of internal injuries suffered in an accident, which occurred during blasting operations on the night shift of October 31st and November 1st. A stone the size of a chicken's egg had ruptured his liver. The doctor said there was no bleeding and the wound only appeared like a superficial cut.

December 1932: A roof fall occurred at the colliery when two men were drawing off timber. Patrick McGinely, aged 36, of 10 The Elms Hersden when extracted from under a roof fall, was found to be dead. Thomas Tate aged 23, who lives at Orchard Villas, Sturry, was seriously injured and was taken to Kent and Canterbury Hospital.

August 1933: Harold 'Harry' Jakes of 6 Nixon Avenue, Ramsgate, a repairer at Chislet Colliery was killed by a roof fall. George Pratt of Oak Cottage, Upstreet, at the inquest, said: "I was engaged with other men including Mr Jakes on no. 21 ripping section, removing stones which had come from the ripping. Mr Jakes was breaking up the stones. George Ball and William Porter were engaged in ripping the roof; all at once we heard a crash and the roof fell in. Mr Jakes died; he was pinned underneath. There were six men found altogether four were hurt; three slightly and a stretcher case."

September 1933. Arthur Davison was fatally injured by a fall on the second day of his return to work after being away ill for 16 weeks. Thomas WM Harris of 41 The Avenue, Hersden, who was working with Mr Davison and two other men, were sitting at the junction of stalls 342 and 347 having a meal when suddenly there was a crash and stone began to fall. One of about 1cwt hit Mr Davison and knocked him on his face, another fell on his left arm and another on his legs. He died but none of the other men was hurt.

February 1934: John T Peckett, aged 50, of 11 The Avenue, Hersden, died from head injuries as a result of a roof fall. Mr Peckett was a native of Towlow, Durham, came to Kent two years ago and played left wing for Chislet Colliery Football Club. Only a fortnight earlier, Mr Peckett's step-daughter, Miss Georgiana (Madge) Dickinson, aged 19, had died.

March 1934: Leonard Thomas Wood, aged 22, of Nixon Avenue, Ramsgate, was killed when four loaded tubs crashed into him.

November 1934: Edward Blunt, aged 47, who lived at 60 Duncan Road, Ramsgate was killed by a fall off the side of the roof. Laurence Eyre of 7 South View said they had almost finished their shift and Blunt had been putting two stones on the pack. "I heard a bump and the fall came instantly. I jumped clear and shouted 'All right?' and (on) hearing no reply I shouted for help and then went back to extricate him. Half a dozen men helped me to find the body which was buried by the fall."

January 1935: An inquest lasting five hours was held at the Black Horse, Hersden, on the body of George Henry

Jones, aged 47, of 134 Hereson Road, Ramsgate; a Deputy who died at the pit. After a telephone call from his home stating he had not returned home from his shift, a search party set out and eventually found the body of the deceased in a hollow in the road marked 'No road', which had been closed since 1934. Martin Benson, Surveyor at the colliery, produced a plan of the scene of the accident, and said that to get to this particular part of the colliery Mr Jones would have had to pull away some strips of wood and squeeze in. This might have been accidental death or suicide.

February 1935: Evan W Evans, aged 57, was crushed by a fall of between 10 and 15 cwts of coal on February 14th. Horace B Bigham aged 20 had his arm caught and torn by a coal conveyer on the night of February 10th–11th. A blood transfusion was carried out from his 22-year-old brother but Bigham died.

October 1936: Alfred John Ryan, aged 21, a haulage hand living in Sturry, was crushed between tubs and fatally injured. An engine was hauling a journey of five tubs. The engine stopped and Mr Ryan was found between the third and fourth tubs with his stomach crushed between the iron edge of the third tub and a low bar in the roof.

January 1937: Nathaniel Dickinson, aged 33, of 2 Marden Avenue, Ramsgate, was run over by a tub. He was a married man with two children. He was found lying on his back, his left leg under the tub; the front wheels had left the track.

May 1937: Thomas Henry Watson, aged 47, of Adelaide Gardens, Ramsgate, died in Ramsgate General Hospital on May 13th, two months after he had been injured in an accident at Chislet Colliery. He had cut himself close to the right knee with a hatchet which weighed about 5lbs when the hatchet had bounced off a pit prop.

September 1937: Bertie Hancock, a single man aged 32 of 5 Poplars, was knocked down by an empty journey of tubs.

December 1937: Runaway tubs on Christmas Eve killed Sidney John Amlin Axford, aged 23, an underground haulage worker of Elvington. Mrs A Axford of 23 Adelaide Road Elvington, said her son had been at Chislet for two or three months after being unemployed for two years; he previously worked at Tilmanstone Colliery.

December 1938: An inquest was held at Canterbury on Joseph Christian, aged 56, of 2 Simmonds Row, Canterbury who was injured at Chislet Colliery on August 11th. Dr G H McCracken of Kent and Canterbury Hospital stated that Mr Christian died from bronchial pneumonia and myocardial degeneration following an injury to the spine. Mr Christian had been pinned down by a fall of debris and had to be dug out. Twenty-two tubs had run away; some girders and props near the pump house had been knocked out and the tubs were derailed and piled up.

June 1939: A Chislet miner, Henry Hulme, a pan turner of 37 Marden Avenue, Newington, who within the previous two years had lost two children in road accidents, was killed instantly by the fall of a roof. His head was crushed by a stone weighing more than 2 hundredweight. He left a wife and two children.

Wherever the pit, whatever the community, every single miner has at least one story of a narrow escape, a crippling injury, a friend whose life was lost. Ross Llewellyn had been at Chislet only a month or two when he had to help rescue someone who was buried, crushed by a rock fall. On Good Friday 1963, the same thing happened to Ross – "I was lucky to get away with it". Les Fordham's father lost fingers in a cog and Les' friend, Rod Taylor, was killed when he fell through the engine house roof

Tilmanstone Colliery Demolition, 1987

at Snowdown. Lyn James from Nantymoel ran the right way when the roof fell in and survived. John Kemp, a third generation miner, saw R o n n i e Foreman, an overman killed while helping him out on the coalface, when a conveyor pinned him to the roof. "He was 59. Lovely man…" Keith Owen watched his father die slowly from silicosis, caused by the dust that wrecked his lungs. His friend, Eric Norton, was nearly killed by a roof fall: "This rock came down on my back and it was a big one. My mate just run up and it was sticking in my chest. I said: 'Jim, I can't move my legs. I can't move them'. Anyway, Jim bent down and he lifted that rock. He lifted it off me. I don't know where he got the strength. And then he carried me out of the pit." George Gibb nearly lost a leg when a conveyor belt started unexpectedly; he got away with a broken bone in his foot.

Stuart Elgar, son of a Tilmanstone farmer, nearly lost his maternal grandfather in a rock fall at the Tilmanstone pit. Though badly injured, his grandfather recovered and worked on until he was 65. Stuart Elgar says: "The danger didn't deter me. When you're young, you're invincible, aren't you? I really wanted to do the job. It's something that grabbed me. Funnily enough, I remember things now that make me want to shiver. But they didn't at the time. No, it was a great job."[149] Stuart Elgar is big, burly and grammar school-educated. He was "unfortunately, the youngest of farmer Elgar's sons, otherwise I might have been a rich farmer

Stuart Elgar

rather than a poor ex-miner."

Elvington's agricultural heritage could not be more distinct. The name itself is derived from Old English and means 'the farmstead of Aelfwine'. Once a manor house, the building is now home to the village bowling club. It is said that Roman invaders used the Ashley Path to Barfreston across the Downs, and, more recently, the village had its own railway station, Elvington Halt, which served the coalmine and other travellers on the East Kent Light Railway. The station, which opened in 1916, closed in 1951.

Those mining families who settled in Elvington and Eythorne seem to have liked it. Mrs Sumner moved there from Platbridge near Wigan in 1931. Her father was a miner and had come south to live in Kent four years earlier, in 1927. He was 60 years old but lied about his age ("I'm just 50")

---

[149] Conversations with author, 2018

and got a job at Tilmanstone. Mrs Sumner, married with one child, moved because her collier husband was on short-time working in the Wigan pit and there was a full-time job in Kent.[150] She and her husband thought Elvington was "heaven".

"We were from an industrial part, up north, lots of smoke and houses back to back. It wasn't a bad place where we lived, it was reasonably respectable – but Kent was paradise. Trees everywhere, flowers everywhere, sunshine. Of course, my boy was just in his glory. Fields for miles and miles. Put him in a push chair and off we'd go every weekend, Sunday morning, Saturday afternoon, every time he was free we'd be off…The people in Elvington were a cosmopolitan lot. They were from everywhere, from Wales, Yorkshire, Lancashire, Somerset. They were semi-detached, yet all together in a village and we were all sort of one big happy family there. My mother was here – that did help because she was another pair of hands. It was a happy life altogether, you knew everybody, everybody knew you. It was 'good morning' every time you met a person and I don't remember any unpleasantness at all…Relations came over here of course, on holiday because it was a seaside place and that kept us all in touch. On the whole we've been very, very happy here."

Eythorne still has its local primary school and, with a handful of colleagues, Stuart Elgar leads the Tilmanstone heritage group in the Elvington Community Centre. Like the Snowdown and Betteshanger group in Aylesham, the archives build a comprehensive picture of the Kent pits and the outstanding moments in the lives of those who served them. Tilmanstone was considered a safe pit. John Kemp also boasts that "it was known as 'the honest pit' because we

---

[150] Oral History, Vol 6, 1978, Gina Harkell

were the only coal mine in Kent that didn't have locks on our lockers. If you put a padlock on your locker, it was quietly cut off."

There is a life-size figure of a miner in the Tilmanstone display at the heritage centre. It is nothing if not authentic. It wears the boots and leather belt once belonging to Stan Whitting, miner and late husband of Doreen Whitting, who is a member of this heritage group: Stan was a rope splicer. He worked in a very dusty area and, unfortunately, that's where he picked up pneumoconiosis that carried him away 14 years ago. Doreen says: "There wasn't many who lived past their retirement age, 65. My dad didn't either. And none of them ever complained – didn't seem to enter their minds. They were content. Strange, isn't it? I guess they came to Kent from Somerset looking for a job and a better life and I think they believed they had found it."[151]

---

[151] Conversation with author

CHAPTER TWELVE
World War Two – A Time to Strike?

*"War is a series of catastrophes that
result in a victory"*
Georges Clemenceau

In July 1926 in Canterbury Cathedral, Neville Chamberlain waved a carefully-prepared regional survey to the decision-makers of Kent, and forecast a new prosperity for the county, based on coal. Thirteen years later, the same Neville Chamberlain, now Prime Minister, returned from a meeting with Adolf Hitler, brandishing a scrap of paper and envisaging 'peace in our time'.

Neither forecast was particularly accurate.

Britain declared war on Germany on September 3rd 1939. Kent prepared once again to be in the firing line of a major conflict. In the four Kent collieries, the miners went along with the national mood and recognised the 'gentleman's agreement' reached between the Trade Unions and their employees – that, for the sake of the war effort, they would work together because coal would be vital to industrial production. The Kent Coalfield had experienced its richest years in terms of production in the mid-1930s. Between 1933 and 1938 for instance, Betteshanger's annual production never fell below 800,000 tons. At Chislet, annual output in the same period hovered around 480,000 tons, with the peak year of 486,192 tons in 1936.

In 1939, Chislet output was still 474,581 tons and all four Kent pits were achieving close to record production.[152] The total coal output from Kent that year was 1,999,400 tons.

Domestically, on the outbreak of war, women and children were encouraged to evacuate. A military exclusion zone was set up, which prevented everyone except essential workers entering or leaving coastal Kent. Rolls of barbed wire wove unwelcoming patterns along the beaches from Margate to Dover. Concrete pillboxes appeared among the cabbages and cauliflowers. Policemen wearing 'tin helmets' manned roadblocks and interrupted journeys to examine identity papers.

Miners were called up and mothers and children had to make the best of it. In a railway tunnel near Doreen Whitting's home, a huge artillery gun was hidden, to be shunted out along the rails when required to retaliate to Nazi shelling from placements in France. Dover and East Kent were well within the range of the German guns and, for years, the residents had to endure long-range and sporadic shelling, as well as attack by aircraft and, later, Hitler's vengeance weapons, V1 'Doodlebugs' and V2 rockets.

Doreen remembers "the horrible noise when the gun in the tunnel was fired. It broke the windows and slates off the roof." Prime Minister, Winston Churchill, came to inspect the big gun. His visit was brisk and businesslike; crowds cheered and neighbours of Doreen's were flattered by the attention Churchill gave to their dog. "I'm not sure if it was a bulldog;

---

[152] For more detailed production figures, see Appendix

Churchill in Kent

it may have been. Anyway, C h u r c h i l l petted it. Unfortunately, the next day, the dog died. When the story got out the next day, there was much laughter among the miners…"

This was, after all, the same Winston Churchill who, as Home Secretary some years earlier in 1910, had called out the Army to quell industrial unrest in the South Wales mining town of Tonypandy.

In wartime Kent, Molly Ramsden, at home in Deal, quickly accepted that "a day out on the sands was a thing of the past. Many beaches were mined and those that weren't, might have been. We just kept away. And I remember the terrible accident with the Earl of Guilford. He was walking along the seafront and he hadn't got his dogs on a leash. So they ran down on the sands, or it might have been pebbles, and mines had been planted there. He chased down to get them back and trod on a mine. He was killed; it was a terrible thing."

Miners worked their regular shifts and, at night, there was a guard at the pits against possible invasion. Some miners joined the Home Guard. At Elvington, the armoury consisted of five Canadian rifles from World War One and five clips of 303 bullets – 30 bullets in all.[153]

Other miners supported the Royal Observer Corps (ROC) as they spotted and reported the Heinkel and Dornier bombers that throbbed to and fro overhead. Betteshanger miners and their families suffered casualties:[154]

26 April 1942	Betteshanger Colliery bombed. Two injured seriously, 9 slightly hurt.
8 May 1942	Convent School, Deal, bombed. Michael Ryan (11) and James Rogan (12) killed.
29 September 1942	Betteshanger Colliery bombed. Two killed and several injured.
27 October 1942	Air raid on Deal. Thelma Nicholls (14), Raymond Giles (14) and Edna Ancliff (16) killed.
5 November 1942	Air raid on Deal. Sarah Anderton (22) killed.
20 January 1944	Air raid on Deal. Gladys Dunn (28), Barbara Dunn (6) and Joyce Dunn (10 months) killed.
2 September 1944	Deal shelled. Ron Jarrett (9) and Frank Jarret (13) seriously injured.
27 April 1941	Evelyn Kirk (nee Coe) serving in the WRNS at Portsmouth, killed.
23 November 1934	George Kirk RN, Evelyn's husband, killed.

---

[153] Those Dirty Miners, JP Hollingsworth, p38
[154] Front Line County, Andrew Rootes; Deal Victoria Hospital Memorial Book

In Dover and Deal, a total of 268 people were killed, 350 suffered serious injuries and 626 were slightly injured. In Eastry, 20 were killed, 32 suffered serious injuries and 57 were slightly injured.

Bomb damage at Betteshanger

The Battle of Britain was waged daily in the blue skies above their heads and the workforce dwindled as many miners disappeared into the Armed Forces. The Government urged harder work and set even higher production targets. The number of working miners in Kent dropped from 7,115 in 1938 to 5,784 in 1944.

Sleep was constantly interrupted by enemy air raids, as it was for the entire population. Coal mining is a dirty, dangerous job. In the heightened stress of a world war, it is not surprising that the tension of everyday survival should spill over into the cut and thrust of industrial relations.

Altogether, between September 1939 and March 1945, there were 2,458 air raid alerts in East Kent; Betteshanger Colliery was bombed five times and, in one raid, the fan house was demolished by a direct hit. The fan house is the key to a pit's ventilation system. A full shift of miners was working underground. Many continued to work even though air was no longer circulating. The winding gear was also destroyed. They were trapped below ground for 18 hours. All emerged unhurt. Betteshanger was closed down while the damage was repaired. Some of the 1400 men were transferred to other Kent pits but many miners remained unemployed and, therefore, unpaid. The unemployed men were not happy and they volunteered to work the pit without the fan-driven ventilation. This was contrary to mining regulations. But the country needed coal and a government mining inspector was sent to Betteshanger to take regular samples of the air. On the basis of these readings, permission was given for the pit to reopen and, for two weeks the men worked in the bowels of the earth without a ventilating system. One of the miners said: "It was as hot as hell. We worked wearing just a loincloth and a pair of boots."[155]

Amid this pressure to produce coal for industry, two other matters became apparent. First, the miners realised the vital part they were playing in the nation's war effort; second, they recognised that the potential power they possessed needed cohesion if it was to be used effectively. The coal miners needed to speak with a single voice wherever they were employed. Nationalisation of the mines would be a prime objective, just as it had been since the 1920s. Coal would become a national asset, owned by the

---

[155] Ibid

nation. The idea drew increasing support both inside the industry and beyond. In 1941, the Government issued the Essential Work Order. This legislation tied the miner to the colliery in which he was working. He could not be sacked – but nor could he choose to leave. In addition, Order 1305 of the Conditions of Employment National Arbitration Order (1940) outlawed all strike action and, in May, this was extended to include miners. It was not the first piece of legislation in the 20th Century to criminalise strikers; emergency measures setting up an industrial truce had been attempted during World War One, but it had not prevented strike action. In World War Two, Order 1305 specifically opened the way for strike action to be punishable under Defence Regulation 92 by a term of imprisonment. There were those who warned from the outset that this was ill-advised, and probably, unenforceable.

Frederick Leggett, then the Government's Chief Industrial Commissioner, declared that prison sentences under Order 1305 'would probably be shown to be useful, only if a considerable body of work people chose to defy it'.

Further, the extension of the Essential Work Order to miners which governed the hiring and dismissal of men, bound miners to their industry more closely than for a century.[156]

Ernest Bevin was Minister of Labour and National Service, a champion of the trade unions. It was he who would have to sanction the imprisonment of would-be strikers. Fortunately, there were no prosecutions during the first six months after the establishment of Order 1305. In an on-going debate, Bevin argued in Cabinet that the Order could be useful against a small "subversive minority," intent on "mischievous ends."

---

[156] Historical Studies of Industrial Relations, Adrian Tyndall, 2001, p112

But the aim of the Order was not to penalise those in dispute, he said, rather to ensure conciliation. He chose to ignore warnings that mine owners could use the Order "as a big stick" against would-be strikers. Within the Ministry of Labour, there were growing calls for penal sanctions to be considered in certain circumstances. Order 1305 should be used. It was not simply "a paper penalty."

Ernest Bevin

In 1941, there was continued unrest in the mining industry; coal output was declining, threatening the whole foundation of Britain's wartime economy.[157]

Compared with other industries, miners' wages were still relatively low and working conditions were poor. In November 1941, in response to what many saw as these new restrictions, there was a dispute at Betteshanger between the employers Pearson and Dorman Long and the miners, who were then represented by the Kent Miners' Association. Feelings ran high; air raids were, if anything, on the increase.

Joe Methuen, who came to Kent from Ynysddu in Monmouthshire, said: "After we'd been bombed and trapped underground, they shook hands and called us bloody heroes.

---

[157] MW Kirby, The British Coalmining Industry 1870–1946, Macmillan, 1977

But when it came to working conditions in the pit – ah! that was different."

The issue centred on a new coal face at Betteshanger – Face 2S. It was a difficult seam, with a line of rock running through it. Kent miners' wages were calculated on a complex series of bonuses. The bonuses for the miners working on Face 2S were estimated partly on the presumption that they would dig four tons of coal per man, per day. But production was falling below that figure. Methuen says: "Management said the men were malingering."

It was not a clever allegation to make. The miners' word for working to rule is 'Ca-Canny'. In their eyes, they were being asked to achieve a target that was impossible, purely because of the nature of the seam they were working. They were making great efforts, they said, but they could not achieve four tons per man, per day.

In November 1941, management took the matter to arbitration. Methuen says: "They sent down an old fellow who knew as much about a coal mine as my dog." The inspector's name was Sir Charles Doughty. He collapsed from the heat at the pit. He found for the management and said that the shift terms offered by Pearson and Dorman Long, 15s 3d based on four tons of coal per man, per day, was, if anything, generous. This did not improve morale at the coalface. By December, production fell to 1.3 tons per man, per day. On Thursday January 8 1942, the men on Face 2S were paid 11s 9d for some shifts, instead of 15s 3d.

A delegation of three men from the Kent Miners' Association went to see Betteshanger management the next day. Joe Methuen was joined by William Powell, originally from Sheffield, who was branch secretary, and Tudor

Davies, from Wales, a Justice of the Peace and the branch chairman. Tudor Davies did most of the talking. Either the men on Face 2S got the 'normal' wage or they would strike. Management refused and reiterated that the men were working Ca-Canny. Whether or not that was the case, Davies said: "That's it. The wheels won't turn on Monday." And they did not.

Unquestionably, to strike during wartime was illegal. The National Arbitration Order forbade it. In Whitehall, there were discussions at the highest level. "In the wartime Cabinet, (Lord) Beaverbrook, who really didn't understand industrial relations, took the attitude: 'They've broken the law; do something about it'. Winston Churchill was of the same view. Ernest Bevin was against bringing the law into these things. It was Dai Grenfell, who was himself once a miners' leader, and now Secretary for Mines, who took the decision. The miners would be prosecuted."[158]

Taking the decision was one thing; implementing it was quite another. Three men had put the miners' case in a delegation to management – Tudor Davies, Powell and Methuen. But 1600 miners had followed their lead and taken illegal strike action. The Ministry of Labour decided to prosecute 1,000 miners who worked underground, including the three leaders. The decision immediately threw the Kent system of justice into chaos. There were not enough forms available simultaneously to take action against 1,000 people. Extra Justices of the Peace had to be found to sign the forms. In duplicate. Extra police had to be drafted in to serve the summonses. And there were two separate actions against the miners – the strike action summonses from the Ministry of

---

[158] Historical Studies of Industrial Relations, Adrian Tyndall, 2001, p112

Labour, and the summonses taken out by the owners against 1,007 miners for breach of contract under the Employers' and Workmen's Act of 1875.

The hearing took place at the Sessions Magistrates Court House in Canterbury on Friday January 23rd 1942, amid more than an element of farce. Clearly, more than 1,000 men could not all be prosecuted at the same time; there wasn't enough room in the building, let alone the dock. The union solved the problem and agreed to abide by the outcome of a few test cases.

Hundreds of messages of support flooded into Kent from collieries all over the country and miners set out for Canterbury to express their solidarity. In wartime, petrol was rationed and the Regional Petroleum Officer faced a dilemma: Should they authorise petrol for miners to travel to Kent? He asked the Department for Mines, who asked the Department of Transport, who asked the Ministry of Labour, who said 'for heaven's sake. There'll be such ill feeling if we refuse'.[159]

The mine owners then withdrew their summonses, which reduced the workload of the justice system by half.

The three accused, Tudor Davies, William Powell and Joe Methuen, arrived at the court amid a huge crowd and to the accompaniment of cheering and a vigorous brass band. The Ministry of Labour first made their case. Of the accused, their solicitor said: "Their actions beggar description in such times." The reasons for their dispute with the coal owners, he said, were irrelevant. The men were being charged because they had broken the law by failing to give the Ministry 21 days' notice of their intention to strike. The defendants then

---

[159] Sir Harold Emmerson, Sunday Times, 1971

spoke in turn. Powell said: "Whatever is decided will not bring peace to Betteshanger." Tudor Davies said: "The men went on strike to defend something sacred – the minimum wage." Finally, Methuen said: "If the proper wage wasn't paid, I, as a union official, cannot ask the men to go back."

The chairman of the magistrates, Lord Hawarden, told the miners as he passed sentence: "We are at war and coal is a very important commodity and as much as possible must be turned out. That, I am sorry to say, has not been the case at this particular colliery. Therefore, we have to consider this matter as very serious indeed and the penalties we are going to announce are serious, too." Powell, Davies and Methuen were considered ringleaders and he sentenced Powell to two months hard labour, and Davies and Methuen to one month each.

He fined the 35 men on 2S Face, where the dispute had started, £3 or one month in gaol, and the remaining men – more than 1,000 – £1 each or 14 days. Methuen, Powell and Davies were led away to start their sentences. The three men served time in Maidstone Prison, 'picking oakum and sewing bags'.[160]

The sentences were considered unfairly harsh by the mining community and by the striking miners. 'People say we were unpatriotic to go on strike in wartime. But, legally, the management were in the wrong as well. They broke the contract because they didn't give us 21 days' notice before they altered our wages. That's why we took direct action',[161] said one miner.

Terry Harrison, former secretary to the Kent NUM commented: "All the talk about miners being unpatriotic

---

[160] Sunday Times, 1971
[161] Oral history, Betteshanger Museum archive

was ballyhoo, an attempt to create prejudice in the minds of the public. These men were on the most exposed part of the coast, nearest to the German planes to the continent, and during the Battle of Britain they remained at their posts and kept the colliery at full production, even when the bombs were actually dropping in the pit yard. And a year before, at a meeting in London, I heard the Minister for Mines tell the Kent Miners' Association executive that the Prime Minister himself had expressed extreme satisfaction at the way the Kent miners had carried on. Moreover, about 250 of the strikers are in the Home Guard."[162]

Emanuel 'Manny' Shinwell, MP who, as Secretary for Mines, had attended the opening of the Betteshanger pit, described the sentences on the three men as 'harsh, vindictive and a travesty of justice compared with mere fines imposed on black marketeers the previous day.

Attitudes at Betteshanger hardened. Two days after the court hearing, on January 25th, a mass meeting decided unanimously to continue the strike. The Government's priority was how to get the men back to work and to reopen the pit. But the three men with whom they would have to negotiate – Methuen, Davies and Powell – were all in prison. The mine owners and the politicians rapidly altered their stance. Secretary for Mines, Dai Grenfell, joined by the secretary of the Miners' Federation of Great Britain, Ebby Edwards, set out for Kent on January 27th. They met the mine management and the Kent union leaders. They performed a complete U-turn and offered the men exactly what they had asked for before they withdrew their labour – a full rate of pay for the men working on the difficult seam Face 2S.

---

[162] Conversation with the author

The next day, January 28th 1942, a mass meeting on miners at the Deal Welfare Club accepted those terms and Betteshanger went back to work that evening.

The Ministry of Labour felt compromised. Ernest Bevin had opposed prosecution from the outset. The dispute ended with 'complete surrender to the men' and this 'might encourage other strikes which are in progress and being threatened'. Then the King became involved. Home Secretary, Herbert Morrison, contacted Buckingham Palace and the miners were given a pardon by King George VI. The Home Office sent a telegram on February 2nd 1942 to the Kent Miners' Association to confirm the royal intervention.

The same day, Monday February 2nd, the three accused leaders were released from Maidstone Prison. They travelled home by bus, having served one week of their sentences. But the farcical element of this wartime strike continued. More than 1,000 miners had been fined. How would the fines be collected as, to date, only nine fines had been paid?

The Clerk to the Justices, whose task it was to prepare 1,000 commitment warrants, inquired if it was proposed to recommend remissions for the 1,000 miners. After all, the men were now back at work. The mine owners, Pearson and Dorman Long, were also anxious to avoid further disruption and they offered to pay all the fines themselves. The Government immediately told them that on no account could they do this. Home Secretary, Ernest Bevin, intervened with a typically British compromise: The fines were not cancelled – but the warrants would be held in abeyance! They were never issued.

The men returned to work with a will and output at Betteshanger trebled in the following week. The dispute further scarred relationships, however. The colliery agent was Charles Magee. He'd been in the job eight years. The men did not like him. He'd come from the Featherstone pit in Yorkshire, where he'd kept the men on strike, they said, for two-and-a-half years and had "gone round turning the women and children from their homes into the street." Even the landlord of the Deal pub which Magee frequented said: "He's a hard man; you can see he's tough." The way he had handled negotiations leading to the strike did not endear him any further to the men. Security in the pit had been so tight, the miners said they had been forced to make their arrangements to act in unison, by secretly chalking messages on the tubs as they travelled through the underground roads. Magee was not to be trusted.[163]

After the strike was settled, Magee called in at the Welfare Club and shouted, "Give the lads a drink!" Joe Methuen recalls: "I think he was a bit taken aback when the bill came to £160. Tudor Davies told him: "If you don't pay that, you'll never come into this club again."[164] He paid up.

This strike in the corner of Kent became a national issue. It is often portrayed as a moment when disloyal Kent miners chose this national emergency to hold the country to ransom in order to take home more money. This is a distorted portrayal. It ignored the leaden thinking of the Government and mine owners' negotiators, who, had they foreseen the impact of their intransigence over a reasonable request by the men, could have avoided the conflict altogether. It ignored the fact that these men and their families, from the outbreak of war, had been shelled from France, bombed from the air and in fear of invasion, so much so that the streets were emptied of residents as women and children were evacuated. Schools were closed. As one woman, who stayed in Aylesham, said in 1942: "Most of them have gone. I am the only one left in this road. All my friends are gone. I parade up the garden and have a good cry. I cry a lot."[165]

It also ignores the fact that the industry itself was changing. Talk of nationalisation would lead to the formation of the National Union of Mineworkers in 1944; a year later the Kent miners would form their branch of the NUM, with an initial membership of 5,100.[166] The face of the workforce was also getting younger. Given the demands of the armed forces, able-bodied men were in short supply. Retired miners were being encouraged back to work, school-leavers were made attractive offers to make mining a career. But, the pits were still short of miners.

In December 1943, Ernest Bevin set out to find thousands of men to work in Britain's mines. He did it through conscription. Britain's young men at the age of 18 had to register for National Service. Bevin used a ballot system of selection. Each young man had a registration number. If that ended in 9 or 0, it went into a ballot and, for these young men, National Service would take place in the coalmines rather than in the armed services. They became known as 'Bevin Boys'. Britain had too few miners even at the start of the war; a government review estimated a 40,000 shortfall in the workforce in 1939. By May 1941, that shortage of men had risen to 50,000.

Ernest Bevin approved two schemes to try to remedy what

---

[165] Betteshanger Museum archive, Oral History
[166] Those Dirty Miners, JP Hollingsworth, p39

Bevin Boys at Chislet

was, by now, a critical situation – the 'Bevin Boy' ballot system, and the Mining Optant Scheme, under which those younger than 25 could simply volunteer to go underground as a miner rather than into the armed forces. The 'Optants', as they were called, were permitted to choose between khaki or coal black. For the 'Bevin Boys' there was no choice. If your registration number ended in a 0 or a 9, it was the coal mine for you.

The target figure for the 'Bevin Boy' campaign was 50,000 men. There was no psychological test to find out if the young men were temperamentally suited to work underground, nor any test for claustrophobia. A total of 47,859 Bevin Boys were selected for National Service.[167] In the first year, 500 were prosecuted for refusal to obey the Direction Order to go into the pits; 147 young men were actually sent to prison. It was generally thought, writes Warwick H Taylor in his comprehensive book 'The Forgotten

---

[167] The Forgotten Conscript, PRO/LAB 37/16, 1995 pp X1 and 5

Conscript', 'that a Bevin Boy was placed into the coal mining industry because of his convictions as a conscientious objector. Facts show that there were only 41 (conscientious objectors) out of the total number...'[168] Training centres for the fresh-faced Bevin Boys were set up in 1943, at 11 collieries all over the country. Kent's Bevin Boys were trained at Chislet. Each of the centres had between 280 and 520 places and the courses ran for four weeks, involving physical training, classwork and mine visits, surface training and underground work. Failures were relatively rare; in the first year there were 1,800 rejections out of a total of 45,300 ballotters, optants and volunteers. There then followed two weeks' further training at a working colliery. Chislet claimed its training scheme was 'the best in the country', with 'two special training galleries underground...physical training was under direction of Corporal ADS Hamilton, a

Part of the Bevin Boys' training was underground

---

168 Ibid

Dunkirk veteran…all the lads seemed keen to do their best… (though) some were naturally disappointed they had been unable to join the forces…but they were all determined to make the best of it.'[169]

The boys' reactions were mixed. Peter Muncey from Tunbridge Wells, having spent the years from 16 to 18 in the Junior Training Corps at the Company School was "horrified" to learn that he would go through the war as a miner. Joe Evans, however, came from a family of builders and had been in the building trade since he had left school. Like Muncey, he became a Bevin Boy through the ballot system – and remained a miner for 27 years. He was one of the last miners to leave the Chislet pit when it closed in 1969. "I came up on the last cage. There were seven of us on it. I actually built a retaining wall on the pit-bottom to keep the water back, the last thing I did before we came up. Sad day."[170]

The Bevin Boys scheme did not produce the anticipated 50,000 extra miners. It gave the industry 15,000 in 1944 and a little over 20,000 altogether. Nonetheless, this injection of young men enabled 11,000 more experienced miners to be released from other duties, to be upgraded to the coal face as colliers. The network of training centres also provided high grade training for about 21,000 optants, volunteers and conscientious objectors to join the war effort.

How good were they? No figures or assessments are available for Kent, as many records relating specifically to the Bevin Boys were lost or destroyed at the end of World War Two. But in South Wales and Monmouthshire, 94 per

---

[169] Hersden by Ross Llewellyn, p57
[170] Ibid, p56

cent of the 1,630 Bevin Boys working in the pits were found to be 'satisfactory'.[171] The majority of Bevin Boys were not interested in joining a union. For most, this was, after all, not their chosen career. The majority of seasoned miners were relaxed about working with this 'non-union labour', although as with all newcomers, sledging and teasing were part of the currency of the working day. Some union representatives took a harder line, however:

> *Dear Friend,*
>
> *I think by now you should have almost become accustomed to your new sphere of working life (not a very kind way of getting a living, is it?)*
>
> *Anyhow I am instructed to inform you that everybody working underground at this pit are in the Union with the exception of a few of you newcomers to the industry, and we think that you have now been here long enough to have joined the (union).*
>
> *So don't be different to all the rest of the pit, and please come and join at once, otherwise unfriendly decisions may be taken against you.*
>
> *Signed on behalf of the committee*[172]

At the end of the war, there was a General Election. A Labour Government swept to power. Political giants emerged in Westminster set on reforming the British way of life.[173] For five

---

[171] The Forgotten Conscript, p89

[172] Ibid, p90

[173] Many monuments were proposed for Churchill in 1945, including an effigy on the White Cliffs of Dover, with a cigar lit as a warning to shipping. The appeal raised £50,000. (Churchill by Andrew Roberts, p887). The monument was never built

years, some of Britain's best brains, staunchest hearts and acute political skills had led the effort to curb and destroy Hitler and the Nazis. Churchill and Butler, Attlee and Bevin, Bevan and Sinclair, Beaverbrook and Morrison and Shinwell had buried political differences in defence of a liberal democracy. They had worked together during some of Britain's finest hours.

With a Socialist government now in power, Clement Attlee became Prime Minister and Ernest Bevin Minister of Labour, while Aneurin Bevan took the two portfolios of Minister of Housing and Minister of Health, assuming responsibility for creating and launching the National Health Service, at the same time as building 350,000 houses a year; they would be homes fit for heroes who were back from a war and who had voted them into power. The nation drew breath and surveyed its assets, ignoring the fact that winning the war had bankrupted Britain, leaving a £4.34 billion debt to the United States, through Marshal Aid, that would take 60 years to repay.

The Kent Coalfield also took stock. The Minister of Fuel and Power, Gwilym Lloyd George, produced a report that was surprisingly optimistic.[174] It declared that the total coal output from the Kent field, arising from planned 'intensified' development, would be four million tons a year. It listed the immediate hopes for each individual pit; Betteshanger and Snowdown could produce 1,500,000 tons a year, which 'relates to 1935…a representative year of high output for these two collieries'. Chislet's immediate target was 480,000 tons a year, which was 'the average annual output from

---

[174] Kent Coalfield Regional Survey, HM Stationary Office, 1945, 9 pence; men who had been on either side of the 1942 Betteshanger strike, CS Magee, agent for Pearson and Dorman Long; and William Powell, secretary of Betteshanger NUM, were among the 13 authors of the Survey

1936 to 1939'. Tilmanstone would need to produce 360,000 tons a year to match the figure mined in 1939. The report then looked to the future. Potentially, it said, Betteshanger and Snowdown could produce 2,250,000 tons annually (an increase of 750,000 tons), Chislet 750,000 tons (an increase of 270,000 tons) and Tilmanstone 'at least 1,000,000 tons per annum (an increase of 640,000 tons)'. This section of the report concluded that 'reserves were sufficient…to justify new sinkings…' and 'Guilford Colliery, now temporarily abandoned…could be sunk to a lower seam with a view to achieving very considerable output tonnage'.

This optimism echoed the calculations on which Abercrombie had based his plans 20 years earlier, in his Regional Report of 1925. The 1945 survey went on to praise the Kent Coalfield's foresight in quickly seeing the advantages of mechanisation and the aerial ropeway from Tilmanstone was '…an expeditious method of transport of coal to Dover, where it can be loaded on to ships at the rate of 400–500 tons an hour'. It suggested that, once there was a working pit at Guilford, a new branch of the ropeway should be opened from Guilford to Tilmanstone.

This optimism extended to industries other than coal. The survey pointed out that no factories had been opened in East Kent since 1933; 'as a vulnerable area, no wartime developments have occurred which might greatly change the occupational picture. There are no industries of any importance other than mining or agriculture'.

But this could change. There were huge deposits of iron ore in Kent, in the same areas as the coal seams. 'The extent of the deposits indicated a life of 100–150 years, on an output of a million tons a year'. Specially designed blast furnaces would be built in iron and steel works which would be positioned close to the Kent pits. Already 'a local site is available'.

The report confidently forecast a boom in employment based on Kent's mineral riches just as Abercrombie had done in 1925. And, again, as Abercrombie had done, it outlined the challenge of attracting and accommodating a new workforce to run this expanding industry. The survey assessed the current 'social situation'.

It drew attention, in particular, to the plight of women, whose 'only opportunities for employment are in the distribution trades or, seasonally, in hotels and seaside boarding houses'. The lack of a broad industrial base exacerbated 'one of the adverse features of mining communities…the segregation from the general community'.

In short, mining communities were 'different'. But they were also 'different', the report reassured its readers, 'in South Wales and Durham, where the (coal) industry has existed for generations and it can be fairly said that a like feeling of segregation and isolation also exists'. It then considered Abercrombie's meticulously planned new town, Aylesham, and found it wanting:

'The settlement (Aylesham) suffers from arrested development, with many of the sites in the centre of the town still rough grassland. There is no public building of any architectural significance, except the central school, …the houses present a marked degree of monotony'.

Then came the sentence that must have hurt Abercrombie and a decision that undermined the completion of his vision:

'Accordingly, we are led to the view that new house sites (estates) should be in the neighbourhood of towns such as Deal, Dover, Canterbury, Ramsgate, Herne Bay and Folkestone'.

This new policy of grouping the new housing as suburbs of existing towns, would have three important results, said the survey. Firstly, the impact of unemployment in the pits, which 'breeds an air of dereliction and hopelessness' in mining villages, would be less severe because there would be alternative trades available in the towns. Secondly, education would be better in secondary and senior schools in the larger towns, for 'ambitious or promising children'. Thirdly, career opportunities would be greater and more valued if larger, mixed towns were created, offering to members of mine workers' families 'at least some measure of employment' which is, of course, lacking, for instance, in the mining villages of Hersden, a village of 165 houses, housing Chislet's miners, which has no facilities or shops and has some of Aylesham's sense of isolation'. This contrasted with Betteshanger, served by the Mill Hill estate, compromising 950 houses, where the mining population had 'intermingled with the normal residents of Deal and have generally struck roots'. The same was true of the village of Elvington where the residents of the 230 houses 'have a social life of their own'.

There was an immediate need to build a further 1,050 houses to serve Betteshanger, 517 to serve Snowdown, 950 for the Chislet miners and 400 at Tilmanstone. These figures 'presumed the repair where possible of war-damaged houses'. The survey also foresaw 'a further provision of some 1,200 houses for Tilmanstone if the Millyard Seam and the Deep Seam are to be worked to the maximum capacity of the shafts'.

Patrick Abercrombie would have approved of the optimistic estimates for the productivity of the East Kent Coalfield. Little had changed in the intervening 20 years since he had written his survey. The new report echoed much of what he had said. He would not have disputed the projections of an increase in the workforce. But the discarding of his revolutionary plans for eight new towns, would have been a disappointment, both because it ended his 'great experiment' in planning that they had embarked upon in 1925, and, even more so, because the judgment of the 1945 survey was that 'the experiment' had failed. Abercrombie could justifiably argue that an economic slump and a world war had prevented a more rapid and extensive growth of the Kent Coalfield, and therefore, of Aylesham, which now, according to the 1945 report, 'suffered from arrested development...a sense of isolation and a feeling of segregation'.

That was a judgment made 70 years ago, as I write. I first visited Aylesham 50 years ago as a young journalist and I found a community more complex and complete than the impression Lloyd George had been given by his inspector in the 1945 Report. The village was overseen by a man named Ianto Hill,[175] chair of the Parish Council, who seemed to know everyone and everything that was going on in the town. He ran Aylesham from his miner's home in King's Road, rather in the manner that the mayors of Chicago used to run their city from Tammany Hall. Everyone was encouraged to express a view but some views carried more weight than others.

Aylesham was not a beauty spot. Not too many people from other parts of Kent visited Aylesham for a day out. But plenty of Aylesham people made the journey to nearby towns to work and play. Much of what the residents of Aylesham needed or wanted, existed in Aylesham itself in sport, recreation, schools and a shopping centre. How much of what Lloyd George's inspector reported was an example of self-sufficiency, rather than isolation? Though the town plan

---

[175] Ianto Hill, see Chapter 16

Abercrombie had made had been discarded by 1945, much of what he would have seen in Aylesham would have given him pleasure, even though the town in 1960, was still only half-finished.

On January 1st 1947, 'Vesting Day': more than a thousand collieries in Britain became nationalised and the property of the nation. It was 29 years since the Sankey Commission[176] had recommended nationalisation; 29 years since the Scottish miners' leader, John Robertson, had proposed a resolution at the annual conference that 'the time has come when this country should no longer be dependent for its coal supply on a small number of capitalist colliery proprietors, coal merchants and dealers…by which the consumer is made to pay a quite unnecessary price for coal…the government should at once take over all coal and other mines…and work them as a national enterprise…'

That day, a notice appeared on the gates of every Kent colliery; 'This colliery is now managed by the National Coal Board on behalf of the people'.[177] The chair of the NCB announced: "We are one family now…if we all work hard and work together we can make nationalisation a great success."

Emanuel 'Manny' Shinwell, who, as Secretary of Mines in 1924 had attended the grand opening of the Betteshanger pit, and who was now Minister for Mines, offered the leaders of the National Union of Mineworkers seats on the National Coal Board. They refused. Although this was a realisation of a Socialist dream, they reasoned they needed to keep their independence – wisely, as it transpired. There is a debate about exactly how many collieries came into public ownership.

---

[176] Sankey Commission 1919 on the Future of the coal industry
[177] Open cast mines were taken over in April 1952

Emanuel 'Manny' Shinwell

NCB records say 958, with compensation of £164,660,000 being paid to current owners and £78,457,000 to former owners. The *Encyclopaedia Britannica* puts the number of pits at 1,647, plus 100,000 dwellings and transport formerly owned by 85 private coal companies. Under the new regime, the country was split into divisions and then smaller areas, each with an average target output of roughly four million tons. George Gibb at Betteshanger remembers: "There were a few pints drunk that night but I can't recall huge celebrations. I think we were all quietly pleased and hoping for improved working conditions and less friction. We thought we would wait and see."

It was bitterly cold, that winter of 1947. The mines were short of men and still recovering from under-investment during World War Two. There was a coal shortage and coal was put on the ration. Exports were temporarily suspended and Attlee's Socialist government had the bitter task of arranging – for the first time – to import coal.

Between 1947 and 1956, the NCB spent more than £550 million on major improvements and new shafts. But as output improved, the demand for coal was dropping. The number of pits had decreased to 822 by 1957.[178] The NCB and the Government pursued a pit closure programme. 'The great Socialist ideals of public ownership were not working out as the

---

[178] Those Dirty Miners, JP Hollingsworth, p30

miners had envisaged…and many miners were disillusioned and felt that the Government had let them down'.[179]

Year on year, the demand for coal continued to fall. There was increasing competition from oil and gas. The demands of World War Two had galvanised British industry, including coal, and there was now a problem of over-capacity. Despite the NCB's claims to the contrary, investment was low and productivity in the mines was dropping. In a booklet 'Plan for Coal' published in 1957, the NCB claimed that 'when the National Coal Board took over Britain's mines on January 1st 1947, they became responsible for an industry that has been shrinking for a quarter of a century'. It cited national production figures to illustrate the improvements achieved since nationalisation: 1949 – 197 million; 1955 – 221 million; and in 1960 – 228 million (estimate).

But the NCB's production statistics of 197 million tons in 1949 were misleading. Although the figure of 197 million is itself accurate, under private enterprise the industry had produced a much higher output in almost every other year in the preceding century; for instance, coal output in 1914 was 287 million tons; in 1923, 276 million tons; and in 1924, 267 million tons. More recently, in the three years immediately before the outbreak of war, 1937 to 1939, output had averaged 233 million tons. By choosing to use 1949 as a baseline year, the NCB's claim of a steady increase in production was badly flawed.

In 1959, the NCB revised its estimates for both the demand and production of coal and, as had been forecast, the 'less profitable' pits were closed down during the 1960s. To ease the financial pressures, Harold Wilson's Socialist government

---

[179] Those Dirty Miners, JP Hollingsworth, p29

passed the Coal Industry Act in 1965, permitting the NCB to write off £400 million of debt. In Kent, the late 60s were years of unrest as the miners disagreed with management over pay and, predominantly, piece rates. Nationally, a demand for an eight-hour day for surface workers led to an unofficial national strike.

In Scotland, the miners argued that, in its strategy document Plan for Coal, the NCB had presumed that miners would still be working '7 ½ hours a day plus winding time'[180] for the next 15 years. They could not accept this, because 'unless we secure a reduction of hours for the miner, we shall never succeed in getting sufficient recruits into the mining industry'.[181] In Yorkshire, miners passed a similar resolution. Within days, 130,000 miners had withdrawn their labour. The TUC and the NCB chairman, Lord Robens, eventually agreed that, if the miners returned to work, the NCB would agree 'within a few months' to introduce an 8-hour day for surface workers. They kept their word.

The miners had won the day with a short, sharp, unofficial action. It was a famous and significant victory. It confirmed in the minds of the miners that coal could take on a Socialist government and the TUC, and still be King. And, perhaps they could be King-makers, as well…

---

[180] Time the Scottish miners spent reaching the coalface and returning to the surface
[181] The Scottish Miners, R Page Arnot, 1955

CHAPTER THIRTEEN
The Sutcliffes and Yorkshire

"No one would remember The Good Samaritan if he had had only good intentions. He had money as well."
Margaret Thatcher, 1980

Kay and Philip Sutcliffe live in a miner's house in Aylesham. The mine owners and the Coal Board built hundreds of them in Kent and there are many houses just like the Sutcliffes' – end of terrace, three up, two down and a conservatory leaning close to the back door. It is a neat house, full of photographs and memories, though the garden isn't as neat as it was before Philip suffered from cancer in 2016 and 'had to slow down a bit'.

Philip and Kay Sutcliffe outside their home in Aylesham

Sometimes in this immigrant community, romantic matches were made across the cultural divides and Kay and Philip are an example of that. Kay's family has its roots in Derbyshire and South Wales. Both Kay's great-grandfathers were miners. Isaac Roberts in Druid Village, Goginon, South Wales and Samuel Boulton in Clay Cross, Derbyshire. Philip's forefathers dug coal at the Worsbrough pits in South Yorkshire.

Kay's father, David (Dai) Roberts, came to Kent in the late 30s with two mates from South Wales, who all found lodgings in the village of Aylesham, where Dai met and married Kay's mother, Jessie Hall.

The Halls first came to Kent in 1934 and Kay's mother was 24 when Kay was born. "Mum had been in the Auxiliary Territorial Service (ATS) during the war. When they married, mum and dad continued to live with my gran. Mum worked in the fields and our gran helped to bring us up. Gran was also caring for my cousin, Alan, who had been left with her when his mother, Dorothy, and his father, my Uncle Sam, had separated. It was a crowded house but we were happy. There was me and my sisters Suzanne and Annette. We didn't have enough money for posh holidays but I'd go off with my dad to relatives in South Wales and mum would take Suzanne and our younger sister, Annette, to her relatives in Chesterfield. It was a funny arrangement but it worked and I learned a lot about South Wales, because I'd never lived there, had I?"

For six days, Kay's family worked and the seventh day was the Sabbath. "They weren't particularly religious but it was church and Sunday school every week. I wasn't forced to go; I enjoyed it. There were good stories and the annual outings to the seaside… I tried the Baptists, and the Catholics but I ended up at St Peter's Church (C of E) where I was in the choir and got confirmed. I was a Sunday school teacher for a while."

It would have been at St Peter's Church that she first noticed Philip Sutcliffe. This was at his confirmation ceremony – "at one time," he says, "I thought I'd like to become a vicar."

Philip's family had initially come to Kent on a week's holiday. That was on August 17th 1945 – the day that Philip's elder brother, Peter, celebrated his fifth birthday. Philip says: "They must have liked it here because my Dad went straight back to Barnsley and began to work his notice, while Mum and the two kids, Peter and my sister Rose, who was two, stayed down here. Apparently, the place was like the Klondike – miners coming from all over the place from Yorkshire, Scotland, Northumberland, Durham, Wales and Nottingham. All sorts. In Barnsley, for instance, there were pits everywhere. It really was the Black Country. To come from the industrial north to the Garden of England to do the same job was a dream. The people who came liked what they saw and they stayed. They could breathe again."

Philip Sutcliffe met Kay Roberts when she was 16. Their families were aware of each other as both fathers worked down Snowdown pit. Philip's mother had six children by the time she was 28. Philip was one of four brothers, the quiet one. His two brothers, Peter and Paddy, both played soccer; Peter, well enough to become a professional footballer with Gillingham and Paddy, a star with the colliery football team, Snowdown. Brother, Alan, was good at sport too. All became miners, following uncles and cousins down the deep shaft, though Philip's father thought Philip was hardly cut out for it. "I had other ideas anyway. I wanted to be in the Merchant Navy and I had an interview to go on the tugboats in Dover Harbour. But I didn't turn up for it. I had already been offered a job at Snowdown and I accepted it. I decided I wanted to stick with my mates.

"My dad always said he was surprised I went down the pit and stuck to it. I think it was because I didn't play football and he thought I was the softest of his four sons. But I stayed down right to the end. So, I think I proved him wrong."

These two families, the Roberts and the Sutcliffes, typify the importance of the male breadwinner in the family, not simply as a provider but as a role model. It mattered to Philip Sutcliffe that he 'proved his father wrong'. For Kay Roberts, it was a special experience to go with her father and to be embraced by the Welsh community values, that had made him what he was.

There's a very defensible argument that the Kent Coalfield community was a patriarchal society. Certainly, looking back, most of the men think so. Though women were indisputably the home builders, the men established a family's place in the town's hierarchy.

The Sutcliffe men enjoy long life. Fred Sutcliffe was 91 when he died. His brother, George, was also 91 and brother, Henry, 89. Not even capture and torture by the Japanese for three years in World War Two could shorten George's lifespan.

Fred, Philip's father, and his two brothers were cut from the same seam. Born in 1917 at the end of World War One, Fred was the youngest of 13 children. Only six of them reached their teens and one was then killed in World War One. Fred was 14 when he first went down Woolley Colliery near Barnsley beside his brother, Mark. He was to be a miner for 48 years. Fred married Philip's mother, Veronica, in 1939; it was a double wedding with Veronica's sister, Emma, also marrying her miner husband, Dick, the same day.

Barnsley is peppered with collieries. The excitement that in 1926 moved Neville Chamberlain to forecast a new Black Country in Kent was based on the fact that large deposits of iron ore had also been found close to the Kent coal seams. So it is in Barnsley. The Sutcliffe family worked most of their lives down the Barrow Colliery at Worsbrough, near Barnsley. It was so-called because of the company that owned it, the Barrow Hematite Street Company. To satisfy the growing demand for coke and coal to make steel, the company decided to buy a colliery of its own. The seam had been worked 40 years earlier by the Edmunds family at Worsbrough Hall, among others, but the pit had been dogged by a series of explosions. The steel men sank a new shaft, much deeper than previously, and it thrived.

Barrow Colliery, Yorkshire in the 1920s

Fred Sutcliffe, 'Uncle Fred', is remembered by Philip's cousin, Tricia Wilson, who still lives in Worsbrough. Three branches of Tricia's family migrated to Kent – the Sutcliffes and two members of the Madden family. Patricia, who was a Pinder before she married Geoffrey Wilson, was too young to recall the impact of this emigration but knows the family was surprised by this fundamental move 'down south'. After all, the mines in Barnsley were successful and prospering. Today, less than a mile from the bungalow where Tricia lives, it's hard to believe there was ever a coal mine in Worsbrough. The green hills of South Yorkshire are unscarred, the broken tarmac of the road that led to the site of Barrow Colliery has no sign to indicate that men ever worked there. The sun breaks through trees and bushes heavy with berries red and black where once stood the corner shop among the houses in Pit Row. The street lived in the shadow of thousands of tons of freshly dug coal piled close to all the back doors. The houses huddled around a turning circle in the road where busses once disgorged thousands of miners, day after day, to go to their place of work underground.

Tricia says, "I know the family were surprised when they all went to Kent because we barely knew where Kent was. It might as well have been the other side of the world. And, of course, we lost touch. Auntie Veronica (Philip's mother) wrote to me lovely letters which I've still got in a little box. Personal, family letters about weddings and rolls of lino, and about Peter who was still at school scoring goals at football and then one day going to see a man at the Labour Exchange to get a job. Auntie Veronica said: 'I think he will go down the pit like his dad'. They exchanged snapshots, taken on box

Brownie cameras and Auntie Veronica enjoined her to 'look after the snaps, won't you?'"

Which, of course, Tricia has done.

"I met Uncle Fred and Auntie Veronica (Philip's parents) when they came back to Worsbrough. But, of course, I've never met Philip..."

When they first married, Philip's parents lived in a terraced house in Thomas Street, Worsbrough. Fred served in the Home Guard during World War Two, and, despite his protestations that at 5ft 2ins 'he would have difficulty carrying anybody', he was made a stretcher-bearer. That first year of World War Two was odd. They called it the Phoney War and those who expected *blitzkrieg* and cataclysm found that daily life changed very little.

In Yorkshire, there was time for brisk exchanges between the military and the owners of Worsbrough Park, the land surrounding the Barrow Colliery. On April 17th 1939, the secretary of the Barrow Barnsley Main Collieries Ltd acknowledged that 'the 71st Field Regiment Royal Artillery would be billeted at Worsbrough Hall in the event of mobilisation'. That same month, permission was given for 'a gas chamber and an incendiary bomb chamber' to be built at the Hall. By 1940, however, the relationship between the colliery and the Royal Artillery was increasingly strained by the requirements of the conflict yet to come. Barrow Colliery's managing director, Douglas Hay, wrote to his Assistant Sub-Area Quartering Commandant noting that the troops would be accommodated in tents and huts and pointing out to him that 'this park is used for the grazing in summer of a herd of cattle under instructions from the County Agricultural Committee. We have received instructions to harrow, lime and otherwise improve the grazing in the park....

It is most desirable in particular, therefore, that you should not cut up the land by sending tanks or bren gun carriers over the ground...In summer, when the cattle are grazing, the entrance gates require to be shut and I shall be glad to have your assurance on this point. I also believe we are entitled to some rental for the use of this place'.

There is no reply on file, nor to a later exchange over whether 'shooting rights' on game in the park extended to troops 'now billeted there'.

When the Sutcliffe family moved to Kent in 1945, the diminutive Fred brought with him a broad Barnsley accent and became known as 'Yorkie'. He had been born in the same year as the Russian Revolution and believed that this had set him on the road to Socialism. He worked hard, door-to-door, for the Labour Party and earned an award for bravery when rescuing an elderly woman who had fallen and broken her ankle when her house was threatened by burning coals falling from a blazing open fire.

Fred Sutcliffe introduced his sons to the world of work underground. Philip remembers his first day on leaving Aylesham School:

"I was shocked as a 16-year-old lad to hear my dad swear. Once he'd put on his pit helmet, and grabbed his lamp, he was a different man. Here was my father coming out with F and C words...so I said to him early on, 'What's that all about?' He said: 'Look, son. Down the pit you're not my son first, you're my mate. But back home, in the house, It's different. You'll not hear me swear in the house – and I don't want to hear you swear in the house either.'"

Many of the miners lived by this rule that separated the two aspects of their lives – the mine, and the home and family.

Philip remembers: "My dad was only a little bloke, five-foot-tall, but he was a grafter at the coalface and he worked when the only tools were a pick and a shovel. He and an uncle of mine were taking eight carts of coal off in a single shift. And someone said to me, 'If you're half as good as your dad, you'll be a good 'un'.

"I'm proud to be a miner and come from a mining family. Proud, because the people you work with are your mates, your comrades. You have disagreements down the pit like everywhere else. They were settled with bare fists behind the bathhouse after work. But you quickly realise that your safety down the pit depends on the person you're working alongside. You can work with the same group of people for years. You may not like them but you could trust them and you'd go drinking together afterwards; so you grew up together, you socialised, you became an extended family."

At 18, Philip was working with miners twice, three times his age, with years of experience at the coalface. The age gap seemed of no concern. "All anyone ever talked about was women and sport. You'd do it to take your mind off work, though sport didn't interest me much.

"Someone once said to me 'That girl you're going with is a bit of all right'. They got to know I was taking out Kay and I happened to be working alongside Kay's dad, Dai Roberts, and some of the lads knew we were courting. They said, 'You want to be careful when you take Kay home tonight. It's so hot that three of the lads' wives or girlfriends have got pregnant. You want to watch what you're doing'.

"And I was going 'shut up' because I knew Dai could hear. And he was a strict Welshman and you wouldn't want him to know that you're messing around with his daughter. But he didn't hear it. Or, if he did, he pretended not to hear…"

Philip says it was Kay who first made the running and Kay lets him get away with it. Philip lived in the nearby village of Woolage and had a much admired motorbike. "The girls used to hang around. Kay was more aware of me because, to me, she was just a young girl, a few years younger than me." They used to hold an annual dance at the local shirt factory where many of the girls worked. That year it was at Dover Town Hall. Philip remembers:

"These two girls were dancing together and me and my mate said we'd go and split them up. I went to dance with the other girl, Mary, who I fancied, but Kay sort of pushed her out of the way and said 'I'll dance with him'. I knew Kay had been going out with one of my best friends but she told me she wasn't going out with Kevin any more. And that was the start of it…

"I don't suppose I was a good 'catch'. My family were poor. I didn't think so then but, though Dad was working at the pit and earning relatively good money, there were a lot of us to feed and money sometimes ran out. We could get 'tick'[182] at the village shop so we didn't starve. There was Alan and myself and Paddy – only three years between us all. We weren't dressed brilliant and I remember going to school in Wellington boots, even in the summer. Us younger ones got used to wearing hand-me-downs. We used to joke 'first up, best dressed' because we all wore the same clothes. If our Alan wore something practically out, but there was still a bit of wear in it, it was given to me and then to Paddy.

---

[182] 'Tick' – credit

"We paid for our gas by putting a shilling in the meter in the hall. If Mum didn't have a shilling, she would cut a little round ring out of the lino (linoleum floor covering) the same size as a shilling. It worked really well – and when the gas man came to empty the meter you were entitled to a little bit of a discount. And the gasman would smile and push all the round bits of lino across the table back to my mum and say: 'Here's your discount, Mrs Sutcliffe'. When me and my brothers went down the pit there was a little bit extra for everyone."

As a newlywed, Kay had little to learn about life in a mining household. She'd grown up with her father, Dai, going to the pit every day. There's speculation that it's unlucky to allow a woman to go underground, but Kay went. "I had quite a shock. I remember getting out of the cage and seeing what seemed like a big space, like being in the London Underground and I thought *Well, this isn't too bad.* But then we walked and got on a little train car and got to the coalface and that was a total shock. My Philip was working in a space about two feet high. We were asked if we would like to go under but I wouldn't. I didn't want to crawl into that tunnel.

"You know your husband is going down that pit every day. And your Dad has been down there year after year, but you've grown up in that situation so you turn off. You don't think about how hard it must be. You don't think about the danger. It's an acceptance…"

An accident ended Dai Roberts' career as a miner, and almost ended his life. It was the middle of his shift and it had been a hard day. He was near a line of moving coal trucks when one jumped off the rails. It crushed Dai against the wall. First, they thought he was dead, certainly too badly injured to survive. But he was rushed into intensive care at the Kent and Canterbury Hospital and he lived.

Kay says: "It was touch and go for days. He had punctured lungs and a crushed shoulder and broken all but one of his ribs. They had to put a pipe into his throat to help him to breathe. We all prayed a lot."

And that was the end of Dai Roberts' life as a coalface miner. He could never work again. "He was very bitter that he had to retire at the age of 59. He died at the age of 67."

Kay Sutcliffe has been a miner's wife for more than 50 years. She recognises the pain of the homesickness that Philip's mother felt. "I sympathise with it because I've heard it from other families. In the early days, the conditions in the pits were appalling and the men had to put up with that. But some of the women never really settled."

Some wives insisted on 'going home' once a year, even if it meant going alone. One Lancashire miner who worked in Snowdown, reflected on what happened in his family.[183]

"A lot of the women were the cause of husbands going back, because you take Aylesham, seven miles from anywhere. They were stuck there, although Aylesham was a good old progressive village despite all the talk about Aylesham. There were some lovely homes there. There were two clubs, a pub and four churches all going well. But a lot of women got browned off with Aylesham and they were more homesick than what the men were."

This same miner explained: "It was mainly poverty that drove people to Kent in the first place. The women resigned themselves to going where the work was." Once in Kent, the extra money seemed to fade into insignificance beside

---

[183] Oral History, Vol 6, 1978, Gina Harkell

the loneliness they felt. When balanced against the loss of an active social life among family and friends, "those few shillings extra were a hard bargain." He recalled, in 1936, a group decision by a number of families that led to an emotional departure from Dover Priory railway station:

"There were sixty-odd men, Welshmen they were, sang 'Land of My Fathers' and 'Bread of Heaven' one Friday night in the square facing the station, Dover Priory. They were all going back. I can see them now – bits of brown paper, boot boxes, brown paper bags with bits of clothes in, all going back to South Wales."[184]

Philip Sutcliffe's father, Fred, took a similar decision in 1984. He retired from the pit when he was 64. Philip's mother died a few years later. For Fred, now a widower, the memory of life in Yorkshire, the county in which he was born, still tugged at him although he had lived in Kent for 40 years. Philip remembers: "Not long after Mum died, Dad went back to Barnsley on holiday. When he came back, he was restless. He saw the rest of his family and had the idea he wanted to stay up there. He was only 67 or 68 and used to joke with them about his days in the Home Guard, guarding the Barnsley brewery. He was happy to go back and he lived until he was 91, which is a good age for a miner.

"It was a shock when he died. He hadn't been in the greatest health so I was up in Barnsley. He was in hospital but I wasn't with him when he passed away. I was there within an hour but he'd already gone. I regret that. And we still miss him, though I wasn't close to him when he died. Though we didn't see him much in the last few years we miss thinking, 'Oh, Dad's still in Barnsley', and now he's no longer there.

---

[184] Ibid

"He was an important part of our lives, at home and down the pit. Politically as well. He was a very motivated man. He had good Socialist principles. He meant a lot to me and my brothers and sisters. We're all on the left of politics and he guided us all the way.

"He may have been one of 13 children, and only 5ft 2ins tall and seven-and-a-half stone. But in our eyes, he was a colossus."

* * * * * * * *

Yorkshire describes itself as 'God's own country'. Eric Scaife sums up the reasons for this modest assessment in his poem 'Tykes' and, joking aside, Fred Sutcliffe would not have disagreed if what follows had appeared on his gravestone:

Tykes

We're a rare strange bunch 'as live up 'ere
But we've gradely grub and champion beer
An'mony a famous name thou'l see
On Yorkshire own proud family tree

Oor sportin' ways are second ter none
Oor art an' culture speak as yan
Us Yorksheer fowk ev Yorksheer ways
An' when we say we laiks we plays

Oor language is t'English true
Oor thee, thou, tha's are nothin' new

Wi' glottal stops an' aitches dropped
The G at end is allus cropped

So com' thi ways to oor grand county
An' sample sum o' Yorksheers bounty
Oor ales are grand, oor looance too
An' friendly fowk to welcome thoo.

Eric Scaife[185]

Yorkshiremen seldom lack self-confidence. It is no coincidence that many of the most bitter disputes between unions and management have taken place in its Ridings. The nationalisation of the coal industry in 1946 sparked one of the most strident. It involved one of the nation's most unusual buildings, Wentworth Woodhouse.

Wentworth Woodhouse is the largest private home in Britain and the longest in Europe. Its frontage is 606 feet long and it has around 350 rooms linked by five miles of corridors. Its walls have been graced by the art of Titian, Raphael and Van Dyck. When King George V stayed there in 1912, he and his staff occupied 76 bedrooms and were well cared for by a staff of close on a thousand. The size and style of this English country house proclaimed the wealth of its owners, the Fitzwilliams and the Wentworths. In the 1780s, through marriage and inheritance, the Peterborough estates of the Fitzwilliams were joined to the Yorkshire, Milton and Irish estates of the Wentworths, making the new Earl Fitzwilliam's estates the sixth richest in the country. The second Earl was largely responsible for developing the mineral rights of the land, including the

---

[185] Eric Scaife, Yorkshire Dialect Society

Wentworth Woodhouse - with and without excavations

mining of coal. Two centuries later, the 7th Earl, affectionately known as 'Billy', an experienced mining engineer, sank a new shaft near Barnsley, called Elscar. The relationship between the Earls and their workforce was enviable. The nearby cottages in which workers lived were – and still are – uniformly painted in the Fitzwilliam family colours of green. Over the decades, the miners and employees alike have consistently indicated their loyalty to the family in The Big House. It is a relationship that has survived wars, disputes and great political pressures. During the General Strike of 1926, the children of Billy Fitzwilliam's miners' families were provided with a meal every day, all 2,500 of them. Yet the strike undoubtedly left a bitter taste, as the victorious mine owners made little attempt, nationally, to make the reforms necessary to remedy the unrest in their industry. Billy was succeeded in 1943 by his son Peter Fitzwilliam, the 8th Earl, and he confirmed his father's attitude to his workers. "Everybody liked him," says Walt Hammond, a former miner, now 90 years old.[186] The Earl used to take the New Stubbin pit junior football team to the local sweetshop every Sunday afternoon to choose from the shelves of bullseyes and sherbet surprises.

But in 1946, the mining world changed. The coal industry was nationalised, accompanied by a promise from the Government that, as the state assumed ownership, the mineowners would be compensated. The Minister of Fuel and Power was Emanuel Shinwell, the same 'Manny' Shinwell who, 20 years earlier, had attended the lavish lunch at the opening of the Betteshanger Colliery in Kent. There, that day, he had warned the assembled dignitaries, that the days of privilege and inherited wealth were coming to an end. Not yet, he added. But soon. In 1945, a Labour

Miners 1984 on strike

[186] Black Diamonds, Catherine Bailey, p278

Government was elected with a landslide majority. For 'Manny' Shinwell, that moment was now. And Wentworth Woodhouse, and the 8th Earl Fitzwilliam were in his sights.

On a grey, chilly day in April 1946, a column of lorries and huge excavating vehicles thrashed their way across the green lawns of Wentworth Woodhouse. Shinwell's predecessor, Gwilym Lloyd George, had given Peter Fitzwilliam a guarantee that, because of his co-operation during World War Two when a million tons of coal had been mined on 2,000 acres of the Fitzwilliam estate, the garden and immediate parkland surrounding Wentworth Woodhouse would not be touched. Shinwell's attitude was very different:

"We must plan in the interests of the community as a whole, stamping out with ruthless severity any part of the 'interests'; landed, financial, industrial and the rest, to defeat the common will."[187] He slapped a requisition order on the park and the formal gardens. He said in Cabinet on January 24th 1946 that the coal under Wentworth Woodhouse was needed to 'keep Britain's trains running…I desire…371,000 tons, of which 220,000 tons is good quality Barnsley coal, urgently needed for the railways'. This was nearly 'three-quarters of a week's requirements for British Railways', he added.

There was certainly a personal element in this demand. Shinwell had written during the war that, while thousands lived in poverty, 'a toff could go to the Newmarket yearling sales and buy a filly for 8000 guineas; …which represents about 40 years' wages of a…well paid workman'. Shinwell did not name the toff. He was, in fact, Peter Fitzwilliam. Trees, shrubs, lawns and ornamental gardens at Wentworth

---

[187] When the Men Come Home, E Shinwell, 1944

Woodhouse were uprooted. The detritus from the open-cast mining – soil, roots and rubble – was piled outside the main entrance of the house, high enough to be level with Peter Fitzwilliam's bedroom window. The Fitzwilliams had the support of the Yorkshire branch of the mineworkers. Joe Hall, President of the local NUM, wrote: 'The Labour government supposedly stands for the preservation (of heritage) and rural beauty. It is amazing to me that they persist in this scheme at Wentworth…(of) sheer vandalism…I have almost got to the point of asking for a 48-hour stoppage of work in this (entire) coalfield to put an end to this terrible sacrilege'. The message made no impact on Shinwell. He continued to justify the scheme in Cabinet, despite a direct appeal to Prime Minister Clement Attlee who, threatened with a 48-hour strike, now agreed to meet Peter Fitzwilliam. Even after his meeting at 10 Downing Street, the 8th Earl was convinced that the Wentworth scheme was intended to be an example to all landowners, part of what Shinwell saw as a class war.

Peter Fitzwilliam died in 1948 in a plane crash. He had been dogged by the problems of family death duties for years and, combined with the onslaught of the open cast mining, the heyday of Wentworth Woodhouse was over. His daughter, Lady Juliet Wentworth-Fitzwilliam, saw the great house turned into a teacher-training college in the 1950s and twice sold privately, before, in 1982, she decided to leave Yorkshire. She moved south, to Kent, as so many had done before her. She bought Bourne Park, a Queen Anne-style country house, between Bishopsbourne and Bridge near Canterbury, surrounded by nine acres of parkland, with a bridge that spanned the nearby Nailbourne river. It has a 13-bay frontage, an attractive orangery and a fine 18th Century staircase.

What was *not* on the agent's sale details for Bourne Park was that, 60 years before, when coal was discovered in East Kent, boreholes were dug all over the county. One of them was at Bourne.[188] The results were promising but the findings were never developed. Having been plagued by the proximity of coal in Yorkshire, there is probably coal beneath the Fitzwilliam family's new home in Kent.

Plus ça change…

---

[188] See map of boreholes in Appendix

CHAPTER FOURTEEN
Conflict – The Strikes

*'The trouble with a free-market
economy is that it requires so many
policemen to make it work.'*
Neil Ascherson, The Observer, 1985

Frank Redman is a big man in every sense of the word. He stood 6ft 4ins tall when in his twenties and, even now, as he sits sipping coffee in his bungalow home in Deal, there is a certainty about him that discourages disagreement. Frank Redman was a miner for 32 years and he is substantially disabled as a result. He has been elected to responsible positions in the National Association of Colliery Overmen, Deputies and Shot firers,[189] of which he became National President in 1989. Frank Redman, who first went down a pit at Betteshanger in 1957, aged 16-and-a-half, has seen this mining business from the bottom to the top, from the start to the finish. I've known Frank for only four years and it is important that I tell you a story about him that has nothing to do with the East Kent Coalfield...

In 1971, Frank emigrated to South Africa. He had just three years earlier been promoted from the coal face to

---

[189] NACODS. See also Frank Redman in Appendix

Frank Redman as a miner in South Africa

Colliery Deputy at Betteshanger but he had reached a stage, which sometimes happens, when he was "fed up with the routine of life, and wanted to explore fresh pastures." He went for an interview with Anglo-American plc and, out of about 1,000 candidates, he was one of the men chosen to travel to the Transvaal, where he would become a deputy in the Arnot Colliery.[190] He and his wife, Pauline, and their two young sons, Andrew, aged six, and Martin, aged 5, flew from London to Jan Smuts International Airport on November 8th. The next day, Frank was taken to Middelburg, to Arnot, a new mine with three shafts, in the shadow of a huge power station with its four cooling towers. He was assigned to spend a 'familiarisation shift' with the mine captain, third in the mine management hierarchy. Heine van der Vleis introduced himself and Frank's induction began:

> "Fancy a coffee?"
> "Yes. Black no sugar, please."
> "David, go get us two coffees."

---

[190] Arnot Colliery was a new mine at that time; it has one of the largest coal reserves in the world; producing around 5 million tons of coal annually

David was one of his clerks. He was black. He left the room and, as he did so, van der Vleis said: "They're all animals, you know. Yes, you know they're all animals." Together, Frank and van der Vleis then went underground.

The conveyor carrying the coal suddenly stopped. It had jammed. Everyone ran to the junction and there was coal piled high with a "little black lad, digging, digging", trying to move a huge piece of coal that had got stuck. Frank remembers: "van der Vleis started screaming at him. Really swearing at him. Deputies carried sticks and he had one with a knob on the end of it. He started hitting the lad with the heavy end, across the back and shoulders. Then, across the head. The lad was on his knees." Frank picked the Afrikaaner up by the collar. "I saw red. Next thing I knew, van der Vleis was on the other side of the junction – and the screaming had stopped."

Van der Vleis was disciplined, "but the incident set the tone for what was to follow," says Frank. He was put in charge

Frank Redman's wife and two sons in South Africa with the cruise ship behind them

of explosives and his 'senior boss boy' was a bright Zulu worker called Jacob. Jacob spoke four languages and was excellent at his job; careful but shrewd. "But he was treated extremely badly, particularly by the Afrikaaners. During a morning meal break, one of the white instructors called Roberts, sent a worker from Mozambique to fetch the drinks. Then he said to me: 'Would you eat bread with that black bastard?' I indicated I would have no problem with that and to substantiate it, asked a colleague to fetch the lad back, and I reached into my sandwich box. Roberts said: 'You do that and I'll send for the police'. I looked at him and said: 'You've just made my mind up. I'm out of here'. I realised I and my family were going home. This was not a society in which I wished to work."

Six weeks later, Frank Redman and his family were on the Pendennis Castle, sailing from Durban, bound for Southampton. As it called into Port Elizabeth, the Kinnaird Castle was at a quay opposite. On board was Frank's furniture, still on its way to South Africa! Furniture and family would be reunited some months later.

Frank Redman was one of the collier's champions during the strike of 1984/5, when the miners confronted the government of Margaret Thatcher, and the story of the Kent Coalfield drew to a slow and bitter close.

* * * * * * * *

The 1980s was one of the most violent and disturbing of decades. It began with the assassination of Beatle John Lennon in New York on December 8th 1980, and the attempted assassination of US President Reagan in Washington DC, on

March 30th 1981. It embraced the Falklands War, the AIDS epidemic, the realisation of global warming, the great council house sell off, and the survival of Prime Minister Margaret Thatcher in the bombing of the Grand Hotel, Brighton in 1984, plus, in Britain, the year-long miners' strike.

When two sides prepare for a war, they would do well to consider their assets, the relative strengths of the positions they occupy. Despite the world-wide drop in the sale price of coal, the feeling among the leadership of Britain's miners was one of some confidence. In 1972–74, they had won confrontations with the Government and the National Coal Board, involving strike action, mainly over pay rates and working conditions. They had successfully forced the Government to implement a Three-Day Week on the nation, and in 1974 had vanquished the then Prime Minister, Edward Heath.[191]

In Kent, this confidence was also based on the richness of the minerals beneath the surface of the Garden of England. Although the Chislet pit had closed almost without comment nationally in 1969, the forecast reserves at the three remaining collieries were high, with a potential annual output of close to two million tons. But the demand for coal was falling, with a commensurate rise in the use of oil and nuclear power, and the Conservative government, now under Margaret Thatcher, were very obviously taking steps towards a third confrontation with the unions.

In the aftermath of the 1973–74 strike, the Conservative government had drawn up a battle plan. Its author was a free-market Conservative MP, Nicholas Ridley, who believed

---

[191] From January 1st 1974 to March 7th, industrial action forced Edward Heath's government to restrict commercial users to three consecutive days' use of electricity each week. Television broadcasting ended at 10.30pm every night

that a Conservative government could win a major strike in a nationalised industry and 'break the stranglehold of the unions'.

The key to victory would be a carefully-planned avoidance of confrontation until all the facets of the plan were in place. In summary, the 'secret' Ridley Report recommended:

- Grading the unions into three groups of possible opponents which could be defeated; the NUM was in the second group, and were rated tough adversaries
- Building up coal stocks at Britain's power stations
- Importing coal from non-union foreign ports
- Recruiting non-union truck drivers from haulage companies
- Installing dual oil/coal firing generators in Britain's industries
- Cutting off the money supply to strikers, to force the unions into bankruptcy
- Creating a large mobile police squad, riot police, to uphold the law against violent picketing.

The Government and the National Coal Board began to stockpile coal and to implement Ridley's other recommendations. Then, on May 27 1978, the 'secret' report was a secret no longer. A copy was leaked to *The Economist*, and subsequently given wide publicity. Strangely, it seemed to have little impact on the NUM or on the miners' leaders.

The Government continued to pursue the recommendations of the Ridley Plan. Despite the NUM's assertion that they would limit the National Coal Board's ability to stockpile, stocks rose from 37 million tons in 1980 to 58 million tons in 1983. Sir Walter Marshall, former head of the UK Atomic Energy Authority (UKAEA), and a staunch Tory, was appointed chairman of the Central Electricity Generating Board (CEGB) in July 1982 and encouraged foreign imports to increase Britain's hoard of coal. He implemented a strategy by which power stations could be switched from coal to oil in the event of a crisis – such as a national miners' strike. He declared that a "70 percent dependency on coal is excessive." It gave miners a "monopoly of power." Margaret Thatcher now had like-minded men in key positions if she were going to take on Britain's trade unions.

In 1981, Kent miners had reasons to reflect on their lack of action over the closure of Chislet two years earlier. Mrs Thatcher had arrived in Downing Street in May 1979 and had immediately insisted that subsidies to the mining industry should be cut so that the National Coal Board would be financially independent by 1983. Two years later, Derek Ezra, then Coal Board chairman, revealed that between 30–50 pits would close over the next two or three years, among them Snowdown in Kent. Arthur Scargill responded: "We are in a battle to save our jobs and…bring about the conditions for an early General Election

Arthur Scargill

Margaret Thatcher

and an end to the Tory government once and for all.[192]"

The initial political chips in this conflict had been laid on the table.

The *Daily Mirror* declared on its front page on February 18th that 63 pits all over the country were to be closed. Strike action received unanimous approval from miners in Kent, Scotland, Yorkshire and South Wales. Mrs Thatcher, only four months after her 'The Lady is not for turning' speech to the Conservative Party conference decided, as Ridley had suggested, to step back from the confrontation. A pit closure programme would not be launched. The *Daily Mirror* declared: 'The Government gave in to the miners without a fight because the alternative was to give in *after* a fight. Beneath the tough words, the Iron Maiden has a velvet fist'. Kent NUM chairman, Jack Collins, warned: "The Government is looking for breathing space and after the dust has settled they will pick us off one at a time."

Arthur Scargill, now NUM President, visited the Snowdown Colliery, still threatened with closure, on October 7 1982. He was loudly cheered. Terry Harrison of the Kent NUM warned that the battle was not over.[193] Mrs Thatcher would come again…

---

[192] Morning Star, 13th February 1981
[193] Kent NUM minutes, 23rd November 1981

In February 1983, a mass meeting of Kent miners accepted the Coal Board's proposal to spend £3.5million on Snowdown Colliery in return for 250 voluntary redundancies throughout the coalfield. The workforce would be cut from 830 to 450, but the promised investment in Snowdown was seen in Kent as a gesture of confidence in the coalfield.

In June, 1983, Margaret Thatcher's Conservatives were re-elected with an increased majority. That September, the Government discussed again a plan that included the closure of collieries. Energy Secretary, Peter Walker, warned of 'the considerable problems in all this if the closures were to be

Ian MacGregor

implemented'. Three months later, in January 1984, Ian MacGregor, now chairman of the National Coal Board, declared that to remain effective, 'the rundown of the British coal industry should be accelerated. This would imply the loss of 45,000 miners over the next two years'. The assumption was that this would be accompanied by the closure of 45–50 'uneconomic' pits. There would be generous compensation. This confirmed the leak to the *Daily Mirror* two years earlier.

There was now undoubtedly a 'hit list' of pits due for closure. One of them was Snowdown, one of the remaining three pits in the Kent Coalfield.

Tension mounted during the autumn of 1983. On October 31st, the miners began a national overtime ban. This led to sporadic strikes throughout the coal fields with a particularly fierce confrontation in Scotland in February 1984. Then, on March 1st, the closure of the Cortonwood pit in Yorkshire was rumoured. More than 55,000 miners were called out.[194] On March 5th, the Coal Board confirmed 'accelerated closure' of Cortonwood and four other pits, including Snowdown in Kent. It also announced a four million ton reduction in coal production. Two days later, the NUM gave its official backing to the Scottish and Yorkshire miners. The stage was set for a struggle – political, emotional and economic – that would last almost exactly a year.

March 12/13 1984: Strike begins – 100,000 of the 183,000 miners working in the NCB's 174 pits down tools

In Kent, on March 11th, a branch meeting of the Kent NUM is held at Deal Welfare Club. It endorses the strike in support of the Scottish and Yorkshire miners, and pledge to resist pit closures. Philip Sutcliffe was on the union's strike committee. He and his wife, Kay, had three young daughters, all at school. "We could see the strike coming. Everything was building up to it. Obviously, at the beginning, we didn't know how long it was going to last."

That month, at a meeting chaired by Malcolm Pitt, the threat of closure to both Snowdown and Tilmanstone was discussed and the importance of solidarity in this strike

---

[194] London Evening Standard, March 2nd 1954

action was stressed and given unanimous support. The meeting was 'in quite high spirits.'[195] The Kent union also called for a national ballot on strike action 'under Rule 43'[196] – a request that went unheeded by the NUM leadership and by Arthur Scargill. The request was repeated at a special meeting the next day (March 11th) and it was agreed that a ballot was 'both necessary in custom and practice.'[197]

March 16 1984: Nottingham miners vote against strike action
In Kent, volunteers were mobilised to picket power stations and collieries. On March 15th, Yorkshire miner David Jones had died while picketing at Ollerton in Nottinghamshire. Kent miners identified, and aimed to cover, 41 picket points. They drew up plans to maintain 16 'permanent pickets' at Dungeness, Littlebrook, Grain, Northfleet, West Thurrock, Tilbury, Richborough, West Drayton, Shell Haven Oil Refinery, Dover Eastern[198] Docks, Ramsgate Docks, Corralls (the coal distributors) at Brighton, Hobart House, Reeds Paper Mills and Hoo Junction. They would also provide mobile pickets where needed, soon to be nicknamed 'flying pickets'.

March 18 1984: Police set up road blocks on major roads around the country to monitor and prevent 'flying pickets' reaching pits in Nottingham and the Midlands, where miners were not on strike
In Kent, the NUM decide legally to challenge the right of this police action. They lose the case, on March 21st.

---

[195] Minutes of NUM Kent meeting, March 10th 1984
[196] Ibid, request made by Trevor Bell
[197] Kent NUM minutes, March 11th
[198] Now Port of Dover

Flying pickets (Orgreave, 1984)

March 25–28th 1984: Vehicles taking 'flying pickets' from Kent to working coalmines in the Midlands are stopped at the Dartford Tunnel

Kent miner, Brian Foy, asks one of the policemen who refused entry to the Tunnel why they were not allowed to drive through. He is told that the Chief Constable of Nottinghamshire had reason to believe that, if permitted to travel through, there would be a breach of the peace. If he tried to 'take the long way around' and finish his journey, he (Foy) would be arrested as he left the county of Kent.[199]

Philip Sutcliffe, who was vice-chair of the Kent NUM and a regular picket, was arrested three times during the strike.

"The first time was when we were picketing Wyvenhoe Docks in Essex. They were trying to bring in coal from Poland so a big bus load went to try to stop these lorries coming through. We didn't do much, just sat in the middle of the road. But we were all picked up and put into police vans. My brother, Alan, was arrested too, and he was kicking off in the van so

---

[199] Miners' Strike, 1984–5, Early p4

Picket on the Betteshanger Colliery

they took him first, two coppers dragging him off. Then they came for me, the same policeman. He asked my name 'Philip Sutcliffe' I said. He misheard me, I guess, and thought I'd said 'Peter Sutcliffe'. Well, it was the time of the Yorkshire Ripper Peter Sutcliffe. And they called my brother Alan (Sutcliffe) back to the desk, and Alan said I was Philip Sutcliffe, not Peter…but he added, 'The Ripper is our cousin and he's dead scared of Philip'. Which wasn't true, of course. As far as we know, I'm not a cousin but we all come from Yorkshire."[200]

The Sutcliffes, Alan and Philip, went to court the next day. "The bail conditions were that we couldn't in future go to any port importing coal."

April 8th 1984: NUM moderates in national executive vote 14−10 in favour of a national ballot on strike action

April 11th 1984: NACODS, the managers' union, vote 7,638 to 6,661 in favour of strike action but rules require a two-

---

[200] Interview with author

Dawn picket at Betteshanger

thirds majority. They stay at work

In Kent, Frank Redman, a member of NACODS national executive, is angry and dismayed. "The strike got off on the wrong foot. While some pits were working, the country and the Government were getting mixed messages. This was a strike about jobs. About keeping pits open, and, in Kent, our ballots were always in the high 90s in favour. We needed unity, urgently. Unfortunately, some in the mining unions failed to grasp that fact."

In Kent, miners march from Deal to Nottingham, led by Terry French and Jack Dunne, former general secretary of Kent NUM.

April 12th 1984: Arthur Scargill rules out a national ballot on the strike

April 13th 1984: Labour Party leader, Neil Kinnock, backs a national ballot to unify NUM. He criticises Arthur Scargill

In Kent, Frank Redman says: "There were some who thought that having the approval of the majority of delegates was sufficient to justify the strike. But it didn't have the strength, the unity, that would have come with a majority in a national ballot. Some leaders didn't foresee that a faction of the union would renege on the decision to strike."

April 19ᵗʰ 1984: A special delegates' conference of the NUM votes against a national ballot
Frank Redman says: "I didn't know what they felt in the Midlands and Nottinghamshire, but in Kent and in other parts of the country, we were fully aware that we were going to be decimated if we didn't do something about it. If you looked at Yorkshire, you'd be working at one pit one week, and, as it was threatened with closure, you'd be transferred to another pit. Then, that would be threatened. The pit closure programme was already under way. The big problem was that they wanted to do away with 70-plus pits in one go."

May 1ˢᵗ 1984: May Day march from Clerkenwell to the Jubilee Gardens, Colchester. Sixty-four pickets arrested; 57 of them are from Kent. Two days later, 40 more pickets are arrested. Photographs are taken by police and filed
In Kent, Philip Sutcliffe is proud of the fact that no one at Snowdown has crossed the picket lines. "There was one lad who went back to work at Tilmanstone. He lived in Woolage Green, near my parents and we all turned out to try to intimidate him, if you like." Philip Sutcliffe was arrested and fined, by Canterbury magistrates, and given bail – "on condition I didn't go within five miles of a working miner's house. I said, 'look, Mum and Dad live five doors away from that bloke. Are you saying 'you

Frank Redman at his last NACODS conference, Blackpool 1989

can't go and see Mum and Dad?' And they said: 'yes.'"

May 11th 1984: National Union of Railwaymen resume coal train shipments to Ravenscraig
In Kent, 32 pickets arrested at Ramsgate. All released, except two who were breaking previous bail conditions.

May 16th 1984: Inter-union feud over coal shipments in Scotland
In Kent, copies of the *Daily Express* circulate bearing the banner headline 'We'll topple Maggie, pledges Scargill'. The miners' leader says of the Prime Minister: "She may have been successful in the Falklands but she won't win this battle. If we have to stop out until November or December, we will beat this Coal Board and this government…We want to save our jobs but, more, we want to roll back the years of Thatcherism."

It echoes an earlier *News of the World* headline: 'We will win – Our cause is a noble one – Scargill'.

May 17th 1984: National Coal Board reports 121 pits idle, 43 pits working normally

In Kent, two days later, Malcolm Pitt arrested while showing Japanese delegation picket lines at Richborough Power Station.

May 29th/30th 1984: Violence at Orgreave – 7,000 blockade coke site – 82 arrested, 69 injured

Kent pickets, who had been occupying Hobart House, the Coal Board head office in London, the previous day, travel north to be part of the Orgreave flying pickets. Arthur Scargill is among those arrested. It is a precursor of even worse violence, for what happened on…

June 18th 1984: Nearly 7,000 pickets and 3,400 police clash. Ninety-three men are arrested, 79 injured (51 pickets, 28 police). Miners now block steelworks but coal trains resume supplies to Ravenscraig and Llanwern

In Kent, Philip Sutcliffe said: "There's still a lot of bitterness against the police. There were miners who had sons in the police force. Some of these coppers said 'look, I don't want to be standing against the pickets, possibly against my dad'. But I remember one guy in particular who said: 'It's my job. If I've got to be there, I'm going to be there' and I've seen him standing up proud and doing his job. I didn't agree with that. There's one miner whose daughter married a policeman and he came up to me one day and said: 'Come on, Philip. Let's shake on it and forget it'. Well, I believe in live and let live. But don't ask me to shake his hand. Because I'm not. No way."

Philip is married to Kay. Kay's cousin went back to work just before the 1984 strike ended. He said before he crossed the picket line: "It's all finished, Philip. And I want to be on the winning side'. He meant the Coal Board's side. It didn't do him any good because he lost his job just like the rest of us. Well, we've met at family weddings and get-togethers. But I won't talk to him. I can't."[201]

On June 17th 1984, Betteshanger Colliery was occupied by striking miners. Eight men sat in, down the pit; 50 men occupied the office and lamp cabins. Overman, Tony Neilson, part of the middle management keeping the pit safe while the men were on strike, remembers "surprise when the door opened and they marched in. There were no hard feelings, though; we were on their side and Terry Harrison (NUM) had been negotiating with NACODS so that there were no difficulties." Frank Redman was on the same shift. The miners occupied the pit for three days. Twenty-nine miners received dismissal notices on June 26th. All but two officials of the branch NUM were among those sacked.

June 21st 1984: Ian MacGregor, chair of the NCB, writes to every member of the NCB[202] stressing 'the damage that will be done if this disastrous strike goes on for a long time'. It is the 14th week of the strike

In Kent, the miners note that MacGregor denied that the Coal Board planned 'to do away with 70,000 jobs' and 'close around 86 pits'. Frank Redman says: "Even if it's half that number, it's too many."

July 2nd 1984 Nottingham miners hold council elections. A landslide for moderate candidates

---

[201] Interview with author
[202] MacGregor's letter is reproduced in Appendix

In Kent, Philip Sutcliffe says: "We knew the Nottingham and Leicester miners were producing coal hand over fist all the time we were on strike. If they had come out with us, the strike would never have lasted a year. It would have been over in months. As miners, we should all have stuck together. You know: United we stand, divided we fall'. And that's exactly what happened."

Coal production continued in Nottingham, Leicester and elsewhere throughout the strike. It is estimated that they mined 20 million tons of coal in that time.[203]

July 18th 1984: Peace talks at the Rubens Hotel in London, between the NCB and the NUM collapse
In Kent, Tilmanstone pit is occupied by 12 miners. Ten of them are sacked.

July 19th 1984: Prime Minister Margaret Thatcher says in the House of Commons that 'giving in to the miners would be surrendering the rule of parliamentary democracy to the rule of the mob.' She compared the strike, in a speech to backbenchers, to the Falklands War. "We had to fight the enemy without in the Falklands…we now have to be aware of the enemy within, which is much more difficult to fight and more dangerous to liberty."
In Kent, on July 20th, a group of children from Nottingham miners' families is welcomed by Kent miners' families to stay for a seaside holiday. On July 26th, five Kent miners on picket duty are arrested at Colchester. On July 27th, folk singers, Peggy Seeger and Ewan MacColl, give a concert at Deal Welfare Club. Kent miners' picketing programme continues vigorously. Right wing journalist, Auberon

---

[203] Guardian, March 5th 1985

Waugh, urges the police to offer a £50 bounty for every miner's scalp.

August 16ᵗʰ 1984: £707,000 is sequestrated from South Wales miners' funds

August 21ˢᵗ 1984: The Trades Union Congress General Council discuss the strike for the first time. It has been running for eight months. Len Murray says it is the TUC's purpose to "bring the concentrated power of this movement to bear on the National Coal Board and the Government." The TUC are at last supporting the strike

In Kent, Frank Redman says: "It is too little, too late. Arthur Scargill has taken a lot of abuse for his leadership of the strike and I'm sure he realises his mistake. But the plain truth is that the Government won the propaganda battle. Scargill was blamed for telling a lot of lies, but letters released under the 30-year rule show a deliberate misrepresentation of the facts by the Government and the NCB. In fact, 70 pits *were* going to be closed with a loss of thousands of jobs and the Government convinced the country that it was Arthur who was using underhand tactics."

After the Orgreave fracas in May, Scargill had said: "The intimidation and the brutality that has been displayed (by the police) are something reminiscent of a Latin American state." But the union fail to stop the movement of lorries and, as Redman said, were losing the hearts and minds of the electorate. A Gallup Poll revealed a 79% disapproval of the NUM's methods. In late June the number of miners at work had grown to 53,000.

September 18ᵗʰ 1984: TUC becomes directly involved in the dispute as peace talks fail

The print workers support the miners. *The Sun* is not published for five days as it wished to carry an article headed: 'Miners used to be the salt of the earth. Too many have become the scum of the earth'.[204]

September 20ᵗʰ 1984: Derbyshire miners win a 'right to work' injunction

In Kent, 'scab' working now becomes an issue. Six scabs are discovered working on the Betteshanger tips, 12 at Tilmanstone. A picket of 250 challenge the working miners; there are 34 arrests. On September 7ᵗʰ at Dover, 12 pickets are detained in custody of one week.

September 30ᵗʰ 1984 Labour Party Conference: Scargill is well-received. Neil Kinnock fails to prevent motions from the floor criticising police behaviour

October 9ᵗʰ 1984: Conservative Party Conference: Ministers Leon Brittan, Peter Walker and John Gummer predict a 'fight to the end' against the miners

In Kent, on October 13ᵗʰ, a food convoy from the French unions arrives in Dover. It carries 400 tons of food on 40 vehicles; 800 attend a rally at Snowdown. A total of £60,000 is raised to support strikers.

The days are getting shorter now, and the nights colder. Among the families of striking miners, there is great hardship. Philip and Kay Sutcliffe were fortunate in that Kay had a job with a security company in Canterbury. But

---

[204] Terry Harrison interview with author, 2019

for the children of Deal and Aylesham and surrounding villages, the miners' soup kitchens were often providing the only hot meal of the day. Philip says: "Everybody had a food parcel made up for them. If we were desperate, I would take one home but, often I'd think *We don't need it, so I'll leave it for someone else.* Then, we had to keep our houses warm and, you wouldn't think it, but we ran out of coal. So we sent gangs of lads out to get logs. We'd ask farmers and landowners and they would give us wood. They were very good like that. Men would put their names down for wood at the picket meeting in the morning and you'd get some that day. It was brilliant. We not only fed people but kept them warm as well.

"And if they happened to do a bit of poaching, with their ferrets, that put meat on the table, as well. Personally, I had no ferrets. I used to feel sorry for the rabbits. But those who did, helped their families – and probably sold a few rabbits for a couple of bob."

Favours from shop keepers were appreciated and still remembered. The Sutcliffes had hired a television form Radio Rentals. They couldn't keep up the payments. Philip was told: 'Keep the set and pay what you can, when you can'.

November 5th 1984: Price Waterhouse announces seizure of NUM assets. NUM delegates' conference unanimously votes to continue strike

November 12th 1984: Worst violence yet in Yorkshire. Petrol bombs thrown. At Lord Mayor's banquet in London, Mrs Thatcher links pickets with IRA bombers

November 20th 1984: Government asks Parliament for an extra £36 million 'to cover the costs incurred by the Coal Board and the police in the dispute'

November 21st 1984: £1 to be deducted from benefits paid to striking miners' *wives and children*

In Kent, the miners' women have been drawn into the conflict. They cooked millions of meals in the soup kitchens and kept their homes and families together amid financial hardship and intense political pressure. They also formed groups and associations to support their men as week followed week, deep into the conflict. The movement became a national network; Women Against Pit Closures. They organised collections outside supermarkets, communal kitchens, concerts and other fund-raising activities. Kay Sutcliffe said: "We're fighting to save our communities. We're not fighting for women, or women's rights. We're fighting to make sure the family has somewhere to live and that there's a future for us all."

For some miners, the energy, political nous and organising ability of their wives and girlfriends came as something of a surprise.

Kay Sutcliffe is a passionate woman. When there's talk of the militancy of the Kent Coalfield it is the image of flying pickets and the clashes with police that flash into the mind. Kay Sutcliffe's actions draw attention to a militancy just as dedicated, just as influential. She has a way with words. As the bitter strike against Margaret Thatcher's government lurched past its sixth month, she wrote a poem. It was called Coal Not Dole:

COAL NOT DOLE

It stands so proud, the wheels so still,
A ghostlike figure on the hill.
It seems so strange, there is no sound,
Now there are no men underground.

What will become of this pit yard?
Where men once trampled faces hard?
So tired and weary their shift done,
Never having seen the sun.

Will it become a sacred ground,
Foreign tourists gazing round?
Asking if men really worked here
Way beneath this pit-head gear?

Empty trucks once filled with coal
Lined up like men on the dole.
Will they every be used again
Or left for scrap just like the men?

There'll always be a happy hour,
For those with money, jobs and power.
They'll never realise the hurt
They've caused to men they treat like dirt.

The poem was set to music by Chumbawamba and by numerous folk groups. It became the miners' anthem in the 1984 strike. As Philip joined the picket lines, Kay spoke at meetings all over the country, rallying the miners' women to support their husbands in this industrial struggle to the death. Philip says: "I honestly didn't know Kay had it in her. She was terrific. I'll never forget what she did and the moment in which she did it. She managed to bring up the family, go out to work, and fight for the cause all at the same time."

November 27th 1984: NCB offer a further £175 to any miner returning to work that week

December 17th 1984: Pit peace talks break down again. John Paul Getty donates £120,000 to relieve hardship among working miners

In Kent, Christmas is celebrated with the usual mixture of vigour and reverence. SERTUC[205] arrange for turkey and Christmas pudding to be sent to the families of all striking miners. Single men receive £10 each. One of the rugby lads dresses up as Father Christmas in the Welfare Club and there are small presents for all the children.

January 11th 1985: Kent pickets, Terry French and Chris Tazey, found guilty of causing grievous bodily harm. French is sentenced to 5 years' imprisonment, Tazey to 3 years' youth custody

In Kent, Terry French's wife, Liz, whose family came to Kent from Scotland, admits[206] there was fighting in the picket lines but "they reckon he beat a policeman up. He didn't deny having a scuffle but he did deny beating him half to death; he had a broken shoulder, I think. Anyway, my Terry was pretty sturdy, but those coppers were big blokes."

---

[205] South East region of the TUC
[206] Interview with author, see Appendix

Twice previously, Terry had been successfully defended by Michael Mansfield QC over alleged offences related to the strike. Mansfield says: "Terry was a leader. He was conspicuous; he often wore a tartan hat. He was fearless. If there was a need to lead, he was never afraid to do so. It was the sort of quality you would welcome in the front line, if you were at war. And in many senses, it was a war. This strike wasn't about pay or better working conditions. It was about survival. Terry French understood that."[207]

January 25th 1985: NACODS warn they would not agree to the miners' union having to accept the closure of all 'uneconomic pits' as a condition of further talks

In Kent, Frank Redman said: "I remember one cold Saturday morning, going into the Coal Board headquarters at Hobart House and meeting the NCB's former Director in Scotland, Jimmy Cowan. We were chatting and I was making a couple of what I thought were one or two reasonable negotiating points, and he looked at me, and there was a long pause. Then he said: 'Frank, the days of the honest broker are over'. That speaks for itself, doesn't it? There was a lot underhand going on. A lot of leaks and a lot of funny business that wasn't so funny."[208]

February 3rd 1985: Frances Colliery in Fife closes. 500 jobs lost

In Kent, Deal Women's Support Group organise a march on February 9th from Sandwich to Richborough Power Station. The group The Flying Pickets give a performance to raise funds for Kent miners at the Granville Theatre, Ramsgate.

---

[207] See Chapter 15
[208] See Chapter 14

February 24th 1985: Miners' demonstrations in London; 101 arrests

In Kent, the TUC organise a Day of Action in support of the striking Kent miners.

February 25th 1985: More than 3,800 miners abandon the strike

In Kent, Frank Redman says: "You could see it coming. I've got no time for Margaret Thatcher. She was instrumental in closing collieries which could have made a profit for years, and made a tremendous contribution to the prosperity of this country. It was admitted in Parliament that Kent was producing coal which had less than 1% sulphur content – basically a smokeless fuel. What a waste..."

March 1st 1985: Area TUC conferences call for a return to work without a negotiated settlement

March 2nd 1985: Yorkshire miners vote to continue strike

March 3rd 1985: Special delegates' conference votes 98 to 91 to return to work on March 5th. There is no insistence on amnesty for sacked miners. The national strike is over

In Kent, the strike goes on. A mass meeting on March 4th at the Granville Theatre, Ramsgate, emphasises support for the sacked miners and rejects a return to work. The next day, the Kent pickets set out for Wales and Yorkshire. Two days later, they are recalled to Kent.

On March 5th, as miners nationally return to work, the NCB make it clear that no sacked miners will get their jobs back. So Kent miners stay on strike. Philip Sutcliffe said: "We had pledged that no men at Snowdown would go back to work, unless the sacked men were reinstated. But the strike was over. More men were going back at Betteshanger and Tilmanstone. It was an impossible situation. It was a pledge we could no longer keep."

All branch committees of the Kent NUM meet at Dover on March 8th. On March 9th, another mass meeting accept a recommendation to return to work; it is also supported by the men who have been sacked.

On March 10th 1985, defiant Kent miners celebrate the first anniversary of the strike, with a performance of the play 'Garden of England', at the Shaw Theatre in Deal.

On March 11th, the Kent miners march in an orderly fashion, back to work. It is exactly a year since the strike began.

That day, Philip Sutcliffe led the line of men along the road to the pit gates of Snowdown Colliery. Kay Sutcliffe took the day off from her job in Canterbury and walked back with him, step by step, side by side...

CHAPTER FIFTEEN
The Aftermath

*"Very few things happen at the right
time and the rest do not happen at
all. The conscientious historian will
correct these defects."*
Herodotus 450 BC

Winning grants the victor the right to set down their authorised version of history. In the 1984 miners' strike, the memories and observations of the vanquished are just as fascinating and relevant a record of what actually happened in those turbulent twelve months.

First, there is little doubt that Mrs Thatcher's government won the propaganda battle that led to public support for the strike gradually slipping away from the miners. It is also beyond dispute that the Government intelligence of what the miners' leaders were doing, and were about to do, was very much better informed than the unions' information on their opponents' intentions.

The inadequacy of the Government's response to the 1972 strike had led to the creation of COBRA (the Cabinet Office Briefing Rooms) to co-ordinate government reaction to a national or regional crisis. The co-ordination worked efficiently.

If this had been a boxing match, neither side abided by the Marquis of Queensberry rules, and allegations of calculated aggression and underhand tactics flew both ways, thick and fast. The evidence of violent behaviour is, to any reasonable person, proven on both sides of the strike. Who threw the first blow, and who retaliated, varied from confrontation to confrontation. What is more interesting is to examine the evidence that the Government employed the apparatus of the state, to achieve its victory.

The starting point is a sentence that appears in the authorised memoirs of Stella Rimington, former head of MI5. She was in charge of MI5's counter-subversion branch at the time of the strike and she admitted the agency's involvement in the dispute, saying that MI5 had targeted "a triumvirate who had declared that they were using the strike to bring down the elected government of Mrs Thatcher and it (the strike) was actively supported by the Communist Party."[209]

The three leaders at the time were Arthur Scargill (president), Mick McGahey (vice-president) and Peter Heathfield (general secretary). In addition, moles in the National Union of Mineworkers allegedly leaked inside information to the Government. Downing Street indirectly confirmed that the security services were involved in the strike.[210]

Cabinet papers now reveal that copies of internal and NUM memos were being read by Coal Board and Government officials within days of their being written.[211] One of the most widely-held beliefs is that Sir Tim Bell, one of Mrs Thatcher's most powerful advisers, had an informant

---

[209] Daily Telegraph, September 11th 2001
[210] Guardian, May 16th 2005
[211] Ibid

within the TUC. Tim Bell was working for Saatchi and Saatchi during the strike period, 1984–85, and police sources have confirmed that Special Branch infiltrated a spy, nicknamed Silver Fox, into Arthur Scargill's inner circle. The finger has been pointed at the NUM's chief executive at the time, Roger Windsor; an allegation he has strenuously denied.

In October 1984, seven months into the strike, the Government's resolve was weakening. NACODS, the pit disputes trade union, which had strayed out of the strike and were keeping the miners both safe and workable, balloted its members and came close to uniting with its colleagues in the NUM. The Government needed to find out what was happening in NACODS' discussions. On October 16th, NACODS decided to bring its 16,000 members out on strike. An internal Coal Board memo from chairman, Ian MacGregor, reveals that 'Tim Bell called. His informant at the TUC has confirmed…that they (the TUC) are trying to stop NACODS from settling…'[212]

Margaret Thatcher later admitted that this was 'the moment that she came closest to defeat.' But on October 24th, NACODS called off its strike action. Frank Redman, a senior NACODS official, said: "If we had had a national ballot of miners then, even though we were nine months into the strike, I think we still could have won."

When looking for evidence of infiltration of the miners' ranks during the year of conflict, one name emerges with conspicuous regularity. It is Robert McGibbon.

In June 1984, with the strike three months old, the National Coal Board announced that Betteshanger was under threat of closure because it was unsafe. On June 18th Robert

---

[212] Ibid

McGibbon, a face-worker, was one of two Betteshanger miners who said they were going to return to work. Twenty-nine striking miners immediately occupied the pit.[213] They were led by Terry Harrison, Secretary of the Kent NUM, and the next day the Coal Board went to court to obtain an injunction against Harrison. The Coal Board succeeded but the police did not enforce the order, as negotiations between the two sides were already in progress. On June 20th, an agreement was signed by McGibbon and the other miner, Alec Smart, witnessed by Harrison, Frank Redman and John Keenan (NACODS) that read:

> 'In view of arguments put to us by individual members of the unions which would be affected by a closure of the colliery, we have agreed as a gesture to help keep the peace not to return to Betteshanger Colliery while the present strike lasts'.

The industrial action ended and the safety cover for the pit resumed. But the 29 miners were sacked for 'gross misconduct'. Twenty-two of the men were eventually given their jobs back. Among those who weren't was Terry Harrison, NUM's local secretary and lead negotiator.

McGibbon was a late convert to mining. He had come to the Kent coalfields after working on the vehicle production line at the Cowley plant of British Leyland. The *Daily Telegraph* revealed[214] that in March/April 1974, he and his wife, Irene, had led a back-to-work movement during a strike at the Cowley plant. Irene McGibbon had inspired a Cowley wives

---

[213] See Chapter 13
[214] Daily Telegraph, April 27th 1984

Anti-McGibbon graffiti on Betteshanger water tower, 1984

revolt against the strike. In August, she set up the Moderate Miners' Wives Back-to-Work Campaign, and fly-posted its aims in Kent villages, claiming that between 350 and 400 miners were prepared to go back to work in September. Despite his earlier agreement with the Unions, Robert McGibbon turned up for work at Betteshanger in September. He had predicted that hundreds would follow him. In fact, only 24 miners returned to Tilmanstone, four at Betteshanger and none at Snowdown.[215] But there were violent clashes with police in the Kent mining villages, particularly Aylesham and Elvington. Six residents complained of police harassment; 34 miners were arrested. Keith Owen remembers: "If you were from a mining village, you were monitored and questioned

[215] East Kent Mercury, August 9th 1984

about your daily routine by hundreds of police who were drafted in from all over the country. Looking back, it doesn't seem feasible. But it happened and most of us will never forget it. Wives, children, grandmas, uncles, aunts, neighbours and friends fought together for our very existence."[216]

The McGibbons were revealed to be members of a right-wing organisation, the Freedom Association (TFA), led by Norris McWhirter, who made a living as an athletics correspondent. Frank Redman said: "The McGibbons were professional strike-breakers and, after their activities in Cowley, we should have been informed. But there was no exchange of intelligence between the unions."

Irene McGibbon was given a standing ovation on the platform at the Conservative Party Conference in October. In February, she attempted to address a meeting of Conservative students at the University of Kent but was shouted down by students and supporters of the miners' strike, and left the campus under police protection.[217] When the strike ended, the McGibbons left East Kent.

It is difficult to calculate the cost of the strike to the Kent community. Forty-five miners had been sacked. Eight had served, or were serving prison sentences.[218] Terry French, from Betteshanger, was serving five years, reduced to four on appeal. The police estimated the cost of the strike at £14million and Kent's shops and businesses believed they had lost about £23million.[219]

Despite the brass bands and banners that had accompanied their march back to work, most miners knew

---

[216] Aylesham Through the Years, by Keith Owen, p100
[217] Daily Express, March 1st 1995
[218] See Appendix for names of men dismissed and/or imprisoned
[219] East Kent Mercury, March 13th 1985

that they had been defeated. But not a single lump of coal had been produced from the Kent pits in the entire twelve months – and that was a victory of sorts.

The most widespread impact on the community was an ongoing resentment directed at those 'scabs' who had gone back to work. It is a generalisation, but mining communities do not forgive 'scabs'. In Kent, the coalfield which had endured the longest, the scabs were graded. Men began drifting back to work towards the end of 1984, encouraged by an NCB offer of a £1,200 Christmas bonus to a miner drawing four consecutive pay packets.[220] When it became apparent in February that the strike was lost, family and financial pressure tempted even the most loyal union man to consider taking the pragmatic option of going back to work. Kent NUM, remember, had decided to continue the strike despite a national return to work. In the two weeks before the Kent miners ended their industrial action, the numbers of returning miners increased, they called them the 'two-weekers'.

In the final fortnight of the strike in Kent, the union's picket lines were still drawn up outside the three pits. The established 'scabs' were roundly abused, for the time for persuasion was obviously over. The 'two-weekers' and the new recruits to scabbing crossed the picket lines in silence. As one miner put it: "I don't class them as scabs." Philip Sutcliffe takes a more resolute view: "There was a distinction between the hard-line scabs and those who went back when, nationally, the strike was over. But most of us stuck out for those who had lost their jobs. There were about 30 men who scabbed at Snowdown in that last week. I still don't talk to

---

[220] In November, 66 men were working at Tilmanstone, 32 at Betteshanger

them. You shouldn't go back till the majority say so. You shouldn't cross the picket line…"

Canvassing opinion nearly 40 years later among those who had lived through the strike, there are three main reasons given for the miners' failure to realise the importance of the Ridley document that revealed the Conservative government's strategy to defeat the unions. The miners watched as coal was stockpiled to buttress Britain in the event of industrial action on a national scale. The unions failed to realise that the Government was ensuring that the miners' strengths that had won the disputes of 1972 and 1974 would be undermined in the next confrontation.

Jack Collins, the NUM's leader in Kent, had promised that, by picketing, the miners would stop supplies of coal reaching the power stations. But the Government had foreseen this tactic and had stockpiled coal at all the power stations. It had also boosted output from the nuclear and oil-fired power stations. There would be no repetition of the Three-Day Week.

Secondly, Arthur Scargill's failure to put the 1984 strike action to a national vote of the NUM membership was a crucial error. The controversial 'flying pickets' were an abrasive substitute. If unanimous approval from a Delegates' Conference was not the same thing as grassroots approval, the majority of miners faithfully followed the NUM's call to strike. But the fact that the strike did *not* have a national endorsement by NUM members had repercussions both inside the coal industry, and outside in the attitude of other powerful unions. The determination of miners in Nottingham, Leicestershire and elsewhere to continue working meant that the supply of British coal to British industry never halted.

Thirdly, Britain's unions never spoke with a united voice. Scargill and the TUC's Len Murray did *not* see eye to eye on a number of issues. For months, the TUC was less than full-hearted in its support for the striking miners. The seamen and the railwaymen supported the miners but the Electrical, Electronic, Telecommunications and Plumbing Union (EEPTU) actively opposed the strike and according to Ian MacGregor's autobiography, its leaders regularly supplied the Government with information that helped Margaret Thatcher and the Coal Board to defeat the strike.

The behaviour of the steelworkers' union is salutary. At that time, the steelworkers had their own problems. In 1980, there were mass closures after they had lost a strike about a pay increase. The miners sought their support in 1984 but the siren voice of the Government warned the steel union that it was planning to close one of the nation's five steelworks. It is completely understandable then, that each of the five steelworks competed with the others to avoid being the one that would close. The steelworkers offered the miners sympathy and support, but little else.

A united, nationwide call from NUM members might have stiffened the steelworkers' resolve. As it was, annual steel production actually increased during the 1984 strike to 15,135,700 tons. This was 149,300 tons more than in 1983 and 1,431,200 tons more than in 1982. In Kent, NUM vice-president, Mick McGahey, said: "I hope the steelmen appreciate that when the miners win this battle, they will have won the battle for other unions as well. If they lose, the steelmen will lose their battle." The strike had six months to run but McGahey's warning contained some substance.

Neil Kinnock, who led the Labour Party during the strike, blamed Arthur Scargill for its failure: "The greatest gift that Mrs Thatcher has had (while in office) was in having the right enemies. Galtieri was a good enemy to have (in the Falklands), a fascist dictator. Scargill was a good enemy to have because he didn't have a (national) ballot…and he tried to excuse illegal actions. The script was written for the Conservatives."[221]

Michael Mansfield QC

Michael Mansfield QC, who defended many of the flying pickets, has a different take on Arthur Scargill's role in the strike. "He was certain the miners could win. He felt the delegates' vote had given the miners' leaders the authority legitimately to lead the men out of the pits. He felt he (Scargill) embodied the spirit of the miners. There had been a vote and he had the authority to lead a united coal union. He was wrong of course; he may have had the authority but the union was not united."

Mansfield knew Scargill probably as well as anyone. Years after the strike ended, Mansfield supported Scargill's bid to form a political party. He shared a platform with him and advised him behind the scenes. It was called the Socialist Labour Party. It advocated re-nationalisation of industries that had been privatised by the Tory Government,

---

[221] Iron Lady: The Thatcher Years, 2012

but a return to radical socialism and a withdrawal from Europe. Its message failed. Its share of the total votes in the seats where SLP candidates stood in 1997 was 3%. This had dropped to infinitesimal by 2017. For a socialist, Arthur Scargill was curiously conservative. "He had to be persuaded that women could make a valuable contribution to a cause," says Michael Mansfield. "The women were so effective in 1984/5 that he simply had to recognise that they could lead, and they could work and win. As we discussed the formation of the SLP, some of our fiercest conversations were over the need to broaden the appeal, embrace others. Simply being Arthur Scargill wouldn't guarantee success – and matters were much the same during the strike. He wanted to get into Parliament but, frankly, he wasn't really suited to formal politics."

The strike ended in March 1985. Of the four Kent pits, Chislet had closed in 1969 and Tilmanstone would close in 1986. But Betteshanger was now thriving. Output increased from 6,104 per week in September 1985 to 10,365 tons in December. This 'turnaround' caught the imagination of Fleet Street. The *Daily Mail* recalled Betteshanger's militant reputation and splashed the story as the front page lead in December: 'Reprieve for 'Trouble Pit'.

But nearby Snowdown was losing £6million a year. It was obviously a risk and, in 1987 British Coal's management decided to halt further investment, but to transfer 90 miners to Betteshanger and begin a partial closure of Snowdown. The unions rejected the decision. The mine manager then announced that Snowdown would close, and the unions went to appeal. What happened at, and during the appeal, is cloaked in controversy. Arthur Scargill presented the union's case, describing British Coal's action as 'dishonest and almost sinister'. Frank Redman, for NACODS, criticised the way investment in Snowdown had been used; it was "incomprehensible" that it should be run down when it was producing "clean, almost smokeless coal." Outside the meeting, Redman had had a private talk with British Coal executives. "We could have reached an agreement to keep Snowdown open, perhaps for a couple of years. But the unions played their cards badly.

"British Coal was murdering a pit with a possible long-term future."[222]

Snowdown closed in October 1984.

On August 25th 1989, this letter was sent by British Coal (the former National Coal Board) to the last working miners in Kent, at Betteshanger:

Dear Colleague,

As you may have already heard, it is with great regret that I have to advise you that Betteshanger Colliery will close on Friday 25th August 1989. The announcement was made this morning by Mr Wheeler, Director of Group Operations, and I attach a copy of the Press Statement that has been issued by British Coal.

The counselling of individuals will now, as a matter of urgency, be carried out by the Assistant Manager (Personnel) and his staff. In order to assist him in arranging counselling interviews, it is essential that anyone wishing to take redundancy on the terms currently available (only until Friday of this week) should register their name with him urgently, so that the necessary paperwork can be put in hand before the

---

[222] Colliery Review minutes, July 22nd 1987

interview. This will speed up the process for everyone.

Yours sincerely

D Bell

Colliery Manager

A salvage company was appointed to remove all the equipment which could be used again in other pits. The last job for a handful of Betteshanger colliers, fitters, safety workers and electricians was to destroy the pit, which had provided a living for thousands of men for more than 60 years. It took six months. The pit headgear, the iconic evidence of a thriving Kent industry, was the last to be dismantled. It took four hours to bring it crashing down into what had been the pit yard. The moment was filmed and on the soundtrack can be heard faintly amid the din, a voice saying: "There goes our livelihood."

When the deed was done, one of the workforce, a former Betteshanger miner, said slowly: "It was like being at the funeral of an old friend."

In 1983, before the strike, Britain had 174 working collieries. By 2009, there were six. The last deep colliery in the UK, Kellingley Colliery, closed just before Christmas, 2015, bringing an end to the country's deep mining industry.

CHAPTER SIXTEEN
Champions

"I live in the centre of the universe, so why would I want to move anywhere else?"

Derek Garrity

Ianto Hill, one of Aylesham's leaders, at a social occasion

Aylesham, the brainchild of Patrick Abercrombie in the 1920s, is still the beating heart of the community that served the Kent Coalfield. It is expanding now, fuelled by the demand for housing in the prosperous South East of England. An army of planners, architects and builders are developing the town along the lines that Abercrombie laid down so many years before, which would have both pleased and surprised him, because Patrick Abercrombie was nothing if not a realist.

When the last pit closed in 1989, Aylesham suffered sorely. Not only did the men lose their jobs but the shops and the sports and social clubs – the whole structure of society could have collapsed. A way of life was at risk. It is at a time like this that communities discover their champions. One was obvious – Ianto Hill, chair of the Parish Council. Welsh, emotional, yet organised.

Ianto Hill died in 1979, having served as a councillor for 27 years. Who better to assess his contribution to this unique community than a second 'champion', Derek Garrity, who sustained and developed everything that Ianto Hill had established in Aylesham. Garrity says:

Derek Garrity

"Ianto wore his heart on his sleeve. He was a hard man and if you crossed him, you had trouble but he was a very fair man. Ianto would fight tooth and nail for the good of the village. He was one of our heroes and even when the pits were closed, he never gave up. He believed in miners and their strength, both in debate and at the coal face."

Garrity says: "Life was quite structured in Aylesham for the first 50 years. You didn't get a house unless you were down the pit. The miners went to work and got their wages and pretty well everything was deducted on the miner's docket – your rent, the cost of your water and electricity, a shilling for the welfare and, if you were a Catholic, two shillings and sixpence for the priest and the church. The men took their 'pocket money' and the rest came back home, to the wife.

"Ianto ran everything else. He was on the District Council at Eastry and he was on the Housing Committee and you never got a house unless Ianto said so. That's a bit of an exaggeration, but you know what I mean.

"After the strikes, Aylesham's men went off to other jobs. Some dug the Channel Tunnel, some became postmen or railway workers. And that's where some families got into debt. Wages were lower and budgets had to be managed more carefully. There were times when people got evicted but Ianto usually got them back into their houses, one way or another."[223]

Garrity has great admiration for Hill, both as a man and as a politician. He is from much the same mould. Unlike Hill, he is not a miner – though, strong and stocky, he could have been. His parents came from Newcastle and his wife's family from South Wales – all miners. Derek's father died from silicosis at the age of 52 and his mother did not want him to go down the pit, so he joined the Army, the Junior Leaders' Regiment, and spent two years as a boy soldier. He served with the Royal Engineers for nearly 30 years, in Germany, Libya, Denmark and with the UN Peacekeeping Force in Cyprus.

For the last 20 years, Derek Garrity was in the Army Reserve living in Aylesham and working as an electrician, the trade he had learned in the Army. "When the pit closed it told us that we weren't required by British industry any more. Then they closed the school. That told us we weren't even fit to educate our own people." Aylesham School figures large in Derek Garrity's life even though he left at 15, with no qualifications. "I said to my mate, Percy Wilson: 'Percy,

---

[223] Interview with author, 2019

they've closed he school, they've closed the pit but they can't close our hearts. We're going to reopen that school and train the people of Aylesham." And so they did.

The dramatic closure of the school, according to Garrity, "said to us, as a community, that we have no place in the working life of Great Britain. The Government had failed us in work, and failed us in education. So a group of us got together and set our own agenda. In our hearts, we knew that the people of Aylesham were trainable. We were untrained but we were not untrainable. We were setting out on this journey for our children but also for ourselves. We were aware of our heritage even if no-one else cared about it.

"We came here in the 20s as immigrants. Not a lot different from those immigrants who these days risk their lives to find a new life in Britain. And we were a lot less popular. We came to Kent for jobs and a better life; other people will be coming here for the same reasons and we will welcome them into our community."

The British working class, and miners in particular, have always had an affinity with the arts, usually in words and music. "The Snowdown Colliery Male Voice Choir still sing as they did when formed in 1926," reflects Garrity. "We have a brass band, a pigeon club, a bowls club, a rugby club, a number of soccer teams and Snowdown chose to play in black-and-white stripes, because it was the same kit as Newcastle United and many of the players' families had travelled from the north-east. The choirs came from the Rhondda, the brass bands from Yorkshire – families fetched their traditions with them."

This, for Garrity, is long-standing evidence of what he calls the "spirit" of Aylesham, the community spirit which, when the pits closed, encouraged a single group of optimists to create an agenda for survival. It was an agenda based on community action, business and education. They assembled their thoughts in the 1990s amid an economic recession. As he sought funding for the project, Garrity remembers being asked, 'Where are all these miners going to go? Will they go back home?'

"It was a good question. But they'd been here 50 years or more. This *was* their home. Only one family relocated to another coalfield and he came back pretty quickly. Because his heart was in Aylesham and because one of the best places to live is Aylesham."

Garrity and the group needed to find powerful friends. "I remember one prominent Dover District councillor saying when we floated the idea to the council: 'It's a dream. It's not a possibility'. And I thought: *You're wrong. It's a probability if we all believe in it. It's something that can happen.* They worked with Kent County Council, Dover District Council and Aylesham Parish Council and the Aylesham Community Workshop Trust was formed – in the same school building that Garrity had left at the age of 15.

In 1997, a Labour Government created eight Rural Development Associations (RDAs) and the South East of England Development Association (SEEDA) brought substance to this flickering Aylesham recovery.

Politics is not only about ideology. It is also about relationships. Ebullient John Prescott was the Minister in charge of the RDAs. Sir Sandy Bruce-Lockhart,[224] urbane and a one-nation Conservative, was chair of Kent County Council. Prescott, the deputy Prime Minister, and Bruce-

---

[224] Later Baron Bruce-Lockhart

Lockhart, representing one of the country's biggest and most important shire counties, formed a partnership which was as successful as it was unlikely. And Aylesham was among those who benefited.

Garrity says: "SEEDA and Paul Wookey supported us one hundred percent. We worked hard and found many supporters, but without SEEDA we wouldn't be where we are today."

Today, from his office on the first floor of the Aylesham School in which he was educated, Derek Garrity runs the Aylesham Community Project, just as he has been doing since 1996. There's a Garrity House office building occupied by 17 businesses, including East Kent Housing which manages the housing stock of Dover, Folkestone, Thanet and Canterbury. The units on the site are occupied by a stone mason, a vet, a hairdresser, a coffee wholesaler, a builders merchant, a dentist, the London Underground Defence Administration and many other entrepreneurs. The project has provided work for some 300 people; it injects £4.5 million every year into the local economy. Outside working hours, a boxing club, a dancing class, a women's choir and many other local organisations fill the old school with sound and energy. And the café is, appropriately named 'Sunshine Corner'.

Derek Garrity MBE says: "Aylesham is essentially a working-class community. It still has its roots in a coal mining fraternity but it's a melting pot of the Welsh, Geordies, the Scots and Yorkshire folk who have formed a unique community. They've got a different attitude to 'outsiders' than most Kentish people, I think. We were regarded with suspicion when we all arrived, and we remember that. We've got at least a thousand new houses being built as we speak.

We say to the people who want to come to live here, to the new 'immigrants', that they will find the better life they're looking for. They're welcome. Enjoy our community and we will enjoy you."

I wondered, if Derek Garrity didn't live in Aylesham, where would he like to live? "I wouldn't know. I live in the centre of the universe so why would I want to go anywhere else?"

Aylesham, as Garrity acknowledges, is as it is today largely because of the huge investment in East Kent made by SEEDA. John Prescott's strategic idea was based on the realisation that, surrounding Britain's dying industries, including coal, were acres of land that could be developed. Snowdown sat in a 200-acre site. Betteshanger occupied nearly 300 acres.

Betteshanger's problems were more intractable than Snowdown's. The site was difficult because the spoil from the pit had simply been cable-carried across the main road and dumped in a huge pile. The land was wet and largely marshland, and, once the pit was closed, it became a desolate eyesore. Boldly, SEEDA invested an estimated £25million into Betteshanger. It constructed miles of high-class roads, grassed over the spoil, landscaped the ground and waited for businesses to occupy this new business park, which they named 'Fowlmead', a poor idea for which no one admits ownership.

Nobody took up SEEDA's invitation. By 2007, Fowlmead had still attracted no businesses. Dover District Council unsuccessfully wooed a number of prospective partners – but they then received an unexpectedly encouraging response from the other side of the county.

Hadlow College were intent on expansion. A land-based college that specialised in agriculture, its headquarters were based near Tonbridge in the west of the county and as everyone who lives in Kent knows, East and West Kent are two tenuously-linked entities with no actual frontier between them. Hadlow had a small campus in Canterbury but were looking for a modest home in East Kent. A group of Hadlow executives came to Betteshanger by bus and liked what they saw. The then Deputy Principal, Mark Lumsdon-Taylor, recognised 'an opportunity'.

Hadlow would take advantage of the tens of millions of pounds already invested in the 300-acre site and build a mining museum to record the history and heritage of the Kent Coalfield; a healthy living hub, and a sustainable energy centre on the former fossil fuel site. The first thing they did was to change the name to Betteshanger Sustainable Parks. The whole thing was an ambitious concept, dogged by difficulties when deep piles had to be driven through the reclaimed land and spoil, to stabilise the building.

The Betteshanger Project, said Lumsdon-Taylor, would create close on 1,000 jobs and inject £6.2 million every year into the economy of East Kent, one of the most deprived communities in the whole of Europe.

The mining museum was within two months of opening when financial difficulties in the Hadlow Group led to the project being delayed. If and when the museum is finished on the site of the old Betteshanger pit, they plan a service to mark the occasion which will be both a remembrance and a thanksgiving.

It will, they hope, be at Canterbury Cathedral where, in 1926, the story of the life-changing East Kent coalfield really began…

THANKS

My sincere thanks for the patient help given by so many friends in the creation of this book. Every single former mining family has given generously of their time and, if I thank particularly, Jim Davies BEM, for his constant attention to my questions, I know his colleagues will understand.

The mechanics of writing a book falter without secretarial help and my gratitude to Megan Kimber, Marina Dunlop and Brooke Sterland is limitless. My thanks, too, to those who have guided me to source material and/or allowed me to quote from their work: they include Professor Gerald Dix, who worked with Patrick Abercrombie and was able to give personal insights into the life of one of Britain's great planners; David Doig and George Proudfoot who patiently shepherded me around Fife and Cardenden; Patricia Wilson and her local history group at Worsbrough who helped so much in tracing the story of the Sutcliffe family – because she is herself a Sutcliffe!; Granville Hale, who guided us through the Sirhowy Valley and Blackwood, establishing the Welsh link with Kent; Derek Garrity and The Aylesham Project and to Elizabeth Pitt who, with her daughters Catherine, Marcella and Rebecca, shared with me their memories of Malcolm Pitt's fascinating life. We are also grateful to Michael Mansfield QC, Liverpool University, Dover Library and John

Iveson, Blackwood Library, Barnsley Town Hall Library, the Elvington Heritage Group and Stuart Elgar; Keith Owen; Ross Llewellyn; Darran Cowd, curator of the Betteshanger museum collection; my friends at the Aylesham Heritage Centre; Frank Redman and Terry Harrison; and to Sandra Dymond and Lynn Divine, who revealed the secrets of those pies and pasties.

SOURCES

The East Kent Regional Planning Scheme Survey, Patrick Abercrombie and John Archibald, Hodder and Stoughton, University of Liverpool Press, 1925

Ibid, Final Report, Austen's Canterbury 1928 Town Planning in East Kent (speech by Neville Chamberlain) Eastes, Canterbury, 1926

The migration of mining families to the Kent Coalfields, Gina Harkell, Oral History Society, 1978

A comparative study of community and militancy in two coal mining settlements in Britain by Adrian Park. (Adrian Park is the son of Jimmy Park, a Snowdown miner and musician)

The Forgotten Conscript. A History of the Bevin Boy by Warwick Taylor, Pentland Press. 1995

Wot Nah! Memories of Worsbrough, Worsbrough Local History Society, Jayne Dowle, 2006

Coal, D Anderson, 1982, ISBN 0-7153-8242-X

The Challenge to Democracy, Ronald McIntosh, 2006, ISBN-10: 1-84275-157-3

Turbulent Times, Ronald McIntosh, Biteback Publishing, 2014, ISBN 978-1-84954-804-5

A Bevin Boy's Story, George Ralston, Impress Print, 2005, ISBN 0-9550991-0-2

Folklore of Blaenau Gwent, Old Bakehouse Publications, 1995, ISBN 1-874538-85-9

Pioneers of British Planning, Gordon Cherry

What I Saw at Bethesda, Charles Jones, Gomer Press, 2003, ISBN-1-84323-324X

Blackwood Yesterday, series by Ewart Smith, Bakehouse Productions

A History of the Scottish Miners, R Page Arnot, Allen and Unwin, 1955

Once a Miner, Norman Harrison, OUP, 1954

Fife, the Mining Kingdom, Guthrie Hutton, Stenlake Publishing, 1999, ISBN 1-84033-092-9

Auchterderran Yesteryear, Local History Group, 1985

The World on our Backs, Malcolm Pitt, Lawrence and Wishart, 1979

Industrial Eden, article by Richard Tilden Smith, 1926

Those Dirty Miners, JP Hollingsworth, Stenlake Publishing, 2010

The History of the Kent Coalfield, JP Hilton, self-published, 1986

The Militancy of British Miners, VL Allen, The Moor Press, 1981, ISBN 0 907698 01 8

Iron Lady: The Thatcher Years, Michael O'Mara, New Upd edition, 2012, ISBN: 1843179113

APPENDIX

1. BOREHOLES

The locations of boreholes and shafts, during the search for coal in Kent, as recorded in the Abercrombie Survey of 1925. Abercrombie's accompanying notes are included:

The Borings

"Even after the discovery at Dover, the process of boring, which was embarked upon, at first met with little encouragement. An unsuccessful boring at Netherfield appeared to exercise a westward pull upon geological advice. Godwin-Austen, whose prescience was amazing, had suggested, as an alternative to Dover, a site in the valley of the Stour a short distance from Canterbury. The actual position was never determined; had it gone ahead, Chislet or Stodmarsh might well have been chosen.

Two explorations companies in 1897–8 sank unsuccessful borings, which proved to be clean west of the coalfield – at Ottinge, Hothfield, Pluckley, Old Soar and Brabourne. Penshurst was selected as another site.

One early boring, at Ropersole was very nearly a success: it was certainly on the coalfield, near its western (productive) limit: it struck the coal measures at a depth of 1,581 feet, but was abandoned, chiefly for financial reasons, after penetrating them for 548 feet, meeting some thin bands of coal and one seam of 1'3". There is little doubt that deeper boring would have shown more coal. The same fate overtook yet another too-westward boring at Ellinge in 1901.

Anyhow, Ropersole and Ellinge proved that the coal measures were not confined to Dover, and the next attempt must be counted as the first really successful boring (after Shakespeare Cliff) and the one which has actually opened the Kent Coalfield. It was at Waldershare, near Lord Guilford's park, that a new boring was put down in 1909, and Mr Arthur Burr's name must always be associated with this economic discovery of Kent coal. Not only were the coal measures met with 500 feet nearer the surface than at Ropersole or Ellinge, but three seams of over 3 feet thickness and two more of more than a foot were found.

Henceforth the field has been pegged out as systematically as a variety of concessionary companies would allow. When later borings appear on the plan outside the coalfield they were definite attempts to discover its limits, or to try for ironstone." It then listed 39 points:

1. Dover (Shakespeare Cliff)
2. Ropersole (stopped too soon)
3. Ottinge
4. Ellinge
5. Waldershare
6. Fredville
7. Goodnestone
8. Barfreston
9. Woodnesborough
10. Walmstone

11. Mattice Hill (Sandwich)
12. Oxney
13. Trapham (Wingham)
14. Maydensole
15. Stodmarsh
16. Ebbsfleet
17. Ripple
18. Stonehall
19. Chilton
20. Lydden Valley (Deal)
21. Herne
22. Chislet
23. Chitty
24. Rushbourne
25. Betteshanger
26. Bourne (Bishopsbourne)
27. Harmansole
28. Hoades
29. Herne Bay
30. Beltinge
31. Ash or Fleet
32. Bere
33. Reculver
34. Elham*
35. Folkestone*
36. Standen*
37. Cliff*
38. Farthingloe*
39. Adisham*

  *These boreholes were sunk primarily seeking ironstone

2. In 1945, a geological survey made by the Ministry of Fuel and Power as part of a Kent Coalfield Regional Report, listed the **BOREHOLES AND SHAFTS IN KENT**, including the depth at which coal measures (CM; the coal seam) had been reached:

Dates	Boreholes	Colliery Shafts	Thickness of C.M. proved *=base reached	Remarks
1922	Adisham		2025*	
1907–12	Barfrestone		2122	
1913–15	Berefarm		1647	
1913	Betteshanger		1811*	
1924		Betteshanger	1445	
1913–14	Bishopstone		1857*	
1897–98	Brabourne		C.M. absent	Sunk 5 m.w. of now known western limit of the coalfield
1886–90	Brady Bore			
1914–18		Chislet	374	
1912–13	Chilton		1960?	Record unsatisfactory
1912–13	Chislet Park		568*	
1912–13	Chitty		C.M. doubtful	
1914–15	Elham		641*	
1900–02	Ellinge		146	
1913	Fleet		771*	
1915–16	Folkestone		1903	
1905–07	Fredville		463	
1906–07	Goodnestone		1717	

Dates	Boreholes	Colliery Shafts	Thickness of C.M. proved *=base reached	Remarks
1911		(Guilford)		A pilot bore is said to have reached C.M., but no records have been preserved. Shaft abandoned 1921 before reaching C.M.
1913–14	Harmansole		C.M. absent	Carboniferous limestone below Mesozoic rocks
? date	Herne		C.M. absent	
1913	Herne Bay		C.M. absent	
1913	Hoades		154	
1912–14	Lydden Marsh		1007*	
1909–12	Mattice Hill		1076*	
1910–11	Maydensole		2655	
1910–12	Oxney		2706*	
1914	Reculver		C.M. absent	
1910–12	Richborough		106*	
1911	Ripple		2388*	
1898–99	Ropersole		1547	
1912–13	Rushbourne		415*	
1886–90		Shakespeare	1173	Shaft sunk on site of Brady bore. Some coal raised 1912 and some iron ore
1909–25		Snowdown	1699	
1910–11	Stodmarsh		1075*	
1911–12	Stonehall		2401	Lower part of record unsatisfactory

Dates	Boreholes	Colliery Shafts	Thickness of C.M. proved *=base reached	Remarks
1913		(Stonehall)		Shaft commenced; abandoned during Great War, C.M. not reached
1906–30		Tilmanstone	2293	First sunk to No. 1 or Beresford Seam. Deepened to No. 6, or Millyard Seam, 1930
1910–11	Trapham		1651*	
1905–07	Waldershare		1469	
1908–13	Walmerstone		1200*	
1910		(Wingham)		Shaft sunk 50ft. only; abandoned
1908–09	Woodnesborough		1546*	
1910		(Woodnesborough)		Some plant erected but no sinking done

3. 1984 STRIKE AFTERMATH: The Sacked and Imprisoned Miners Delegation: Liz French, Terry's wife, was a member of a party of seven from Kent that visited Washington DC, Chicago and Los Angeles in the United States in the aftermath of the 1984 strike. It was sponsored by the Communist Party and celebrated May Day 1986 in the US. On the return journey she visited her husband Terry, who was still in Maidstone gaol.

4. The full text of Wilfred Owen's poem **MINERS** (see Chapter 2)

There was a whispering in my hearth,
A sigh of the coal,
Grown wistful of a former earth
It might recall.
I listened for a tale of leaves
And smothered ferns,
Frond-forests, and the low sly lives
Before the fauns.
My fire might show steam-phantoms simmer
From Time's old cauldron,
Before the birds made nests in summer,
Or men had children.
But the coals were murmuring of their mine,
And moans down there
Of boys that slept wry sleep, and men
Writhing for air.
And I saw white bones in the cinder-shard,
Bones without number.
Many the muscled bodies charred,
And few remember.
I thought of all that worked dark pits
Of war, and died
Digging the rock where Death reputes
Peace lies indeed.
Comforted years will sit soft-chaired,
In rooms of amber;
The years will stretch their hands, well-cheered
By our life's ember;
The centuries will burn rich loads

With which we groaned,
Whose warmth shall lull their dreaming lids,
While songs are crooned;
But they will not dream of us poor lads,
Left in the ground.

5. KENT COAL OUTPUT AND EMPLOYMENT, 1945

§ 8. *The Distribution of the Coal Population over Eight New Sites and in several Existing Places*

The following is the basis upon which the Coal Population of 180,000 has been distributed over eight new sites and added to several existing agglomerations.

NEW SITES

Site.	Population.	From Pit.
1. Chislet (north of pit)	8,000	8,000 from Chislet
2. New Littlebourne	12,000	10,000 „ Stodmarsh / 2,000 „ Canterbury
3. New Wingham	20,000	10,000 „ Elmstone / 10,000 „ Wingham
4. New Woodnesborough	12,000	10,000 „ Fleet / 2,000 „ Woodnesborough
5. Ham	31,000	10,000 „ Betteshanger / 8,000 „ Woodnesborough / 8,000 „ Sandwich / 5,000 „ Deal
6. Nonington	20,000	10,000 „ Snowdown / 10,000 „ Adisham
7. Martin Mill	20,000	10,000 „ Ripple / 10,000 „ Langdon
8. Shepherdswell	24,000	9,000 „ Tilmanstone / 10,000 „ Guilford / 5,000 „ Stonehall
Total	147,000	

73

The distribution of the coal population over eight new sites and in several existing places

6. MAP OF EAST KENT LIGHT RAILWAY (from A History of the Kent Coalfield, John Hilton, 1986)

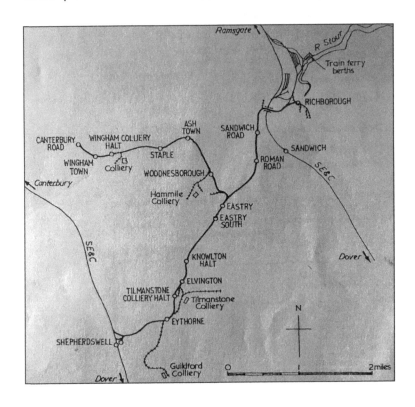

7. LETTER TO ALL MINERS FROM CHAIRMAN IAN MACGREGOR, NCB CHAIRMAN, JUNE 1984

National Coal Board
Hobart House, Grosvenor Place, London SW1X 7AE

NCB

CHAIRMAN
Ian MacGregor

June, 1984

Dear Colleague,

YOUR FUTURE IN DANGER

I am taking the unusual step of writing to you at home because I want every man and woman who has a stake in the coal industry to realise clearly the damage which will be done if this disastrous strike goes on a long time.

The leaders of the NUM have talked of it continuing into the winter. Now that our talks with them have broken down this is a real possibility. It could go on until December or even longer. In which case the consequences for everybody will be very grave.

Your President talks continually of keeping the strike going indefinitely until he achieves "victory".

I would like to tell you, not provocatively or as a threat, why that will not happen however long the strike lasts.

What this strike is really about is that the NUM leadership is preventing the development of an efficient industry. We have repeatedly explained that we are seeking to create a higher volume, lower cost industry which will be profitable, well able to provide superior levels of earnings while still being able to compete with foreign coal. To achieve this, huge sums of money are being invested in new equipment; last year it was close to £800 million and we expect to continue a similarly high rate of investment in the years ahead. Our proposals mean, short term, cutting out some of the uneconomic pits and looking for about 20,000 voluntary redundancies — the same as last year. The redundancy payments are now more generous than ever before for those who decide not to take alternative jobs offered in the industry.

However long the strike goes on I can assure you that we will end up, through our normal consultative procedures, with about the same production plans as those we discussed with your representatives on 6th March last.

But the second reason why continuing the strike will not bring the NUM "victory" is this: in the end nobody will win. Everybody will lose — and lose disastrously.

Many of you have already lost more than £2,000 in earnings and have seen your savings disappear. If the strike goes on until December it will take many of you years to recover financially and also more jobs may be lost — and all for nothing.

I have been accused of planning to butcher the industry. I have no such intention or desire. I want to build up the industry into one we can all be proud to be part of.

But if we cannot return to reality and get back to work then the industry may well be butchered. But the butchers will not be the Coal Board.

You are all aware that mines which are not constantly maintained and worked deteriorate in terms of safety and workability.

AT THE PRESENT TIME THERE ARE BETWEEN 20 and 30 pits which are viable WHICH WILL BE IN DANGER OF NEVER RE-OPENING IF WE HAVE A LENGTHY STRIKE.

This is a strike which should never have happened. It is based on very serious misrepresentation and distortion of the facts. At great financial cost miners have supported the strike for fourteen weeks because your leaders have told you this .....

    That the Coal Board is out to butcher the coal industry.
    That we plan to do away with 70,000 jobs.
    That we plan to close down around 86 pits, leaving only 100 working
    collieries.

IF THESE THINGS WERE TRUE I WOULD NOT BLAME MINERS FOR GETTING ANGRY OR FOR BEING DEEPLY WORRIED. BUT THESE THINGS ARE ABSOLUTELY UNTRUE. I STATE THAT CATEGORICALLY AND SOLEMNLY. YOU HAVE BEEN DELIBERATELY MISLED.

The NUM, which called the strike, will end it only when you decide it should be ended.

I would like you to consider carefully, so we can get away from the tragic violence and pressures of the mass pickets, whether this strike is really in your interest.

I ask you to join your associates who have already returned to work so that we can start repairing the damage and building up a good future.

Sincerely,

Ian MacGregor

8. COAL AND IRONSTONE FIELDS - East Kent Survey, 1925. The lightly shaded portion is the economic coalfield. The darker portion is the probable extent of the iron deposits

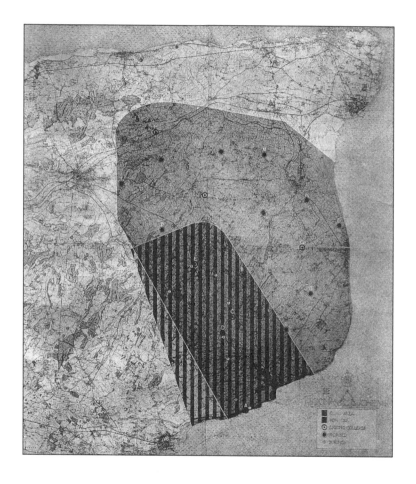

9. FLYING PICKETS 1984

Betteshanger

Men Dismissed

Terry Harrison	*Secretary*
John Moyle	*Chairman*
Jimmy Trice	*Treasurer*
Brian Foy	*Vice-Chair*
Charlie Sheavills	*Sur. Rep*
Peter Fulbrook	*Craft Rep*
Pat O'Donnell	*Committee*
Terry Birkett	*Committee*
Ray Lawton	
Andy Hayward	
Jimmy Waddell	Bob Nicholls
Mark Best	Nigel Pickford
John O'Connor	Wally O'Donnell
Ian Foy	Jack Young
Peter Holden	Steve Simmonds
Les Sweeting	Ken Ridyard
Graham Brace	Alan Hatser
Allan Bell	Mel Thompson
Brian Day	Brian Michael
Billy Leonard	Brian Guy

Men Jailed

Terry French	5 years
Chris Tazey	3 years
Dave Hemmings	4 months
John O'Connor	1 month
Steve Moore	3 weeks

Tilmanstone

Men dismissed

J Bracc

J Jones

D Worthington

I Rodgers

L Kyle

G Almond

M Denny

A Samson (COSA)

J Mills

C Rodgers

10. Frank Redman (see Chapter 14). Frank Redman was born in Germany during World War Two. His father was a Feldwebel in the German *Wermacht* and was killed on the Russian front in 1942. His widowed mother married a British soldier, John Redman, who had been a prisoner of war after being captured in the rearguard defence of Dunkirk in 1940. They came to Britain in 1948 and, after attending Deal Central School, Frank joined the army and later became a miner. Aged 19, he was a 'timber lad' at Betteshanger when he took part in a staydown strike and was fired. He worked as a seaman on coastal vessels out of Dover and was in Hamburg when he was told his job was open again. He returned to the pit.

11. BETTESHANGER CLOSURE NOTICE, August 22nd 1989

British Coal Corporation,
Betteshanger Colliery,
Betteshanger
Deal, Kent CT14 0LU

British COAL

Telephone: (0304) 611944
Fax No: 6000

August 22, 1989.

Dear Colleague,

As you may have already heard, it is with great regret that I have to advise you that Betteshanger Colliery will close on Friday, 25th August 1989. The announcement was made this morning by Mr.Wheeler, Director of Group Operations, and I attach a copy of the Press Statement that has been issued by British Coal.

The counselling of individuals will now, as a matter of urgency, be carried out by the Assistant Manager (Personnel) and his staff. In order to assist him in arranging counselling interviews, it is essential that anyone wishing to take redundancy on the terms currently available (only until Friday of this week) should register their name with him urgently, so that the necessary paper work can be put in hand before the interview. This will speed up the process for everyone.

Yours sincerely,

D.Bell
Colliery Manager

12. POET IDRIS DAVIES (1905–1953) was born in Rhymney, near Merthyr Tydfil. His work captured the essential dignity of the working man and woman. He wrote 'Gwalia Deserta' in 1938.

> In the places of my boyhood
> The pit-wheels turn no more
> Nor any furnace lightens
> The midnight as of yore
>
> The slopes of slag and cinder
> Are sulking in the rain
> And in derelict valleys
> The hope of youth is slain
>
> And yet I love to wander
> The early ways I went
> And watch from doors and bridges
> The hills and skies of Gwent
>
> In Gwalia, my Gwalia
> The vandals out of hell
> Ransacked and marred forever
> The wooded hill and dell
>
> They grabbed and bruised and plundered
> Because their greed was great
> And slunk away and purchased
> The medals of the state
>
> And yet I love to wander
> The early ways I went

And watch from doors and bridges
The hills and skies of Gwent

Though blighted be the valleys
Where man meets man with pain
The things by boyhood cherished
Stand firm and shall remain

Pete Seeger's recording of his poem; 'The Bells of Rhymney' became a folk rock standard.

13. CHISLET MEMORIAL

1915 T Watson (aged 14)

1918 W H Hewes (45)

1919 W Widdett (39)

1920 W Andrews (53)

1920 T Addley (46)

1922 H C Watchan (58)

1923 J Hoskin (60)

1924 J Owens (48)

1925 T Cox (36)

1926 G Clarke (24)

1927 G C Newberry (34)

1927 T Goodwin (34)

1928 T Kinsey (26)

1929 R Dobson (33)

1929 J Banks (54)

1929 G Blundell 942)

1921 G Glover (1946)

1931 J Williams (15)

1932 S Merrett (43)

1932 A G Whitehead (49)

1932 P McGinlet (36)

1932 F Deverson (26)

1933 J Jakes (30)

1933 A Davidson (44)

1934 J T Peckett (50)

1934 L T Wood (22)

1934 E Blount (47)

1935 H P Bigham (20)

1935 E W Evans (57)

1935 G H Jones (47)

1936 A J Ryan (21)

1937 N Dickinson (33)

1937 T H Watson (47)

1937 B Hancock (32)

1937 S J Axford (23)

1937 A Scary

1937 W Ellis (39)

1938 J Christian (56)

1939 H Hulme (39)

1941 S Bridgman (40)

1943 L Bing (21)

1943 A J Moon (20)

1946 A R Gilbert (21)

1946 R Kelly (59)

1950 L Theedon (37)

1954 E R Thomas

1955 F Beckham (67)

1956 W Stutely

1957 A Hougham

1959 F Bridgewater (38)

1960 T Beever (60)

1960 K Hemingsley (32)

1964 J Barnes (59)

Two other miners, A H Purvis in 1929 and T McCullough in 1935, were omitted from this comprehensive list.

14. RECIPE FOR PIT PASTIES

Ingredients:

8 oz self-raising flour
Pinch of salt
4 oz margarine
2 oz water
12 oz boneless beef, cubed
1 medium onion, sliced thinly
1 lb potatoes, peeled and thinly sliced
1 teaspoon dried parsley
Salt and pepper to taste
2 oz water or as needed

Directions:

1. Using first four ingredients make the pastry by rubbing the margarine into the flour until a breadcrumb consistency
2. Mix together with water until a dough is made
3. Divide dough into 2 equal pieces
4. Roll out into circles; use a plate if needed to cut to shape
5. Place half the potato slices in a line down the middle of each circle
6. Leave a space of about an inch at the end
7. Lay onion slices over the potatoes
8. Season with salt, pepper and some parsley
9. Place half the cubes of meat onto each circle and season again
10. Fold the edges over and cut three slits into the top
11. Place the pasties onto a greased baking sheet
12. Bake for 45 minutes in an oven pre-heated to 200°F

13. Remove from oven and reduce heat to 175°C (350°F)
14. Spoon a teaspoon of water into each slit
15. Return to oven for 15 minutes or until golden brown

GLOSSARY OF MINING TERMS AND PHRASES

AFTERS – The afternoon shift, 2pm to 10pm. The other two shifts are called 'days' and 'nights'.

BANK, BANKSMAN – The immediate vicinity of the top of the shaft, the 'banksman' being the man responsible for seeing the cage is safe to descend. His opposite number underground is the 'onsetter'.

COLLIER – Generally a skilled underground labourer. They are usually subdivided into 'colliers' who work on the coalface; 'rippers' who work on the stone, and 'pan turners', who work on the conveyors.

DEPUTY – The hierarchy of the colliery begins with the Manager. Next the under-manager. There is usually an 'overman' in charge of a group of districts of the whole pit on the back shifts. The deputy is the man in charge of one district, which he must inspect twice a shift. Though his wages must not depend on production, he has an immense influence on the successful working of a district.

DISTRICT – The area supervised by a deputy. It should be, though often was not, small enough to be travelled twice in a shift.

GATE – Any roadway leading to the face, though normally reserved for the portion near the fence itself.

GOB, GOAF or WASTE – The void made by the removal of the coal.

HEADING – A narrow section of coal cut out further in advance than the rest of the face.

INBYE – Inbye means going nearer to the coalface, outbye means the opposite.

INTAKE – A roadway or gate carrying fresh or relatively fresh air to the coalface.

LOADER – An apprentice collier.

MANHOLE – A cubby-hole in which to hide in case of danger on the haulage roads.

RINGER – A crowbar.

RIPPER – See 'Collier'.

RIPPING, CHEEKING, and DINTING – Excavating rock in the roof, side, and floor respectively, together with all the ancillary work such as putting up supports.

ROADWAYS – Roadways, levels and gates are the three most common terms for underground tunnels.

SHIFT – See 'Afters'.

SNAP – A snack. It also denotes the 20-minute break halfway through the shift.

STONE PROP – A temporary wooden prop put up by rippers for their own safety when working on stone.

TURN OVER – The distance by which the conveyor advances as the colliers remove the coal. The 'pan-turners' turn the belt over.

1s, 3s, 10s, 60s, 84s, etc. – Names given to districts. The numbers chosen seldom bear any relation to one another.

OLD 2s, OLD 3s, etc. – Disused districts.